# LIFE'S
## Turning Points

## Arthur Sweet

LIFE'S TURNING POINTS by Arthur Sweet

ISBN 13: 978-0615577371
ISBN 10: 0615577377
 LCCN: 2011944886

Book and Cover designed by Ellie Searl, Publishista

PRINTED IN THE USA

DIAMOND OF LIFE PUBLISHING
ENCINO, CA

*TO MY*

*BELOVED BRIDE,*

*WHOSE COMPANY I TREASURE.*

*OUR LIFE TOGETHER HAS BEEN AWESOME.*

*LIFE'S TURNING POINTS WERE MADE*

*EASIER BECAUSE OF YOU.*

*THANK YOU !*

# PREFACE

EVERYONE REVIEWS THE PAST. Each of us has intense emotions about life, especially when making important decisions. That's when a personal computer can help.

The modern era has undergone change as never before. Why? Many of man's activities have been expedited by his using the personal computer. How? The PC's discovery, development, and increasing use is the most important set of events of the 20$^{th}$ century. The PC provides data that influence many areas of individual endeavors. Much of what happens in decision-making involves one's personal data. Why? The PC is a dispassionate tool used to change life's path. When provided complicated questions, it processes millions of bits of information and gives the answers. It does so in an instant.

This impartial tool keeps such decisions unbiased. By doing so, quality is improved when individuals face the Turning Points of life. Having such a tool as the PC at decision-making time boggles one's mind.

Life decisions of what to do and when to do it are difficult to make. Once a choice is made, it is hard to reverse and, in many cases, irreversible. Whether the turn is to the right or to the left, the time now or never, the course of action to take is difficult to decide and even more difficult to follow. The advantages and disadvantages of either choice become life-altering points of no return, but one must decide—thus creating a Turning Point in one's life.

## PART ONE - PROLOGUE

## PART TWO - THE STORIES

## CHAPTER 1 - ACCIDENTS — 25

## CHAPTER 2 - BATTLES — 47

# CONTENTS

## CHAPTER 6 – FAMILY (cont.)

## CHAPTER 7 - HEALTH

## CHAPTER 8 - HAPPENSTANCE

## CHAPTER 8 - HAPPENSTANCE (cont.)

## CHAPTER 9 - PROMOTION — 269

## CHAPTER 10 - RELIGION — 293

# CONTENTS

# CONTENTS

## PART THREE - APPENDIX (cont.)

# PART 1

# PROLOGUE

# *MUSINGS BY THE AUTHOR*

I BELIEVE, AS MANY writers do, that inspiration is better than perspiration. This is especially true now that I have started to write again. I began writing *LIFE'S TURNING POINTS* quite accidently. I had retired four times in my sixty years of business activity. My wife had started to create what she called her memoirs. She suggested that our life of sixty-four years together warranted being the subject of her writing efforts. She added that togetherness had no limitations and asked me, "Why don't you take up writing too?"

Old age is similar to an aphrodisiac. It stimulates the subconscious in asking the mind and the body to perform acts that usually are difficult but are rewarding. One of these is writing a book. The oldster can fill up as much of the day as he wants. He can pick any subject that is of interest to himself and others. He can satisfy his desire to be creative. This makes the effort worthwhile.

I pondered a while, and then I reminded her that I had written several stories, the first about my becoming a pilot during the Second World War. In addition, I had published two books in connection with my business activities. However, I needed a theme for my new writing efforts.

After thinking about what should I write about, I considered my war experiences of being a bomber pilot but realized while it was exciting doing it, writing about it would not be fascinating to the readers. It was then that I remembered I had changed direction during my fifty-plus years of working—being in my own business and meeting interesting people along the way—and that other people had incidents worth writing about.

I had been an employee, had bought a manufacturing company where I ran the show, had sold out to a major conglomerate, and had become a developer of commercial and industrial real estate—all in a sixty-year career.

As an oldster, I can enjoy my leisure time. Such freedom gives me perspective about life in general and my own in particular. I recall my past, peer into the murky future, and live for the present. This introspection has caused me to consider each segment of life in terms of today. Shakespeare lived in the Middle Ages, but I related his seven stages of man to modern times.

Stage one is birth and infancy. It is the first time the baby turns over in its crib, and a life's Turning Point—to a baby, to its parents, and to all others viewing the event. This simple act demonstrates to the world that a baby is independent and a separate being. The other six stages are equally compelling, and challenge the reader to read on.

# THE BOOK: *LIFE'S TURNING POINTS*

## *Background*

THE TURNING POINTS THEME was cemented during the 200th anniversary of Lewis and Clark's three year adventure traveling the Northwest. A Stanford University Travel Study trip down the Missouri River seeing unaltered sights provided the impetus for writing this book.

During the two-week trip, I met a grandfather and his grandson from St. Louis. Around the nightly campfire, the group leader discussed Turning Points in Meriwether Lewis's life and behavior. That led to a discussion of other Turning Points that changed the directions of people's lives.

I reconsidered the idea that everyone had a story to tell. There would be several times in their lives where there was a turn in the road—when their lives changed. Each one of these occurrences was a life-changing incident, a crossroad. No matter which choice they made, it would affect not only their own life, but also the lives of those around them. This theme became the inspiration of my work.

After I retired, I moved my office into our new home. My wife, seeing me writing at my desk, remarked, "You're working too hard."

I replied, "So what's new about that? During the past forty years, I have written and self-published four minor works about my dinnerware, glassware, and gift business, a men's necktie company during the decline of the necktie industry, and a Rotary International Cookbook."

I went from Stanford University into aircraft manufacturing at Lockheed. Then, in the sixties, I joined and operated a nationwide giftware manufacturing company. In the seventies, I became a developer of small shopping centers. In the eighties and nineties, I became an investor in industrial real estate. The turn of the twentieth century saw me semi-retire.  The 21st century has been a period of review and creativity.

As one can see, my career has been diverse, involving many business venues. Each phase of my career was untroubled and ended successfully. Since the twilight of my life, I have served on boards of public and government agencies

I have had more than a handful of major changes of direction. I narrowed them down to major decisions that I would classify as Turning Points. All of them were irreversible, all affected the lives of others, and all materially altered my plans as I travelled down the road to the great beyond.

It occurred to me that I was not unique—that there were stories that deserved telling. I was sure that everyone encountered such crossroads in their lives. All of us eventually reach a point where change is in order. It might be to start some new operation or stop some negative action.

It was at this point that I wanted to expand the concept of Turning Points.  To develop the idea more fully, I decided to interview people of various age groups, career types, financial status, and distinguishing characteristics to discover incidents that caused them to alter their plans and future direction. I developed a one-page questionnaire with fourteen questions.  My focus centered on the important times when people made decisions about their future plans— what to do and when to do it. Some of the Turning Points people told about are universal, like birth and death. Some are unique, such as falling from a five-story office building or winning a national award. The responses were reviewed and followed up with an interview where possible.

The information was classified into categories of Traits and Tendencies—aptitudes, attitudes, characteristics, and opportunities—as observed by the author. The "end all" was material for the stories in *LIFE'S TURNING POINTS*.

# PART 2

# THE STORIES

# 1

# ACCIDENTS

S UNDAY NIGHT AND THE phone rang. The voice on the other end said, "Do you have anything to do with the building on Thompson Street? If you do, the whole building is burning down. You should come over right away."

George got into his car, drove to Glendale, and saw that it was hopeless. His building had burned to the ground. It was an accident waiting to happen. Fortunately, as so often is the case, fire insurance covered the loss. This incident was a Turning Point in George's life. He lost his largest customer because he could no longer meet the delivery schedule. This is an example of how an accident affected a life.

## A SKIING HOLIDAY AND CLIMBING
## THE MOUNTAIN TO SUCCESS

*Being Number Two is Better than Being Number One*

T HE FAST APPROACHING DARK clouds over the Tahoe ski slopes looked menacing. Two helicopters, rotors twirling, waited for the ten passengers to board. It would be the return trip to the Hollywood Burbank Airport.

The pilot of helicopter Number One yelled, "Come on, Frank. If we don't take off right away, we will be snowed in for at least two days. Get four others, and let's take off now!"

Five skiers loaded their gear and hopped aboard. The door closed, and the pilot gave the thumbs up sign. In an instant, the helicopter rose and headed south.

The other five skiers hopped aboard helicopter Number Two. Paul was one of them. He was pissed because he wasn't in the first helicopter with Frank, the president. It would have been a great chance to talk with him about the Disneyland operations and accounting activities.

Flying above the clouds, the two whirlybirds headed back to Burbank. Then Paul heard the first helicopter radioing, "Uh oh, it looks like we're in trouble; it looks like we're going down." And then nothing.

Paul's pilot said, "I can't see Number One ahead."

He swung his helicopter into a $180^0$ turn, and all aboard tried to locate the other chopper. Paul looked down and saw the parts of Number One scattered over the snowcapped hillside. It was a total wreck with no signs of life. Paul and the others in Number Two could not believe it.

This accident was a Turning Point in Paul's life.

Chance changed Paul's life from being one of the CPAs to being the only one! For the previous two years, Paul had been assigned to audit president Frank Wells's functions and records. For two years, Paul had prepared some of Frank's personal information for the 1993 and 1994 tax returns. As such, Paul was in the best shape to get an extension of time to prepare the 1994 Federal and State tax return.

After the funeral, Mrs. Wells asked Paul to be the executor and handle Frank's estate. Paul agreed as long as there would be no conflict of interest and he could establish an investment counseling company that met all legal requirements.

The Diamond of Life qualities that qualified Paul's appointment were education, skill, knowledge, personality, dedication, and familiarity. Paul would manage an estate estimated to be in the millions. He would need to set up a good organization to do this.

Paul felt he was up to the challenge. He accepted the position. While this tale is not a rags to riches story, it shows that Number Two may be the winner after all!

# ACCIDENTS HAPPEN

*A Window Washer's Lucky Break*

D URING THE SECOND DECADE of the twentieth century, Mac, a window washer, ran a crew that cleaned the outsides of windows in high-rise buildings. Mac had a contract to wash the windows for a major department store called Carson Pirie Scott & Co. It was the second largest department store in Chicago. It was housed in a multi-story building on State Street facing Marshall Field & Company.

Mac was washing windows on the fifth floor of the Carson's building. He was suspended in a 'bosun chair' so that he could wash the outsides of the windows. This chair was connected to the top of the building by a rope and pulley. There were two men who pulled Mac up to the window he wanted to wash. Mac had the water, soap, and cloths with him as he was washing the windows. The two helpers would keep the people walking on the sidewalks away from the building. The helpers also moved Mac from floor to floor as he needed to continue his window washing.

One day, the rope holding Mac up to the top of the building frayed and broke. He fell five stories and hit an awning on the ground floor. This awning cushioned Mac's fall and saved his life. In the process, Mac broke both ankles. The doctor told him it would take six months for him to heal.

There was no such thing as workman's compensation insurance, public liability, or any way of having Carson's, the owner of the building, pay for the medical costs of this accident. It was part of the cost of owning and operating any service such as window washing.

This one hundred-foot fall was the Turning Point in Mac's life. He had to decide what to do. The competition and the bad winter weather made reopening the window washing business questionable. His wife wanted him to move, and his customers wanted him to remain. This was to be a life altering decision!

While Mac was in the hospital recovering, he mulled over what to do. There were pros and cons to consider before making a choice whether to move or to stay. In any event, it would be a difficult decision and, once made, could not be reversed.

After several weeks on crutches and talking it over with his wife, Mac decided that it would be best for him to move to California. He realized that this was the time to move. He bought a Ford, and the family drove to San Francisco.

Once there, Mac checked the potential of establishing a window washing business in the Bay Area. He found that the building owners of the downtown buildings were satisfied with the service of Mac's competitors. Mac saw what destruction the earthquake and subsequent fire had caused to the city. He analyzed where, and if, his window washing service would be needed.

After a week of careful review, he talked to his wife, and they both decided that the climate in California and the growth that had occurred in the San Francisco Bay Area were the deciding factors. Staying and opening a new business in San Francisco was the best solution.

Mac reopened his window washing service in the Bay Area. This was a Turning Point in his life. It was so successful that a competitor bought him out.

The one provision Mac did not like was that he could not open another such service for ten years. He sold his business in the early 1920s. Then Mac went to the Los Angeles area and started washing windows for the third time.

Starting up in a new city was not always easy. Mac, being Irish, was a 'hail fellow well met.' Many times he was found in a bar after work—either buying drinks for friends or having somebody buy him a drink. Despite this weaknesses, Mac was successful in the Los Angeles area.

Mac the window washer had arrived at another Turning Point in his life. He had made his decision, was providing a needed service to the Los Angeles area, and had 'out-washed' all the other companies in town.

According to the Diamond of Life review, Mac did not worry. He was religious. He had faith in God and in himself. As an added plus, Mac's courage in performing under hazardous conditions, his trust in the actions of others, and his having the strength of character kept Mac on a positive path. Other traits, natural or learned, had been rated. Such qualities can lead a person to live a successful life or be doomed to failure.

Mac's Irish heritage—being blessed with the gift of gab and having good luck at his side—pointed him toward success. One must believe that accidents happen. However, it is with the thought that a person is far better off being Irish and lucky than just being smart!

# DAMNED IF YOU DO—DAMNED IF YOU DON'T

*Joe Faces Fear in Order to Succeed*

A LMOST ALL OF THE Turning Points in Joe's life were fraught with danger. So it was with his submitting a bid to clean up the Twin Towers' mess in lower Manhattan in September 2001. The Twin Towers, two 113-story buildings, had become a pile of rubble. Thousands had died because two commercial passenger planes had crashed into the upper floors. The subsequent building fires and the 90-foot pile of rubble were added to the collapsed parking structure. A mountain of wreckage was the result.

President Bush declared the incident, and the resulting damage, a national disaster. Rudy Giuliani, New York City's Mayor, prompt in his appraisal of the situation, moved with all possible speed to clean up the mess. It was a Turning Point for all New Yorkers and the rest of the nation.

In order to get the cleanup underway, proposals and bids for demolition, cleanup, and salvage were to be submitted by the end of October 2001. The building owners would make the award of a cleanup contract through the Mayor's office. Joe was one of the major demolition contractors to analyze what had to be done, how to do it, and how much it would cost to complete the job.

Joe had been in the business for years. He knew that the job was so large that it would be given to a consortium of firms. He reasoned that his best bet was to become involved with the disposal of the debris. His cleanup plan was unique, inventive, and a touch of genius. He knew it would be a difficult task unless he handled the trash quickly and effectively.

Joe also knew his firm was at a disadvantage as his business was on the New Jersey side of the Hudson River. The bid was to include segregating the dead bodies from the debris and disposing of the debris and all salvage from the site. The site was to be left so that a new structure could be constructed. Whoever got the job knew he would be 'damned if he did and damned if he didn't.'

Joe spent sleepless nights trying to resolve the problem of how to clean up the mess. He wanted to do the work, but to do it in the conventional way would be impossible. All the other demolition firms were going to bring in equipment to cut the metal beams and load them on trucks to sell as scrap. The rubble would be loaded on dump trucks and driven over New York streets to a dump in New Jersey. Any bodies found would be given last rites by religious pastors and priests and taken to a cemetery.

Finally, the parking structure, which had collapsed in a heap 60-feet below street level, would be very difficult. Dynamite blasting would be used at night. It would break up an estimated one million tons of concrete. This would need to be removed from the site.

Because Joe's yard was on the Jersey side of the Hudson River, it would be a long haul to get everything to Joe's operations. Joe mulled over the demolition, the trucking, and the danger of working on the rubble pile almost 100-feet high from ground level.

The cost of the entire job was to be in the millions because it would be a cost plus contract with a not-to-exceed limitation. The estimated time to complete the job was established that included a completion date. A daily *"late penalty will be assessed if contract completion is not met."*

All bids were due on October 11, and no time extensions were to be given for any circumstance.

About a week before October 11, Joe woke up during a restless night and said, "Eureka, I've got it." He could hardly wait until the sun came up. He went down to the Twin Towers site, which by that time was completely fenced in and patrolled by security guards. Joe was allowed to get additional information and recheck his other assumptions necessary for his bid.

By ten o'clock in the morning Joe had reviewed his inspiration. He had an outline of how he planned to do the job. Using his past experiences, he estimated the cost of the portion of the job that his firm would do. The new idea would reduce salvage cost by 33%. He still had a full week to finalize his bid, including the cost savings provided by his 'new wrinkle.'

Joe was pleased with his Diamond of Life analysis. His new method was Innovative. It was prompted by his ambition. It would give him an advantage by cutting costs 33%, and therefore he could be the low bidder on his portion of cleaning up the Twin Towers debacle.

Joe submitted a sealed bid, which would be opened on October 11, just a week away. If he got this job, he would be able to retire if he so desired. His wife of nearly thirty years could buy the fur coat she always wanted, and the kids and grandkids would be 'in clover.'

The bids were opened. It was the Turning Point of Joe's life—a job so immense that Joe could hardly believe it. He had created a simple solution. Joe devised a way to eliminate the normal way of removing trash from a building site.

Instead of trucking the scrap to the dump using the crowded New York City streets, Joe proposed using barges and the Hudson River as his bridge to Jersey. Joe's not using trucks to get the site scrap from downtown Manhattan's Twin Tower site and eliminating many of the trucks was novel. It required digging a channel wide enough to allow a barge to go several blocks to the site. The barges were loaded at the site and towed to New Jersey. Once there, the barge was unloaded in Joe's salvage yard and sorted there.

This contract would be the Turning Point in Joe's life. He was not to be 'damned if he did.' But he would be 'damned if he didn't' submit a bid to get the job. Joe's brainstorm to clear the Twin Towers site saved New York City and all others affected by the disaster—time, money, and inconvenience! Not only was Joe's solution novel, but it was also the quickest and the best way to get the job done.

# MOUNT HOOD AND THE CLUMSY BUS DRIVER

## *I'm Okay, You're Okay*

AN ELDERLY COUPLE IN their eighties waited for the Breeze Bus Company's driver to get on the bus. It was 7:30 a.m. on an early June day, and the twenty-four people on the bus were getting restive. They were ready to get going, but the bus driver had not finished loading the baggage.

A few minutes later, the driver slowly climbed the three steps of the bus and sat down. While putting the baggage on board, he had tripped and fallen, cutting his forehead. Holding a handkerchief against a bleeding cut, he sat down in the driver's seat. Then he got up, turned, and slowly said to all, "I'm okay, I'm okay, you're okay. I'll get going in a moment." With that, the bus driver lay down in the aisle between the two rows of passenger seats. He raised his feet and put them on top of the dashboard. He was still pressing his handkerchief against the cut on his forehead.

The couple looked at each other, and one whispered, "Should we stay on this bus or wait for the next one? It won't come till 2:30 p.m." This was a Turning Point in the life of the two oldsters. Married, they had been through 'thick and thin' together.

The bus driver was still shaky even after his five-minute rest with his feet elevated. He stood up and returned to the driver's seat. He said, "All aboard! This here Breeze Bus has a tail wind. I'll make up for lost time. Not to worry. I could drive back to Bend with my eyes closed." He added, "Let me concentrate on driving. I'm not hurt bad at all."

The two riders, sitting immediately behind the bus driver, looked at each. They wondered, "Do we get off the bus and call a cab, or do we stand by and wait for the afternoon bus? In any event the bus will be late getting to Bend even if we stay on the bus and continue on our trip to Bend hoping that the bus driver has recovered."

The road over Mount Hood, a very winding two-lane highway, had one lane in each direction. The highway twisted and turned and would be relatively difficult to drive, especially in the late spring when there was still snow on each side of the road above 10,000 feet.

This Turning Point, whether to get off the bus and wait or stay on the bus, was 'the sixty-four thousand-dollar question.' For people in their eighties, this decision was critical. Fearing the driver would hear their discussion, the two seniors talked very quietly about what had happened and what to do.

The bus driver got up, shook his head, drank some coffee out of his thermos, and seemed to have recovered. He said, "All aboard? Let's go."

The two people had made up their minds; it could be the Turning Point of their lives. The road to Bend was not going to be easy to drive. The five hours could be very terrifying.

The bus was unusually silent as the driver headed up the highway over Mount Hood. However, it was an uneventful drive up to Government Camp. The bus climbed to 11,000 feet. The passengers could see the top of Mount Hood. It was a beautiful ride, and the entrance to Government Camp was crowded with cars.

The bus driver pulled in, opened the door, and said, "Be back in ten minutes." He left the bus and walked slowly to the restroom.

The rest of the passengers disembarked and took a trip to the bathroom. There was still snow on the ground. The passengers went into the visitor's center, used the restroom, and bought coffee. The two senior citizens were the last passengers off the bus. They all looked at the bus driver when he entered the center. They wanted to be sure that he was okay. The cut had stopped bleeding. So far, so good.

The ten minutes passed in a flash. The oldsters got back onto the bus along with the others, took their seats, put on their seat belts, and said a silent prayer.

In two or three minutes, the bus driver climbed onto the bus, and said, "Hi ho, and away we go." He had a bandage over his head wound. He smiled a crooked smile and said, "We're ready to roll. We should be in Bend in another couple of hours. I'm okay and you are in safe hands… me!" He backed up the bus and re-entered the highway to Bend.

The conversation in the bus was muted. The twenty-odd passengers had stayed on the bus for the six-hour trip. They all realized that they had gambled and won. If they had waited for the next bus, it would have come along in six hours—not a pleasant choice, but a tolerable one. The choice was safety versus time.

The place where they would stop again would be when they crossed the Deschutes River, and there they would enter the last hour and a half of mountain high desert travel.

As the bus rolled along, it was a beautiful spring afternoon, and the snow had melted off the pavement. The bus driver was maneuvering without any difficulty. The pine and fir trees were white from the recent snowstorm, and the older couple realized that the worst was over. The two would soon be in their summer home at Eagle Crest.

At the last rest stop, the wounded bus driver did not leave his seat. He seemed okay and even assisted the passengers back onto the bus to continue the last stage of the trip. By that time, all the passengers seemed relatively calm, cool, and collected because of the way the bus was handled during the drive.

The Turning Point after the injury was a thing of the past. They had had a stressful six hours. The clumsy bus driver, the frightened passengers, and the decision of how to continue their trip to Bend had been made.

The Turning Point—this risky choice—could have been a headline in the Portland Oregonian, "Breeze Bus Belly Ups on Way to Mount Hood." No one would know the reason why.

The life threatening decision to go on or to wait for the next bus would be an unsolved mystery. The passengers had gambled and won. The oldsters had toyed with fate and won, in spite of snow on Mount Hood, a mountain road, and the clumsy bus driver.

## LIFE CAN BE CRUEL ACCIDENTALLY

*Two Generations Suffer the Same Fate*

WHILE SAM WAS LEARNING to be a 'racing dude,' Sam's father, Marv, was paralyzed during a dune buggy accident. Though doctors said Marv could never talk or walk again, after fifteen years of extensive rehab, he regained his speech and partial use of his legs and one arm. Sam called his father his idol because of his persistence in solving physical difficulties.

1997-1999

Teams Blueprint Racing

LP Racing

Treadway Racing

Starts 26

After his father's accident, Sam did not race for fifteen years. However, the lure of racing was in Sam's blood. At the age of thirty-three, Sam raced at a competitive level, supported by his business income. He dreamed of someday driving in the Indianapolis 500.

At an early age, Sam became successful as a businessman and in the field of racing. Sam first drove professionally in 1995 and won Rookie of the Year honors. In 1997, Sam became a rising star in the Indy league, raced in three consecutive Indianapolis 500s, and finished fifth in series points in 1999.

The Diamond of Life showed that Sam had the necessary Traits and Tendencies of personal courage and the intelligence to organize and

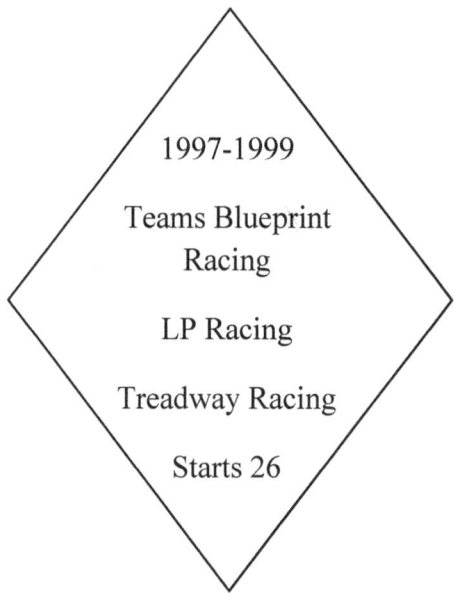

expand his father's business. He also wanted to honor the family name as a racecar driver. His driving efforts were supported by a successful business. Sam's work ethic duplicated that of his father, Marv.

In the 1999 'off season,' Sam was involved in a great tragedy! It occurred while he was testing his racer in preparation for the 2000 Indy Racing season. Sam suffered a horrendous crash at Walt Disney World Speedway. This accident made Sam a quadriplegic. He remained in a wheel chair after his life was spared.

At that juncture, Sam needed to find a new passion, and so he did. He founded 'Sam Schmidt Motorsports,' which became an extremely successful racing team in the Indy Lights Series.

Sam Motorsports entered a full-time Indy Car in 2001 and continued to participate annually in the Indianapolis 500. In addition to the motorsports enterprise, Sam established a Paralysis Foundation to further the cause of paralysis research in its treatment and quality of life issues. Sam now lives in the Las Vegas area. He travels extensively and has a very productive life.

# WHERE IS TED?

◆

*A Mysterious Disappearance*

TED GASSED UP WHILE Myrna went to the bathroom. When she returned, she looked for the travel trailer. It was gone. She was left stranded at a Texaco gas station. She went into the office at the gas station and asked the cashier, "Where is my husband? I can't find him. He was at the pump getting gas. I don't know what happened."

Myrna was in shock. Outside the office, she corralled the station manager and asked him the same questions. "Where is the travel trailer that was at the Number One pump?" The manager looked around and said, "I don't know, lady. A guy came in, paid his bill, and pulled out. It must have been five minutes ago. It must have been accidently. Sorry about that!"

This became a Turning Point in the couple's life. Ted and Myrna named it " A Bathroom Desertion."

First – Ted's wife had no money as it was in the travel trailer.

Second – Cell phones had not been developed yet.

Third – Ted and his wife Myrna were "gypsy-ing" and had no meeting place.

Fourth – Ted drove for three and a half hours before he realized Myrna wasn't in the trailer.

Ted's wife was frantic. Here she was near Joplin, Missouri, on the maiden voyage of a new pickup truck and travel trailer. Ted had driven off without her. She had left her purse in the vehicle and she had no money. What a predicament!

Ted's wife waited for about twenty minutes to see if Ted had realized she was not asleep in the travel trailer. The couple was on their way to Kansas City, Missouri. They had planned to continue driving west for five or six hours until they reached their next rest stop. What was Myrna he to do? No money, no phone, and 1,800 miles away from home.

Ted was listening to the radio as he travelled west. He thought his wife was taking an early morning nap. The sun had come up and he continued on his merry way. Ted drove through Kansas City on his way to Sonia, Kansas. Ted picked up the intercom mike and turned it on and said, "Myrna, Myrna are you there? Wake up—its ten o'clock." Not hearing any response he pulled over to the side of the road, got out of the truck, and went to the travel trailer. He opened the door, and Myrna was gone.

Ted said to himself, "My God, I accidentally left her back in Joplin, Missouri, at the Texaco station." He didn't know the phone number there or anything, so he must turn around. It would mean Ted had to drive the four hours back there to pick her up. He knew she must be frantic: no purse, no money, no way for her to get in touch with him. He said to himself, "I'm in deep trouble. Myna will kill me."

He turned the trailer around and headed back for the Joplin Texaco station, hoping in his heart she'd been able to let the kids at home in Sunland, California, know that she was stranded in Missouri. He stopped the truck at the nearest gas station and got out to use the pay phone to call back to Sunland, California, to see if Myrna had called in. The answer he got was negative. Ted told his oldest daughter, "If Myrna calls, tell her I'm on my way back to Joplin to pick her up."

He got into the truck and headed back to Joplin. He didn't even stop to get anything to eat or drink. It was four hours before he arrived back at the Texaco station. Not seeing her around, Ted asked where his wife was. The attendant said, "Oh, you must be the guy that the lady was asking about four hours ago." He added, "I sent her over to the café across the street to sit there and wait for you. I thought you would be back sooner than this, or I would have gone over and told her to call home."

Ted got back to the truck, got into the cab, and drove to the restaurant across the way. He went inside, and there was Myrna sitting at the table drinking a cup of coffee and talking to the waitress. She looked up and said, "Ted I've been waiting for you all afternoon. How far did you get before you found out I wasn't aboard?"

He said, "My God Myrna, you didn't tell me you were going potty. I would have waited, but I thought you were still taking a nap."

Myrna frowned and said, "Forget it Ted. Remember. We checked your Diamond of Life for raits and Tendencies . You scored high in being honest, upright, and true. You are loyal and loving. All these qualities lead to success, but...well, let's face it. You are a failure when it comes to memory and keeping an eye on your wife. "

So much for the Turning Point in Ted's life. When asked about his trip at his Rotary Club meeting, Ted said, "My deserting Myrna was more like a 'Turn Around.' I had to go back to get Myrna. Now I call it the Turning Point in our togetherness."

# HI-HO THE DAIRY-O, THE FARMER TAKES A LIFE

*Getting Away with Murder*

THE SUPERIOR COURT JUDGE said, "You stand before me accused of committing murder in the first degree. How do you plead?"

Morris, the defendant, answered, "Not guilty, your honor."

A murmur of disbelief passed through the courtroom. Being one of the leading ranchers in the small town of Stockton, California, Morris was being arraigned for killing a drinking buddy in a local bar. This crime was a major Turning Point in his life!

Morris had been owner of a cattle ranch for many years. At sixty-three years of age, he was six feet, three inches tall, and weighed a hefty two hundred forty pounds. Most nights he went to the same bar and sat on the same bar stool.

On the night in question, Morris entered the bar and shouted to the bartender, "Set 'em up Jake! Set 'em up for the house." He went to the bar and sat down next to Frank.

He said, "Hi, Frank," and they started a conversation.

Before continuing to talk, both men took the whisky shot that was before them and gulped it down.

Morris said, "Frank, let's not bitch until we've had another." Both men drank the second whisky down.

Several rounds later, the two men were drunk. Frank got up from the bar, mumbled that he had to go to the john, turned, and knocked over his drink. It soaked Morris. Speechless, Morris got red in the face. Being a big man, he got up and pushed Frank to the ground.

The two friends started to scuffle on the floor. The men pushed each other and rolled around. After a minute or two, Frank ended up on top. He stood up, turned to the bartender, and said, "That oughta take care of the bastard."

Morris, who was still on the floor, pulled his gun and shot Frank through the head. He said, "That oughta take care of that son of a bitch!"

Morris got up and staggered from the bar, which was in an uproar. The cops came and picked up Morris as he wobbled next to his car, trying to get into it and drive away from the scene.

Of course, Morris was accused of first-degree murder. He was put in jail and allowed to get an attorney to defend him. His attorney came the next day and said, "Morris you are in deep doo-doo. They're going to try you for first-degree murder, and you'll be hard pressed to defend yourself. If we lose the case, you will get the chair."

Morris looked at his attorney and said, "You are a smart mouth piece. Figure it out."

The attorney left the room with the following remark, "I'll be back in a couple of days, Morris, after I've had a chance to think over your defense."

After a couple of days, the attorney returned. He entered the jailhouse and met with Morris. The attorney said, "Morris, I'll enter a plea of not guilty. The only defense for your case is that it was an accident. You did what you did in self defense."

At the trial, Morris was asked to take the stand and relate the details of what happened that night at the bar.

His attorney asked Morris, "Why did you shoot your friend, Frank?"

Morris thought a minute and said, "I did it in self defense. I admit I shot Frank, but it was in self defense."

As he said this, the judge pounded his gavel on his desk and said, "Order in the court."

When the hubbub stopped, the judge listened to the balance of the testimony. The case was concluded, and the jury left the room to deliberate.

In about an hour, the jury filed back into the courtroom and entered the jury box. The foreman stood up and said, "We have reached a verdict your honor. Guilty as charged."

The whole courtroom gasped, and the newspaper reporters rushed from the room to spread the news.

The judge asked the bailiff to bring the defendant before the court. The judge looked at Morris for a minute or two and said, "Morris, you have been charged with first-degree murder and found guilty by a jury of your peers. Your defense was that Frank pushed you to the ground and was going to kill you. So you pulled your gun and killed Frank. Since the jury found you guilty, my sentence is as follows."

"You are guilty as charged; however, due to extenuating circumstances, I will grant you clemency. You have been in prison awaiting trial for more than a year. I am modifying your sentence. Your punishment is satisfied by the time served. Case dismissed."

Thus Morris faced the Turning Point of his life—a jury's decision that had gone against him! However, he was a lucky man. He had a good lawyer, and he beat the odds. Morris's defense was that lying with his back against the floor was the same as having his back against a wall without the possibility of escape. Thus, the judge sentenced him to a prison term that was satisfied by his time in jail.

In retrospect, the Diamond of Life trait favoring Morris was his character. He was a first-time offender who had given much to Stockton. He always supported its community needs by belonging to a service club called Rotary International, whose motto was "Service Over Self."

His murder was his first run-in with the law. Morris met his Turning Point during the fight of his life and ended it by 'getting away with murder.'

2

# BATTLES

"**B**OMBS AWAY" WAS THE design painted on the side of the B-24 bomber. The heavy bomber was completing its 50th mission. This mantra was yelled over the intercom by the crew. It was heard over the roar of the engines. It was the last time the 'Bombs Away' logo would be seen in the sky over Italy. The crew was completing its tour of duty.

The Bombardier shouted, "Head for the barn." It was a Turning Point for the B-24 and its crew. It was the last battle this crew would ever fly. It is true that the largest number of battles is the result of wars.

But another type of battle and its Turning Point involve economic issues. An example of this was demonstrated when a young couple escaped the wrath of the Russian Czar by emigrating to the 'Land of the Kangaroo' and their son battled to become Lord Mayor of Melbourne.

Furthermore a social Turning Point is the final example with a different twist. An Austrian serving as an interpreter during the 'Battle of the Bulge' interrogated prisoners captured by the Americans. He saved his company from destruction. This was a Turning Point that he never forgot. Nine of such battle stories follow.

## BORN WITH A STRAWBERRY PATCH

*A Palm Shaped Birthmark Covers Forehead and Cheek*

IT WAS DAWN IN the city of Minsk, Russia, and a young couple stood on the side of a dusty road looking west. Gary and his wife, Minna, had been married for several years. They had one child, a little boy under three. Gary knew he faced an unknown future. They were emigrating to America.

Gary was a fifth-generation plumber, his family's trade. The couple was Jewish, and after the Nazis almost conquered the Soviet Union, Gary wanted to start anew. Going to the United States was Gary's dream. This Turning Point was possible because the future looked promising.

Gary weighed the plusses and the minuses against the Diamond of Life standards. He mentally measured benefits of his planned move to a new country. He wanted the freedom to work as a plumber. His review indicated that this improvement alone would make going to the United States worth the effort.

This move would be hampered by Gary's a birthmark on his face. It was strawberry in color and the size of his palm. Gary had an arranged marriage with Minna, who bore him a healthy son. Gary was not only intelligent but also 'street smart.' Best of all, Gary had the plumbing trade as a skill. He and his wife Minna had scrimped and saved enough money to travel to America.

He had no contacts in the United States except a second cousin who lived in Southern California. Gary had contacted him about his move. The cousin wrote back that construction was slow in the Los Angeles area. He said that Gary's plumbing experience in Russia would not allow him to work as a licensed plumber. It would take three years working as an apprentice to do so. To make matters worse, Gary and his wife spoke no English. Despite these drawbacks Gary said, "Minna, let's take a chance."

The decision made, the family boarded the bus to Leningrad. After the bus trip, Gary and his family boarded a boat going to New York City. Their final destination was Southern California. The travel money was about gone when the threesome got off the Union Pacific in Los Angeles. They had come halfway around the world to find freedom and opportunity. Leaving the Soviet Union represented a major Turning Point!

In a strange country, speaking no English, halfway around the world, and having one contact in Southern California, Gary called up his cousin in Los Angeles.

His cousin said, "Mozel tof! You made it. Welcome to Los Angeles. Ruthie and I will put you up for a few days while you get settled." He added, "Your family members have been plumbers for four generations. There is work in housing construction, but without a Union Card, you can't get a job.

Gary had been involved in the family trade of plumbing since he was sixteen years old. He thought that he would be able to get a plumbing job quickly as it was just before the Korean War. The housing market in the United States had been booming, and Gary had an occupation that was in great demand—that of being a Journeyman Plumber in Russia.

Gary's three-year apprenticeship in the plumbing trade passed quickly. Gary's disfigurement was ignored by the Plumber's Union. Luckily, his experience in Russia made him eligible to practice his trade after getting his city license.

Gary became the plumber of choice in the San Fernando Valley. The Turning Points in Gary's life were leaving Russia, going to a new country, learning English, establishing a successful business, and overcoming a birthmark, the strawberry patch on his face. Hat's off to Gary. He is a fifth-generation tradesman to ply the plumber's trade. It shows that drive, ability, and common sense pay off. Being born with a strawberry patch was no problem. Gary ignored his disfigurement. He and his family lived a full and productive life in the U.S.A. Gary became a success!

# KEEP THE HOME FIRES BURNING

*A B24 Mission by Captain Jim and Crew*

"**K**EEP THE COFFEE POT On The Stove." This was pilot Jim's wish as he turned his B- 24 and headed back to the air field where he was stationed. His bomber, "TO HELL WITH U" and crew had successfully taken out the Ploesti Oil Fields and deprived the Germans of much needed petroleum fuel. Soon the war was over. Jim and the seven men that he commanded returned home to wait until the enemies surrender was received. It was not long in coming.

After military service, Jim studied to become a mechanical engineer. Jim had been a premedical student before his air force gig. He liked the outdoors. He liked lots of danger and excitement. He was 'jazzed' by flying big bombers. He had flown fifty missions before he trekked home.

His girlfriend, who later became his wife, worked in the San Fernando Valley. Their home was new when the newlyweds bought it.

Jim lived in that house into his eighties, when he started to experience poor health. His age and the onset of Alzheimer disease began to plague him.

In the summer of 2007, he could not live alone any more. Jim sent for his adopted daughter. The event would become the Turning Point of his life.

Before Donna arrived, Jim had been calling the local paramedics at least once every month because of gastro-intestinal problems. Occasionally, Jim drove himself to the Emergency Care Hospital when he felt sick, and many times it was a false alarm.

The increased frequency of such incidents and his living alone made his 'tarnished' years unbearable. Jim informed Donna of his worsening health. Although father and daughter had seen each other very few times over the previous twenty years, Donna made up her mind to go to the San Fernando Valley to live with him.

After Jim returned from the war, he and his wife had moved to a new home in Encino. Jim worked as an Engineer at Northrop Aviation. Not being able to conceive a child had become a Turning Point in the couple's life. Jim and his wife began to drink booze. Soon the couple became alcoholics. They found the bottle had no bottom. Drinking problem persisted even after Donna graduated from high school and moved away.

Jim and his wife both became alcoholics. Jim had trouble until his wife died of the DTs in 1971. She had been drinking for twenty plus years, and Jim matched her drink for drink. Jim took the pledge, became a survivor, and kissed alcohol goodbye. He never took another drink. Jim did the impossible. He dried himself out.

In the 1980s and 1990s, after he retired from his job at Northrop, he lived a stress-free, peaceful life. Then Jim needed help. Donna had moved to Seattle, Washington, and out of Jim's life almost twenty years before. She was his only hope. Donna was the closest person he could call on. Jim, in desperation, asked Donna to come to live in the Los Angeles area. He felt that her assisting him during his terminal years would be ideal. Reluctantly, she and her husband-to-be moved to Los Angeles. Their return became Jim's last Turning Point.

With the tail pipes roaring a cloud of smoke, two Harleys roared into the driveway. It was a strange way the two angels from Seattle arrived. Donna's return marked the first time in a year that Jim could relax. Donna assisted Jim by relieving him of all his cares. Her help was a little 'mind boggling' since she had not seen him for so long. He really needed her being there during his terminal years. Jim recognized no one and he was incapable of taking care of himself.

In reviewing Jim's past, Donna had moved out of Jim's life. Despite this and Jim's health difficulties, an unbiased analysis would show that he had courage. He had faced the enemy in World War II and had come back safely. He suffered health problems in his declining years. It made them his 'tarnished years.'

In addition, the Diamond of Life attributes include attention to detail (learning to fly), skill (working as an engineer for many years), and good luck (coming back from WW II without a scratch), to name a few. It is apparent that such traits and abilities served him well during his post-war career. The symbol on Jim's headstone could be, "To Hell With U," he was so independent. May his soul rest in peace.

## RANGER TAKES THE VACATION OF A LIFETIME

*From Para-Trooper to Plumber in the U.S.A.*

R ANGER, A SOUTH AFRICAN plumber, traveled from Johannesburg to the United States for a two-week holiday. It was before Easter week in 1978. He had always wanted to visit the United States. Sometimes a casual glance at a newspaper ad changes one's entire life. Ranger looked at the South African Johannesburg Sunday paper. Staring back at him was a full-page ad showing an almost naked blonde saying, "Stay ten days with me in Los Angeles - See Hollywood and the Pacific Ocean and have fun." South African Airlines ad continued, "We'll fly you there and back for less than one thousand dollars."

Ranger was a paratrooper. He had been on the Namibian border for two years protecting South Africa from invaders. He was tired and a month's holiday was due him from his military duty. After re-reading the offer, Ranger went to his bank and paid for his ticket. He knew his leave would be during April, just before Easter. He wanted to be back by that time. Ranger was completing his stint of a two-year duty, and he had planned to re-enlist when he returned from the United States.

As he settled into his seat on the South African Airline, he sipped a complimentary cocktail. He remembered what the last two years as a paratrooper had been like. Being a young man of twenty-seven, he had felt that he was entitled to this holiday, no matter how much it cost. Ranger thought he might write a book about his experiences in Namibia.

The Namibian rebels on the border had plunged into South Africa immediately north of the post Ranger had been occupying. He had killed nineteen of the invaders personally during his duty. All these thoughts were whirling around in his mind. He was exhausted and went to sleep on the plane with visions of a beautiful starlet racing around in his mind.

The flight of twenty-three hours was over. Ranger got off the plane at LAX, grabbed his bag, and headed for Santa Monica and the beach. The South African Airline put him up in a nice hotel, and Ranger proceeded to 'do the town.'

He went to Warner Brothers Studio, he went to Disneyland, and he went to the downtown area. He saw Chinatown and most of the other 'must sees.' He went to Beverly Hills. He went to Hollywood and walked down Hollywood Boulevard. He ogled the attractive women walking down the street. He ate at fancy restaurants and thoroughly enjoyed the time, so much so that at the end of ten days, he sent a note to his brother who was in Cape Town and told him to pack up the rest of Ranger's personal belongings and send them to California. He was not returning to Africa.

Ranger planned to stay in Los Angeles and make his way in the world. This was to be a Turning Point in Ranger's life. It was an irresistible urge to do something bold and brash before it was too late. Ranger had entered the South African Army. Then he had tried the plumbing trade. Now Ranger looked around the Los Angeles area for an apprentice job while he got a plumbing license.

Ranger moved to the San Fernando Valley because it was more reasonable to live there. He procured a green card so that he could stay in the United States temporarily while his application for permanent citizenship was being processed.

His apprenticeship was with the Moe Plumbing Company. Ranger practiced and learned his trade so he could get his license as a journeyman rather than be an apprentice.

Ranger was "a big guy." He was six feet, three inches tall, and weighed over two hundred ten pounds. He led a clean life, didn't smoke, and worked hard to make his way in Los Angeles. He wanted to be a Success, so much he could almost 'taste it.'

As part of his plumbing activities, Ranger became familiar with the white plastic pipe and fittings that were being used in the United States. He learned how to read blueprints. He learned what items would be on the test he was required to take to become a journeyman in the plumbing trade.

While he was attending night school in Los Angeles, he met an attractive young lady and dated her for a year before getting married. It turned out that this marriage was a mistake and a Turning Point in his life. Even though he had a daughter during this hectic alliance, Ranger finally 'had it' when he found out his wife was 'playing around.' He filed for divorce and it was granted.

During his marriage he changed jobs. He worked with a local plumber in the San Fernando Valley. Ranger then opened his own plumbing business. A few months later he sent for his brother from South Africa. The two brothers formed a partnership in the plumbing business. He was able to arrange credit to buy tools, buy a truck, and support himself as the owner of a business, rather than working for somebody else. This was a major Turning Point in Ranger's life.

During the next ten years of his life, he met a friend from South Africa who knew of his paratrooper experiences in Namibia and Angola. He helped Ranger during the next five-year period as he expanded his plumbing business.

By 1970, he had become very successful. Ranger has had a plethora of Turning Points with personal Traits and Tendencies to match. His coming to the United States was triggered by an ad so this shows decisiveness. His courage and bravery is shown by his service in the paratroopers in South Africa. Ranger's intelligence is shown by his ability to master a plumbing trade, and his initiative is shown by his starting his own business and becoming successful. A review of the life and struggles of Ranger shows he is the epitome of success. All his accomplishments were triggered by Ranger's reading an ad in the Sunday paper.

Ranger felt in his bones that the Diamond of Life's Traits and Tendencies had pointed him toward his goal of success. His courage (serving as a paratrooper), his decisiveness (acting upon visiting the United States), and his hard work (working and learning his trade at night), all contributed to Ranger's success.

Ranger made his vacation a vacation of a lifetime. To sum it all up, Ranger, a South African immigrant, said, "I am really thankful that I read the Sunday ad and vacationed in America twenty-odd years ago."

# STEEL YOURSELF FOR TROUBLE AHEAD

◆

*Family-Owned Business Expansion During WWII*

PEARL HARBOR, HAWAII WAS devastated. The Second World War had started. The Rosenblatt brothers were distributors for United States Steel (USX). They sold steel throughout the Intermountain West. In 1944, the Rosenblatt brothers had a decision to make. Did they want to work directly for USX? Their answer was, "No." They felt that this steel giant would terminate their contract any time. To be farsighted, they went to the eastern part of the United States to find another steel maker to represent. During wartime, the brothers' search was fruitless.

The Rosenblatt brothers faced this Turning Point 'head on,' and they became regional executives for USX. The choice of USX was logical. USX was much larger and better known than Republic Steel and other competitors. Both brothers had ambition, (advancement possibilities at USX), vulnerability (USX was stronger than Republic Steel), and good timing (USX had been waiting in the wings and were anxious to buy the steel plant from the government). Considering each possibility, the brothers chose to work for USX and had used the Diamond of Life method of making a decision.

Their sons, Donny and Bernie, were cousins. The two boys worked at Rosenblatt Brothers during the summer. They learned about steel from the ground up. The two graduated from the University of Utah and each had a different aim in life. Bernie wanted to produce the steel that Donny would sell it.

Immediately after graduating from the University of Utah in 1941, the two got jobs with their parents. Both were exempt from military service because they were in the steel business, a defense industry.

In 1943, the federal government had a steel mill in Orem, Utah. It was called the Geneva Plant. The United States government wanted to either close the steel mill or sell it. U.S. Steel bought the plant.

The Rosenblatt brothers had a decision to make. This decision would be a Turning Point in their lives. If the rumors were true, namely, that USX wanted to buy the Geneva plant and have a production facility there, it would kill the distributorship that the brothers had. Thus, the choice the brothers had was to fight USX (keep Rosenblatt's open) or sell out to USX and join USX as executives of the steel mill.

The elder Rosenblatts were in their fifties and the two cousins were in their early twenties. The steel business was in a 'hard hit' U.S. industry due to excess production capacity. USX was big enough to buy the Geneva Steel Mill from the U.S. government. For the Rosenblatt Brothers to compete with USX was not possible. The two founding brothers decided that there was a niche in the Intermountain West market for the Geneva plant to produce for the market.

Bernie and Donny could make a relatively small steel facility develop into a good business because the big mills, like big steel, could not cut their production to a size that could be profitable the way a small company could. This was a novel approach to a very difficult situation.

Donny and Bernie decided that this was what they wanted to operate. They could make the steel from ore that was available in southern Utah and coke that was available in the state of Wyoming, which was nearby. With USX's capital and the Rosenblatt marketing capabilities, the principle of 'too big to fail' would be changed to 'too small to overcome.'

After careful study with their accountants and finding production personnel that came from steel plants in the east, the two cousins created a clever merchandising scheme. The plant was built and completed just before the Second World War.

Donny and Bernie divided the new company's operations so that one handled the production and the other handled the sales. Bernie would be Mr. Inside, and Donny would be the sales manager for the new firm.

There were many problems in getting started, but by 1939, the glitches had been worked out. The new company, Geneva Steel, was able to make, sell, and deliver small orders of steel. The major firms, such as

U.S. Steel, Carnegie Steel, and Pittsburg Steel, could not handle this business because of the size of the order that they could process.

In the early forties, Henry Kaiser was setting up a shipbuilding program. He needed steel. At this stage of World War II there was a military need for thousands of tanks to be used in the European theatre of a World War. These tanks required steel. Donny and Bernie were involved in expanding their facilities to meet the demand. They had to decide whether and how to expand their steel company to handle the U.S. War Department needs. This growth would require help from the United States government. How fast and how much would depend on raising private capital in the western part of the United States. Such capital investments would come from the larger cities.

The discussions about expansions, and the best way of doing this, brought the two cousins to loggerheads. Donny, who was in charge of sales, wanted to utilize this growth to expand their operations to all thirteen western states with a sales force to match. On the other hand, the production end of the steel mill was involved in providing the steel. The customers' orders must meet schedule if the company was to be production-oriented. It seemed to Bernie that the war effort would be over within a few years. Therefore, such growth should be on a gradual or conservative method. It was strictly the sales viewpoint versus that of the production division. This Turning Point would concern the direction of Rosenblatt Steel.

Fast forward ahead three or four years. The war was winding down, and it looked like Donny's sales' efforts would be increased and production would be reduced because of less warship building, fewer tanks, and the production of other military products. In addition, the size of orders favored the old-line Pittsburgh-oriented U.S. Steel operations. So it came down to which of the two cousins would prevail. The projection for the future was hard to estimate, and it would require the definition of what the goals were for the steel company.

As Donny saw it, his goal would be to build a sales organization and to make the production of steel keep up with the pace of sales. His eventual goal would be to sell the whole company to one of the basic steel manufacturers. He thought that he and Bernie would eventually work for, but not own, the steel company.

On the other hand, Bernie wanted to have the production end of the company be expanded as the sales expanded. Should the war end suddenly, they could lower production and still make money. Bernie's plan would be not to expand production facilities, but to increase the use of overtime and third shift operation as needed until they reached the need for a 24/7 operation. The Turning Point of growth at a tremendous rate required that sales be the factor to establish how big and how fast Geneva Steel would grow.

The other model would be to have production be the basic consideration as the company grew. Such business conflicts and Turning Points are prevalent throughout all industries, but in the steel industry, which requires mammoth capital investment and substantial new plant additions, they put a premium on which model to use.

These Turning Points, emphasizing growth, are tough in a family-controlled, expanding business. They involved the cousins having opposite ideas of which way to go. This applied even in the steel business, in which one must be ready for trouble ahead. Rapid growth was needed while demand varied and supply took time to increase. This was true in the case of Geneva Steel. World War II started in 1940 with Pearl Harbor. Demand was the factor and the government would fund all capital required.

The wartime operations reflected the similarities and differences. According to the Diamond of Life theory, timing was very important— the when of change, the how of financing, and the why of purpose. It was possible because the government was guaranteeing loans for government production plants and equipment. It made supply needs the major factor. The Rosenblatt Brothers, during and after World War II, were made of Steel and found it meant trouble ahead for the company!

# THE SCRAPPIEST MAN IN TOWN

◆

*Tale of Success in a 'Dirty Business'*

THE SHELLS WERE BURSTING overhead, and Bill, a G.I., was engaged in the 'Battle of the Bulge.' He was a member of the Offices of Special Services, the OSS. Even though Bill was an Austrian by birth, he had been a U.S. citizen for several years. He had been drafted for World War II. When the top brass found out Bill could speak German fluently, they transferred him to the front lines fighting the Germans.

Bill had the Turning Point of his life when he was transferred to the OSS and did interrogation and translation for his Army units as they advanced toward Berlin. It was the Nazi's last attempt to win the war.

After the war, Bill went back to the United States. He landed in New York. Thanks to a service buddy, Bill was able to find a job in New York at the Fine Jewelry Building on Fifth Avenue.

After a couple of years of showroom selling, the owners of the showroom put Bill on the road. This meant that he traveled between New York and Chicago, contacting department and jewelry stores in the Midwest.

On one of these visits, he was in Cincinnati, Ohio, showing his line of merchandise in one of the finest hotels. He attended this spring jewelry convention. On the last day of the event, the managers of the show gave a dinner dance. People from the major department and jewelry stores of Ohio, Pennsylvania, Indiana, and Illinois attended. Bill's company, one of the exhibitors, was asked to attend.

Bill went to the party. When the orchestra played, Bill got up and asked one of the ladies sitting at his table to dance. She loved to dance. Bill also loved to dance. The two spent most of the evening dancing their little hearts out. The young lady, Charlotte, was destined to marry him six months after they met. It was a life-altering Turning Point for Bill.

Charlotte, Bill's new wife, told him that she did not want to be a salesman's widow while he traveled the Midwest territory. The young couple chose going to Los Angeles, California. Bill agreed to move if he could borrow money from his in-laws. With this seed money, Bill spent six months while he was out finding a new occupation. Moving to a strange town, even though it provided opportunity and its economy was expanding rapidly, became a Major Turning Point in the life of the couple.

The newlyweds went there in April, and by September, Bill had found a job. It was not in the field that he knew, selling jewelry gifts and other items. It was calling on aircraft manufacturers, such as Lockheed, and picking up the scrap aluminum and selling it back to the aluminum smelters. This scrap was to be reprocessed. Bill was one of the first environmentalists.

The couple moved to the San Fernando Valley, and Bill started storing and selling aluminum scrap. He collected aircraft parts from Lockheed, Martin, Douglas, and the other aircraft manufacturers that were located throughout Southern California. Bill would pick up the scrap aluminum and other metals. He would take the scrap to a fenced yard where it was stored and sold.

After doing this for a year, Bill decided that he could grow his business if he bought a truck and rented a yard near Lockheed Aircraft Company. He borrowed the money from his father-in-law and purchased a truck. Bill started making the rounds of all the manufacturing facilities in the eastern part of the San Fernando Valley. He picked up at Lockheed. He picked up at Industrial Metals, and he picked up in the various firms that were the producers of metal items. These included pots and pans, home building materials, etc. Thus, the establishment of Bill's business was a success.

Furthermore, Bill had selected Burbank, California, as a place to start his scrap metal business. His first customer had been Lockheed Aircraft Corporation, which was a source of aluminum scrap from the airplanes the company produced.

As the years rolled by, Bill became very efficient. His scrap yard was number one in the Valley. The next Turning Point occurred during the Korean War. Eisenhower had been a wartime president, and the aircraft manufacturing in California was winding down. The need for airplanes for the army and air force was bleak. Therefore, Bill, the astute manager, decided to go into other types of surplus materials just as the electronics industry was becoming very active and growing. The expansion into electronic surplus was another activity pursued by Bill.

One of the amazing Turning Points now facing Bill was to buy his own building and scrap yard. Bill expanded his operation. He called it Apex Metal and Electronics Surplus Company.

In his sixty-year career Bill was versatile. He displayed his interest in, and becoming involved with, community activities. Bill joined the Rotary Club and established an annual scholarship award for the Sun Valley Chamber of Commerce. In 1995, Bill became the Man of the Year for the United Chambers of Commerce.

Owning his own facilities meant expanding his scrap yard. It became a vital goal for Bill. He purchased, utilized, and resold the real estate needed to run his business. This was a great Turning Point in his life. Bill was working twelve hours a day. He had his wife run the office. It was a family enterprise.

A new field of endeavor appeared on the horizon. TV shows were on the video screen. These shows had stage sets, which needed realistic furniture and fixtures. Bill's surplus items were real. The writers and directors went to Apex Electronics to select the items they needed for a show. It was Bill's having a tremendous selection of surplus electronic equipment available that brought in these set decorators. TV programs such as "Star Trek" and "30,000 Leagues Under the Sea" used Bill's leased equipment. These were long running TV series. Rent rather than buy became Bill's edge in the movie and TV business. The TV producers saved income taxes in doing so. The studios could write off all the costs if they leased, but not if they purchased. This made Bill's business explode.

In the early 21st century, Bill reached his retirement age, but he felt that he should work a little longer so that his oldest son, Don, could take over the reins. Lengthening his career actually ended his life.

Bill's Diamond of Life attitudes and abilities included intelligence (his command of three languages), personality (telling a joke or good story), knowledge (knowing electronics and thousands of part numbers), and versatility (performing many jobs well). On the other hand, he was rigid in his beliefs, he was an ultra-conservative, he did not take criticism well, he was stubborn, and he worked too hard.

Bill lived a great life, had many friends, and had many Turning Points, most of which led to success. If this sounds like a testimonial rather than a story about Turning Points, Bill deserved all of the accolades he received. He proved to his community, his family, and his friends that he was truly the 'Scrappiest Man in Town.'

## GARBAGE IN, GARBAGE NOT OUT

*Hans Made Lemonade out of Lemons*

"TURN IT OFF! TURN it off! There's water all over the floor. Bert, you better call Hans again!" This happened every day or so. Hans would be called to repair the test model of a newly developed kitchen appliance, the Waste King Garbage Disposal.

Twenty minutes after the call, an SUV drove up to a house in Beverly Hill. A medium-sized, graying man rushed into the kitchen of the upscale home. He put his bag of plumbing tools on the floor, grabbed the mop, and started getting the water mopped up.

Hans came into the living room and in a guttural voice with a heavy German accent said, "Bert, it's the same damn thing. The float is stuck in the 'on' position, but the motor and water valves don't turn themselves off. I'll get a new replacement disposal from the factory!"

Hans left the house muttering to himself. This was a problem Hans never faced in Germany. He had designed many automatic systems on machines that turned the water and motor off automatically. However, this was his boss's home, and he was testing the Waste King Garbage Disposer. It was the second time in a week that the appliance did not operate properly. Given Manufacturing Company was testing the prototype. The test had been a failure so far, and it happened to the owner of Given Mfg., Bert Given.

As an escapee from Germany before the start of World War II, Hans was ineligible to join the United States Military or to be drafted. He had fled the Nazis just before the book burning in the streets of Berlin. He was thirty-two and had left his wife and family while he rearranged his life in the United States. He was very well educated. He had received an advanced degree in engineering while in Germany and had been promoted to assistant plant manager of a small motors electric motor factory in Dusseldorf, a facility that made motors for washing machines, refrigerators, and other home appliances.

Hans arrived in Los Angeles in the summer of 1936. The world was suffering from too much Hitler and not enough business activity. Hans had been supplied with the names of companies who could provide a job so he could reunite with his family. One of the first companies he called on was Given Manufacturing and Machine Tool Company. He had a letter of introduction from his German employer. He had gone to see the president of the Los Angeles Chamber of Commerce and asked him about Given. As so often happens, the Chamber of Commerce members were friends of Bert Given. Bert interviewed Hans and hired him on the spot.

In the twelve years after Hans joined Given Manufacturing as a design engineer, he had sent for his family, worked in the design department of Given, and advanced up the organization to become the head of new products design.

By 1948, the pent-up demand for consumer items, such as household appliances, had been satisfied. However, the demand for housing was still unsatisfied, and consumer appliances that could be installed into the new homes of housing tracts were in great demand.

During wartime, Hans worked on a new consumer product called a garbage disposer. He designed and personally tested the Waste King Garbage Disposal. While working to perfect this device, he became the Plant Manager of a factory being built by Given Manufacturing Company. This building was to manufacture garbage disposers of a new design with automatic shut off when the garbage had been ground up and flushed down the drain.

Hans would not only continue his development efforts, but also be the production manager of the Waste King Garbage disposals division. Production of one thousand units per day could be assembled. The engineered units were tested for a six-month period. The decision was to open the plant and build one hundred twenty-four units per day.

The first twenty-four units were given to friends of Burt Given. They promised to use the disposers in their kitchen for a six-month period. Meanwhile, the plant would produce the units. The tests would take place in the kitchens of the friends, and any malfunction would be reported to Bert in writing. The test involved installation by a licensed plumber in the tester's kitchen, and Given Co. would supervise such installation. Solving the complaints was Hans's responsibility.

Hans was to make the test units functional. He designed the units carefully and initiated the use of an automatic switch to turn off the water and the unit as soon as the garbage was pulverized and flushed down the drain. Hans would investigate any problems to find out what happened and why.

The tests went on during the next few months, and Hans was inundated with calls that the units worked for a while but had jammed up and were not working properly. He was told that the automatic switches were not turning the water and the disposer off. The problem units were replaced and the tests went on.

After several months the second test in kitchens had the same problem. The units would freeze up. The water was not being shut off, and it became a major problem for Hans and the Given Mfg. Company.

A redesign of the unit was undertaken by Hans. He personally went to each house that reported a freeze up of the unit. He'd replace the unit, take the poorly functioning unit back to his laboratory, and repair it.

This test program was a Turning Point in Hans's life because his fame and potential fortune would depend on his solving this problem. Hans checked each incident. In observing a freeze up and the water running, Hans decided to take drastic action to cure the problem. He removed the float system and the automatic water turn-off from the designed unit.

The solution was simple and effective because the simplified replacement unit worked like a charm. The repaired units were retested showed no failures. The units did not freeze up because they were operated manually as far as turning on and turning off the grinding motor. Thus, the problem was solved.

Hans had faced his major Turning Point while in the United States. He was given an award from the Clean Plate Club for developing one of the important household items to make housework easier. So it was with Hans, where his effort to solve the problem was direct, and the way he faced it was a thing of beauty. His Turning Point was to learn from the past (test failures), think for the future (solve the problem), and live in the present (get it done now). Hans disproved the theory of 'garbage in garbage out' by successfully solving the nasty household garbage by washing it down the drain.

# THE THREE JS FROM SALINAS

*Jack, John, and Jerry—Three Young Men, Stanford, and Success*

S ALINAS IS THE SALAD bowl of the nation. It is a small city near San Francisco, California. It has the right climate and the right farms to grow half of all lettuce consumed by Americans. In order to raise lettuce, the farmland near Salinas is ideal. It has sandy soil, and the sky is overcast much of the time providing cool weather.

Jack, John, and Jerry (the three Js) were the sons of a very successful insurance broker during the Second World War. He was located in Salinas, and many of the lettuce growers bought life insurance from him. He had made enough money to send all three sons to Stanford University.

Immediately after WWII, the three Js picked up their lives again. Jack was the eldest son. He was married and had one child. He had attended Stanford and graduated. He continued his business education by getting his master's degree in business administration. He majored in accounting and became CPA. His education, college degrees, and careerwere Turning Points. Seventeen years later, Jack experienced the ultimate Turning Point—dying from a heart attack in his early forties.

John, the second J, also went to Stanford. At the end of WWII, he decided to major in business and entered the retail business in Salinas. John was an extrovert. He was a 'hail fellow, well met.' John's father wanted John to return to Salinas and work awhile before studying law. John agreed. This became a Turning Point in his life.

John decided to open a men's store. He felt, because of his father's reputation in Salinas, he could become very successful and might even start a chain of men's stores throughout California. He opened John's Men's Apparel on the main street of Salinas. Rather than being a success, John's store failed, and it was back to law school for John.

Two years later John graduated from Stanford Law School with honors. A short time later, he passed the bar exam and became an attorney. In his law class, he met two students who came from Fresno in central California. The three new lawyers decided to practice in Fresno.

John liked Fresno. It was a 'boom-town.' John's law practice flourished and a Turning Point of his life occurred. The two friends from Fresno decided to open a cemetery. One pony-upped the land, one came up with the money, and John provided the legal work.

The cemetery became a gold mine. From that date onward, John became wealthy. His move to Los Angeles, his adoption of seven children, and his investment in Los Angeles real estate for his heritable trust, were his attempts to atone for his sins. Success was John's Turning Point, which validated the old saying, "If at first you don't succeed, try, try again."

Jerry, the third and youngest J to attend Stanford, had a different path to follow. With WWII over, Jerry returned to Salinas to find his father at fifty-one suffering from a stroke. Jerry enrolled in Stanford the month before his dad died. This was a life altering Turning Point. He had to go to Stanford and help his mother recover from his dad's demise. Jerry sold the house in Salinas, bought a house in Palo Alto, and lived there while getting his law degree.

Jerry had the most ambitious dreams of success. He wanted to become an attorney. He planned to move to Los Angeles after passing the state bar exam. Joining an established attorney's office to get experience, Jerry became a full-fledged business counsel in Southern California. The choice of where to live and how to proceed on the road of life was the Turning Point for Jerry.

Jerry went to Los Angeles and married a very wealthy young lady he met at Stanford. He entered the field of law, specializing in Real Estate Development. Jerry and John were very close to each other, both as brothers and friends. They both lived in Westwood, California, which is very near UCLA.

Jerry's career blossomed as Mark Taper became one of the most successful developers in the Los Angeles. Taper created Lakewood, a community that eventually had many thousands of homes. This certainly was a Turning Point in Jerry's life because being Taper's attorney and having opportunities to invest with Mark Taper in some of his projects. Jerry became wealthy, and of the three brothers, perhaps the most successful.

Thus, the Turning Points in all three lives, the three Js from Salinas, show that with great education, effort, and persistence in wanting to succeed—the three traits most applicable from the Diamond of Life—led each man to health, wealth and happiness. What more could anyone ask?

## WAR HERO FINDS A LOVE MATCH

*Bill Learns How to Mix War and Peace as Day Follows Night*

"HEAD FOR HOME!" BILL heard his navigator shout over the intercom. Flying over Berlin, the pilot watched as his squadron made a lazy 180° turn and headed back to England. It was May 1944, and the last mission Bill would fly before returning to the States for reassignment.

Bill thought to himself, "I really need some leave. It has been a long haul. This last year—flying twenty-five missions—has been an exciting time in my life. Completing this run will be an important Turning Point in my life, a major one at that!"

As a matter of fact, Bill had saved the money he earned during the Second World War. He had flown his missions over Western Europe. He came back to the Southern California area and a booming economy.

Bill was a war hero returning home to friends and strangers who were ready, willing, and able to employ him, but he thought he should complete his education by returning to university. He was treading water. His savings, coupled with the G.I. Bill, would last him through college. It was buy a business, or go back to school.

Bill was an innovative sort of guy and he took the money he had saved and made arrangements to borrow more if he needed it. He negotiated this potential loan from Union Bank so he was able to become a 'looky-loo.' He spent the next six months looking at businesses, real estate properties, and new home developments in the San Fernando Valley.

Every deal he liked he ran it by his advisor at Union Bank. He soon discovered that the bank was interested in his money (keep your savings at Union) and advised him not to buy properties either developed or undeveloped.

This was Bill's second career-in-the-making and a Turning Point in his life. Did he want to become an entrepreneur, or did he want to go back to school and become an aeronautical engineer?

Bill went to his pastor who told him that he was approaching thirty and should go back to school. He said he based his advice on Bill's character, intelligence and planning abilities as shown by his air force duty and the Diamond of life.

Fortunately, Bill found the woman of his dreams, but she was afraid that Bill would lose all his money by making foolish investments. She said to Bill, "Go back to school, get your degree, get a good job, and I'll marry you." He did as she asked, and he had a happy, middle-class life. His two children, a boy and a girl, became his marriage bonuses.

Bill's was the typical war story—a United States Air Force B-17 pilot with twenty-five successful bombing strikes went home to find his old flame had found a new match.

Major Bill found a new love, returned to university, married, and had two kids. He became a chemical engineer and a family man in his old hometown. Sounds like a dull life, but it was exactly what Bill, the war hero, needed.

# UP, UP, AND AWAY

*Tall Tales of a Pilot in World War II*

"HERE WE GO INTO the wild blue yonder," sang the nineteen-year-old who volunteered for Air Force training. David had wanted to become a pilot. Almost everyone his age wanted to become a pilot. It was the most glamorous career and appealed to the young women that pilots dated. Having made this decision before his birthday in 1942 , he then faced a timing decision. He had come to a Turning Point in his life. It had to do with WW II. Should he volunteer to become an air force cadet immediately, or should he get drafted into the army and request being assigned to the air force? If he volunteered, he would get pilot training. If he waited to be drafted, he might not have to serve his country. He decided to volunteer.

There was a wait before the air force pilot training would start so David got a temporary job at Hill Field, an air base near his home. After a six-month wait, he was called to active duty. David was to learn to fly!

He asked to enter the air force training at Kearns Air Force Base in Utah. The military gave David an order to report to the air base by midnight Saturday. He did and left his car by the entry gate.

It was five minutes before midnight. The volunteer approached the sergeant at the entrance gate. David joked with showed him that it was his last day of freedom.

The sergeant did not laugh but replied, "Welcome soldier. Find any bed without a body in it and sack down." He grinned as he said, "I am the welcoming committee."

The young man did what he was told. David went to sleep with his clothes on.

At 5:30 in the morning, a bugle blew reveille. David jumped out of bed and heard a voice from the lower bunk, "Where the hell do you think you're going?"

David said, "Don't you hear the bugle? It's time to get up."

The voice said, "Get back in the sack. Chow's at 8:00 o'clock…until then, sack out."

David climbed back up onto the top bunk and waited until the others started to dress. It turned out that he had picked a barracks full of men who had just returned from duty up in Attu, Alaska. They had served there two tough years. These men were battle hardened and 'army-wise.'

For David, this was the start of a six-month induction-training period. The process that followed included David's receiving army clothing, personal items, and a WW I rifle. That ended day one.

David joined a training squadron of fifty men. It was led by seasoned non-commissioned officers. They knew how to get the men in shape so as to learn to fly. It would require two months of discipline and control. The next eight weeks were unbelievable.

On the second day, the trainees were assembled and divided into groups of forty-eight. The drill sergeant told David and the others, "Some of you are back from Attu. Some of you are as green as grass. I am your drill instructor. Every time I call your name you will step forward one pace and answer, 'Yes, Sir.' If I tell you to jump up in the air, don't come down until I tell you to. Understand?"

A few brave souls said, "Yes, Sir."

The drill sergeant cupped his hand over his ear and said, "What?"

The trainees yelled back, "Yes Sir!"

They returned to their barracks. Day two was over. That was David's initiation into Attu Squadron.

This began a Turning Point in the life of a nineteen year old. It was sixty days of torture. Squadron Attu was marched everywhere including to breakfast, lunch, and dinner, sometimes marching at double time to get the men in shape. It was 'hurry up and wait!'

On day twelve, David and the Attu squadron were marched to the rifle range. The range officer, a lieutenant, asked if there were any eager beavers to show spirit and who wanted to become pilots. David stepped forward along with another man. The two suffered the other members of Attu saying in low voices "Suckers, Suckers."

The officer said, "Follow me," and took the two men to the fire watch tower. He told them to climb up, watch for fires, and use the phone to report them.

Climbing up the tower was easy. This duty seemed bearable, although the temperature outside was on its way up to one hundred plus degrees. The two men decided that one person watching would be sufficient, and that they would each serve the two-hour stint before the officer came to relieve then. The duty was a breeze. Furthermore, it became a Turning Point in David's life. He discovered that it was better to know for certain what you are asked to volunteer for than to volunteer for the unknown. It was better to be safe than sorry. Saying no could be a turning point in life.

The final Turning Point in the life of a raw recruit required making a fifteen-mile hike during the hot summertime. This duty was supposed to condition each man to march, march, and march wherever they had to go.

By this time in the training program, the pilot to be was skeptical, but he complied with the order to prepare for this ordeal. The drill sergeant had made his own job easy. He had made the hike of sixteen miles in full battle dress, including carrying a rifle, seem to be a miserable duty. The march was around a square, four miles to a side. He told the men to go at their own pace but to be back by two o'clock. The men were to report to him at the recreation center when they returned.

The group leader asked, "David, do you know how far that is?"

David replied, "No sir."

The leader said, "It will be close to sixteen miles, and we're expected to do that in less than four hours. Get ready to kill yourself!"

David started hiking down the road along with two of the other recruits. They walked at a leisurely pace because the four hours they were given included rest time and would be about three miles an hour, which was a normal walking pace for the army.

The three of them decided that if the sarge could goof off, so could they. Then they thumbed a ride. Every time a car stopped for them, they told the driver about the sarge, the hike, and their need for a ride back to the Kearns gate. Using the 'thumb a ride option,' it did not take long to finish the sixteen miles and reach the entrance gate from which they had left at 8:00 o'clock. They got out of the car, thanked the driver, and proceeded to the entrance gate. They arrived just before twelve o'clock. The three were among the first of their squadron to arrive. They were greeted by their sergeant who told them "Good going men. You are the first to get here. Get ready for lunch. It will be at one o'clock when the rest of the men return."

This was the Turning Point of how to make volunteering for the Air Force as painless as possible. David felt that it was 'Up, Up, and Away.' He couldn't wait for flight training. He did not realize how demanding it was to learn how to fly, but it would be worth the effort.

The Diamond of Life review showed that flying a plane was demanding. The aptitudes needed to learn the profession were attention to detail (things happen fast), physical conditions (speed and altitude), intelligence (decision-making), and judgment (it's better to have the right altitude than a good attitude. The traits needed to become a pilot and fly high in the sky were patience, stability, confidence, courage, and character. With the above traits, and good luck, David faced the perils of piloting. It was 'Up, Up, and Away' as David became a pilot, an officer, and a gentleman in the U.S. Army Air Corps.

# 3

# CAREERS

A CAREER IS THE historical record of one's occupation, job, or profession during a working life. It can be embellished during a battle or by serving one's community. It can reflect success or failure. It can involve a productive activity, such as writing, or a destructive force, such as in war on the sea, in the air, or on land. Making tough and unpalatable decisions can change a career. Many of the people interviewed felt that being courageous resulted in their careers being successful. Illegal activities were responsible for a relatively few career changing events. Such tactics were viewed as being detrimental to the reputation. When such behavior is viewed in terms of a career, the effect of such negative actions was disastrous.

In the incidents presented, the entrepreneurs made many career decisions. Judgment as to what to do, and the timing thereof, appeared to be an important part of having a successful career. Such was true in the lives of three brothers. One was involved in the Flamingo Hotel Affair. Belonging to the Dragma Mob terminated his career by his ending face down in the desert. Other stories in this chapter, while not as earth shaking, include a variety of careers with major Turning Points.

# I BOUGHT THE STORE

*From Mortician to Florist Overnight*

THE ORGAN WAS PLAYING "Ava Maria" as background music before the funeral service began. Don, the mortician who had prepared the body for the viewing, looked at the flowers around the altar. He thought they were exceptionally beautiful. Don saw Jim Bardwell, the florist, positioning the arrangements. Don walked over and greeted him. This meeting was a Turning Point in both men's lives.

Jim Bardwell owned the florist shop in Sun Valley. His health was failing, and his doctor had told him to take it easy or he would kill himself. Jim had consulted another physician and had heard the same thing. His health was failing!

Jim Bardwell asked Don if he knew anyone who wanted to buy his flower shop in Sun Valley. Don told Jim that yes, he knew of one man, and he pointed to himself. He said that he would look at the books. If Jim could see his way clear and was able to give him good terms to buy, Don would buy the store. This single act became a life-altering Turning Point in Don's life.

This chance meeting at the Eckerman Heisman Mortuary in San Fernando, California, resulted in both parties taking actions they hadn't even considered before. Here's what happened.

It was in the 1950s, and Donald had come from his hometown Atlanta, Georgia, by way of Charlestown, South Carolina. Once there, he spent twenty years as a mortician in a Charleston suburb. Don was tired of the odd hours that were required by the owner of the mortuary. Though he had learned his trade well, preparing bodies for burial, the hours of preparation, and the sameness of the job were getting to him. In addition, his wife, who came from Detroit, liked cooler weather. She did not like the humidity and the heat of Charleston. She told Don to move or she would pass into the 'great beyond.'

The couple had three children, two girls and a boy. The boy was almost ready to enter high school. Don knew if they were going to move, now was the time.

In the summer of 1952, Don decided to move to the Los Angeles area and surveyed the scene. He was looking for work as a mortician. Don ended up finding work in the city of San Fernando. The job was with Eckerman and Heisman, a leading mortuary in town.

Don and his family loved southern California, especially the San Fernando Valley. However, Don was starting over. The hours were still difficult. He had to get a California license to practice his trade. It required a year of apprenticeship and going back to school.

Every day, as Don drove down Glenoaks Boulevard to his mortuary job, he would pass by Jim Bardwell's flower shop. Don remembered that many of the floral arrangements he displayed came from Bardwell's shop. He got to know Jim Bardwell because his flowers were displayed at the funerals.

It was shortly after Eisenhower's election to the presidency that Don purchased the florist shop. He became the sole owner and proprietor of Bardwell's Florist. This was in the year 1959 before the election of President Kennedy.

Don was concerned that he did not know anything about the florist business, but as part of the deal, Jim Bardwell agreed to introduce Don to all his vendors in the Los Angeles floral district. Jim Bardwell agreed to give him his customer list in the San Fernando Valley. He also agreed to take Don to see the ten most influential business people he knew in the East Valley so he would have a smooth transfer of ownership.

Don's wife, Marilyn, loved flowers and agreed to work in the shop keeping the books. This move to the San Fernando Valley, the change of occupation, and the purchase of a strange business in a strange town definitely was a Turning Point in the life of Don and Marilyn.

Don found out he had an artistic talent and could do the floral arrangements. If it was necessary to get a little help from employees, Jim Bardwell agreed to help Don if he wanted him part time. This transfer of ownership and hard work made Don a successful businessman. His wife was the bookkeeper, and his kids grew up in the florist business as the business expanded.

Some fifteen years later, the gas station across the street from Bardwell's Florist became available. Don liked the location because it was on the corner of the two most traveled boulevards in Sun Valley. Bardwell had never owned his own real estate, but Don was willing if he could get financing.

Don called up the U.S. Small Business Administration to find out if he could borrow the money to purchase the lot to build a freestanding florist shop. The SBA business office in downtown Los Angeles came out with the loan application, reviewed the site, and looked at the potential plans. Don agreed to finance not only a construction loan, but also the permanent financing based on Don's previous business record.

This would be another Turning Point in Don's life. He consulted his accountant, consulted his attorney, and filled out the application to the Small Business Administration. He was given a two hundred thousand dollar loan to cover the construction of a four thousand square foot building, doing all the site work, and allowing twenty-five percent of the new building to be built for expansion purposes.

This was in the 1970s and the deal was struck. The local Chamber of Commerce arranged to have an area contractor build the new Bardwell's Floral shop, and it opened in 1978 with fanfare from the Chamber of Commerce, the Small Business Administration, and the business itself. Don, his wife, and their three kids were eagerly willing to help the family succeed. Don joined the Chamber of Commerce and became a vital new member.

The Diamond of Life showed that Don and Marilyn had the courage of their convictions, the ability to run an independent florist shop, the expertise to train new workers, and the foresight to get it all together.

Thus, it was possible for two strange occupations to intermingle in terms of experience, training, and success. Certainly one would say that Don had successfully changed from being a mortician to the new owner and entrepreneur of Bardwell's. Don had a beautiful business— being the leading florist and proving 'it is not how you start the game, but how you finish that counts.'

# FROM COMPUTER SALES TO FISHING GUIDE

*Sometimes It Pays to Flip a Coin and Lose the Toss*

THE COIN SPUN HIGH in the chilly Alaskan air. Tails came up. Dick won the toss. He said, "Since I won, I'll buy the two of you out." Thus, Roger received $51,000 cash from selling his one-third of the business partnership, but he was now out of work. One of the most successful computer sales and service businesses in Anchorage, Alaska, was but a memory to Roger, its former owner.

Roger knew that Anchorage, Alaska's largest city, had a booming economy in the early 1980s. Its downtown area, which had a number of banks, department stores, and other smaller retail and financial service operations, was the center of activity. Roger was one of the three partners of the leading computer sales and service firms in the state of Alaska. He was single, had a good job, and was happy with it.

As was the case of many small businesses, the XYZ Company was in the red, as was the rest of the state's economy. The business was not able to earn enough to support all three of the partners, so they agreed to get a fair price established by a local appraisal company. The valuation would take about three months to complete.

During these three months, the partners thought about the prospects of the business and who would own it and buy the other two out. This would be a Turning Point for the business and for each partner who would have cash instead of a share of the operation.

While the three waited for the appraisal to be completed, the men debated how to handle the transaction and how to make the decision of who would be the lucky owner of the business. All three agreed that a coin flip would be held the day the appraisal was received. It would be witnessed by the appraiser, and the winner of the toss could buy the other two shares. Roger was a partner in the business, and this transaction would be a major Turning Point in his life. Would he be the sole owner of a computer sales/service operation, or would he be looking for another job opportunity?

The day the appraisal was completed, the appraiser called and said he was bringing his finished paperwork to the store. All three agreed that the odd man out would have a choice of taking ownership of the store or taking the money.

Roger watched as the appraiser flipped a coin. It fell to the floor. His heart sank as he lost the toss. The three looked at the appraisal. It was for $153,000. Roger's share was $51,000. He was crest fallen, so much so that he said he would take a few days off and go fishing.

It was a great time to fish for king salmon. It was just before the summer solstice in late June in 1983. Roger went home, gathered some clothes to wear, and picked up his fishing gear. He had heard from his customers the week before that the king salmon were running in the Kenai River. So Roger headed south around Turn Again Sound and went to the little fishing town of Soldatna on the Kenai River.

The town contained a number of motels. Roger had fished in the area before, so he knew the lay of the land. He registered for a room. He grabbed his fishing equipment and headed up the river. Even though it was past 9 o'clock at night, it was as light as it was at noon. It was hot and muggy, and the sun was up for twenty hours during that time of year. It never got very dark, so Roger was able to fish.

Roger loved to fish. He went up to the power lines, which crossed the river. He started fishing. As he waded down river, he came to a spot on the riverbank where there was a log house. It was set back from the river about sixty feet. It had river frontage. Roger said to himself, "I am going to come back tomorrow and find out if I can buy this house and river frontage."

The rest is history. It turned out a widow owned the property. Given that the economy was bad, the property was ready to sell. She sniffed at Roger's offer but said she would sell her property for $169,000 cash. Roger went to the local bank and borrowed the balance of the cash. The deal was done.

Roger became one of the three hundred licensed king salmon guides on the Kenai. He married the high school principal and began thinking of running for Mayor. All of this happened after a major Turning Point in Roger's life and his losing the flip of the coin. Sometimes it pays to lose!

# WHERE WERE YOU WHEN YOU HEARD PRESIDENT KENNEDY WAS SHOT?

*On the US 5 Freeway Going to Important Sales Meeting*

THE CAR RADIO BLARED. "Attention! Attention! This is CBS, Dallas, Texas. The President of the United States, John F. Kennedy, has been shot while in Dallas, Texas. We have no news about his condition. CBS will update this announcement when we get further information. Attention! Attention! President John F. Kennedy has been shot."

Gene pulled off US Interstate 5. He used his car telephone. He told the receptionist that he was making a sales call and would be there shortly. He had a sales meeting with an important customer.

Gene was a star salesman who sold Christmas gifts for DCT Inc. This sale would make Gene's year a great year if he clinched the order. Gene thought, "And now this." If he failed to make the sale this year, 1963 would be a downer. Gene faced this Turning Point with trepidation.

Gene called his company where the meeting was to be held. The client of Gene was on his way to the meeting. The client would be notified that Gene would be a little late. Immediately Gene got back on the freeway and headed to Anaheim.

Gene greeted his customer with, "This is a Hell of a mess. Let's postpone our meeting until we can get together without being distracted."

Gene's client nodded his head. "Yes."

Gene proceeded back to his San Fernando Valley office. As he was driving, he contemplated the effect of such a national emergency. It was a Major Turning Point! If the president died, it would call for one course of action. If the president was injured, it would call for another plan. If it was a minor injury, life probably would go on as usual. In any event, this was a Major Turning Point in Gene's life and here is why!

Gene was in his early twenties. He had not gone to college but had wanted to learn to become a salesman. He had found that salesmen were pretty much on their own, and he would be lucky to make a living until business conditions improved.

On the positive side of this equation were the following facts as Gene saw them: he was young, he lived at home, he had an office in the guest house, and he was eager to make his way in the world. From his review of the Diamond of Life, he knew he had enthusiasm, he had youth, he had sales ability, and he looked forward to the future. He was egotistical enough to know in his own heart that he would be successful.

On the negative side was the Kennedy assassination. It had disrupted Christmas giving. The important client Gene had been meeting was impressed with him and had selected him to arrange his Christmas giving to his customers. Now this plan was disrupted, and it added another factor to the equation— uncertainty is not a friend, but an enemy. The assassination put Gene's plans on hold. Gene knew that within six months he would have to look for another job working for somebody else. He could not be on his own. This was a Major Turning Point in Gene's life.

It came from external sources and was not within Gene's control. Gene felt that he had the basic Traits and Tendencies in his make-up to overcome any obstacles he might find blocking his path to success.

Gene gave this Turning Point his all. He decided to go ahead as planned. He contacted his customer and indicated that he would go to his own bank and get financing for the gifts if cash flow was a problem. He told his customer, "In trying times, one should do everything—including giving gifts—to maintain his customer base."

Six months later Gene had solved his problem. The Christmas gifts selected by the customer were properly packed and distributed to the hundred plus firms scheduled to receive them. The delivery went off better than expected, and Gene's client had been surprised at the response he had received. All in all, Gene's actions had promoted his new career, had given him a base from which to expand, and had given him confidence in his sales ability and business acumen.

A second Turning Point in Gene's life occurred a number of years later. It occurred in January 1984. Gene had become a successful salesman and a manufacturer's representative. He worked independently out of a commercial office and had an administrative assistant who answered the phone and did the paperwork.

During the twenty plus years of business activity, Gene became an ardent pro football fan of the L.A. Raiders, the 'Silver and Black.' The Oakland Raiders moved to Los Angeles. The Raiders had won the Western Division, and the Washington Red Skins, the 1983 Super Bowl champions, had won the Eastern Division.

Why was this important in Gene's life? It had to do with a new career in which Gene would become a sports announcer and PR person for the Raiders. He had approached Al Davis, the owner of the Raiders, with such a proposal, and Al Davis, still quizzical, was investigating the possibility of hiring and utilizing Gene's talents even on a part-time trial basis.

Gene had had a successful twenty years in the advertizing specialty field, and he felt it was time for him to find a supplement to his advertising specialty career. He thought that he could sell season tickets to major business firms throughout the Southern California area. His business had grown to where he had a three-person operation, and he was anxious to have a shot at this new activity. Al Davis wanted to wait for a review of Gene's efforts.

The game day approached, and Gene, his wife, and another couple flew down to Tampa Bay. They arranged for scalped tickets. It was not too difficult because the Washington Red Skins were favored by almost two touchdowns.

Game day arrived and the two couples, Gene and his friend, went to the stadium and found out their seats were in the middle of the Washington Redskins' section of the field. The Washington Redskins were called the Hogs by their fans, and upon entering the stadium the two Raider couples noticed that all the Washington fans had plastic snouts covering their noses so that they did look like hogs.

The kick-off took place. The two couples settled back in their seats and the Redskin fans with snout -like noses were sure that the Silver and Black Raiders would go down to defeat.

Such was not the case. By the end of the first half, the Raiders were thirteen points ahead and it was no contest. By the end of the game, the Raiders were victorious. It was a great upset, and of course, Al Davis was ecstatic. This game and its outcome proved to be the Turning Point in Gene's life.

The Diamond of Life analysis showed that Gene had certain Traits and Tendencies that would put Gene on the path to a successful new career. It gave him an entrée to Al Davis. It gave him an opportunity to get involved in L.A. Raider functions, and it improved his financial position. These Turning Points in Gene's life pointed the way to success and it turned out that everybody (including Gene) knew where they were the day President John F. Kennedy was assassinated.

# A SMALL TOWN, A GREAT CAREER, AND A MISTY FUTURE

◆

*My Life Is as Easy as One, Two, Three*

PETE, AT SIX FEET, two inches tall, was born, raised, and hoped to die in Sun Valley. He was born after the little town of Roscoe, California, had its name changed to Sun Valley. This occurred immediately after the end of World War II. It was while Pete was still in grade school, but yet he remembers the 'hoopla' when the town called Roscoe was renamed. This became a Turning Point for the residents of the area, including the kids in Roscoe Elementary School.

The Friday involved was a community holiday declared by the Los Angeles City Council. Schools were out. Mayor Bowron came out and led the parade. The dedication and erection of the road sign saying Sun Valley started the event. Thus a community was born.

Pete remembered when Sun Valley was just a water stop for the steam locomotives on the Southern Pacific railroad line going to San Francisco. He remembered when Sun Valley was referred to as the chicken capital of the United States because of the great number of chicken ranches in the area. Pete's parents were involved in raising chickens and selling fresh eggs.

Pete attended primary and secondary schools in this small suburb of Los Angeles. He played football at 'Poly High.' At seventeen, Pete was a hefty six feet, two inches tall, and weighed two-hundred fifty pounds. And yet he didn't want to continue his football career in college. At twenty, he was doing odd jobs, taking any kind of work he could get. Finally, he worked as a letter carrier for the U. S. Post Office while he waited to get into the army.

He then entered the U.S. Army. After basic training, Pete was shipped to the Philippines, where he spent nearly three and a half years with an army-engineering unit.

In 1969, he was briefly sent to Viet Nam where his military service ended. Then came another Turning Point.

Pete returned to the States and resettled in Sun Valley. Pete had worked in the U.S. Post Office in Sun Valley for a few weeks prior to his entering the army. When he was discharged, he went back to the U.S. Post Office in Sun Valley. Pete well remembered Zip Code 91352 because he started his career as a letter carrier. This was a second Turning Point, and it represented a second phase of Pete's life. It was the beginning of thirty-nine year career in the U.S. Post Office.

Pete's Traits and Tendencies from the Diamond of Life demonstrated that he was very, very successful. He was diligent (always gives his all), persistent (thirty-eight years with the U.S. Postal Service), and had a great attitude (greets every day with a smile). The one blot on his record of success was a poor relationship (the divorce from his first wife).

Starting as a letter carrier in Sun Valley in one of the most difficult areas to work, Pete walked the walk and talked the talk of being a mailman. He suffered the tortures of the damned without a whimper. He was up at six, arrived early to sort mail for his route, walked nearly fifteen miles, and sometimes carried twenty pounds of mail. Pete did this in the Sun Valley summer heat, which sometimes reached $110°$ and in the winter when frost was on the ground.

Pete continued delivering the mail for the postal service until his middle fifties when he replaced Bill Wilson, the assistant postmaster, who became ill and retired. Pete was appointed as the Sun Valley Postmaster. This was another major accomplishment and a Turning Point that proved his leadership abilities.

Pete really liked responsibility coupled with authority. He proceeded to take on more functions until he was supervising and directing fifty employees.

Not only was Pete attending to his position as postmaster, but he also developed his social skills. How? By joining the Sun Valley Rotary

Club. The Rotary Club was an important organization in town. In addition, he became very active in the Sun Valley Chamber of Commerce, which then had several hundred members. He was elected president of the Rotary Club and also president of the Sun Valley Chamber of Commerce.

The third part of Pete's career was his continuation of his activities for nonprofit public organizations. He supervised the Los Angeles Anti-Graffiti Program, and he ensured that public functions of the Sun Valley area were handled properly.

In addition, certain civic improvements were made. These involved the Beautification Project in downtown Sun Valley. The City of Los Angeles provided funds to revitalize the area. These improvements were finished in 1984. The Route 5 Freeway, with all its activities, was built during Pete's tenure in the post office, and of course, he introduced the Anti-Graffiti Program on the Interstate 5 Freeway that passed through Sun Valley on its way to San Francisco.

The third phase of Pete's life was a misty future. He was President of the Sun Valley Neighborhood Improvement Council appointed by the Mayor of Los Angeles and officiated at the Sun Valley Fair, which happened every year in May.

This misty future for Pete showed that the Turning Points in his life have been drastic. He could have continued his work at the post office in 1965 rather than volunteering to go into the army and being shipped to the Philippines and later to Viet Nam. On his return in 1969, he faced a Turning Point of what to do once his army service had been terminated. He made the choice of returning to his former job as a letter carrier for the U.S. Post Office, and he continued at that job until he changed positions to that of postmaster.

The Diamond of Life showed Pete's perseverance and dedication to a public service job rather than seeking out a different career. Further analysis of Pete's career showed that he had the ability to direct people, having dealt with the Sun Valley Post office staff of almost fifty people. He had good luck because he did not get hurt during his military service in the Far East. He spent three and one-half years breaking his back loading C-130s. Pete had leadership capabilities, as shown by his being able to assume a position of U.S. Postmaster in Sun Valley and directing the activities for the next ten years.

Pete used to say, "My life was as easy as one, two, three," and although the future was dim, the prospects looked very promising for Pete, postmaster extraordinaire!

## SUNGRO CHEMICAL AND THE TRIPLE WHAMMY

*The Environmental Protection Award of the Year 2006*

THE APPLAUSE WAS LOUD and long. The administrator of the U.S. Small Business Administration smiled as he motioned to the crowd of businessmen and women to take their seats. It was the annual meeting of the nation's most productive economic sector—small business and its agency, the SBA. The Small Business Administration had completed its 52nd year of existence. The meeting included announcing the winner of the 2006 Regional Environmental Protection Award.

The winner was Harold. He stood up and went to the podium. He could not believe his good luck. He had consulted the Diamond of Life to find out the characteristics that would make him a hero to the nation. What he found was that good luck, his imagination, and his attitude were very important Traits and Tendencies and the characteristics involved in his selection.

On the other hand, he felt he had some negative factors that might have held him back. One was his being located in the 9th District, which included the state of California. The second was the size of the pool of small businesses from which he was selected. There were twenty-five million plus small business organizations and companies throughout the United States. He also felt his age was detrimental to his being selected, which could have led to failure.

Harold stepped up to the podium to receive the award from the administrator and briefly said thank you for selecting him as the environmental person most useful in protecting our country's health, wealth, and safety. Harold returned to his seat and noticed his palms were sweaty.

As president of Sungro, he went to California in 1945 after his discharge from the Army. His first job after graduating from college was with Allied Chemical's subsidiary located in Sylmar in the East San Fernando Valley. A year later, Harold was faced with a major Turning Point in his life. He had to decide whether to move back to Chicago, Illinois, or to stay in Southern California and find another position. He mulled over his choices and decided that he would start a small business, name it Sungro Chemical, and produce garden chemicals to be sold in California. This was a far cry from working for a gigantic chemical manufacturer like Allied.

This was a major Turning Point in Harold's life. He reasoned that the Diamond of Life characteristics that would lead him to success were his usual good luck, his ability and his inspiration. These traits would go far in developing new products used in the garden chemical field.

Harold opened his company during the 1970s and continued to operate it for fifteen years. In 1988, he joined an organization that became a Turning Point in his life. It was called California Small Business United. It was a group of small business owners who had banded together to be eligible to participate in a White House Conference for Small Business.

This Turning Point in Harold's life occurred during the second term of President Ronald Reagan. It was important to Harold's career because it gave him national stature and an opportunity to have his abilities and philosophy presented on a national scale.

The organization that was represented would have the 2010 delegates at the conference. Harold became one of the delegates. Environmental Protection was one of the subjects being considered important to the United States of America. But this was an important Turning Point in Harold's life since it gave him and his Sungro Chemical Company national exposure for the first time.

Fast forward to the year 2006. It was the final Turning Point of Harold's life. His achievement was recognized by receiving the

Environmental Protection Award. It was given to Harold in Washington D.C. He was excited with this prestigious award as it capped a fruitful career.

The Diamond of Life showed that Harold often made the proper decisions. Many of the Traits and Tendencies he possessed led to his success. One can argue that luck, both good and bad, was a factor, but his successful companies and his success as a proponent of the Small Business Environmental Protection Movement, demonstrated that Harold avoided the triple whammy most small business leaders encounter—the rules, regulations, and laws governing the manufacturer of garden chemicals. And he did all of this after reaching the ripe young age of eighty-four!

## THE FICKLE FINGER OF FATE

*Federal Government and Its Price Controls*
*Between 1972 and 1987*

"OH MY GOD! WE'RE in a financial depression. My business has gone to Hell! I'll be looking for a new job." These were Bob's thoughts as he drove to the high desert near Redmond, Oregon.

He realized that at fifty-two, his lifetime choices were limited. He had faced them head on. He had married after the Korean War and had become an Oregon Lumberjack in the vast forest surrounding Salem. He had continued this vocation until President Nixon's second term. At that time, the foreign imports of plywood used in home building had severely impacted Oregon's lumber mills. Thus Bob, though worried, faced this Turning Point with the Diamond of Life traits of good timing, luck, and ability.

In 1972, commodity prices for lumber and plywood was fixed by the federal government through price controls. This applied to all lumber mills except those with sixty or fewer workers. The larger mills did not want to sell at a loss so, of course, they closed their doors. This law enabled Bob to change from lumberjack to lumber salesman. This change of occupation in the lumber industry was a Major Turning Point in Bob's life.

Bob formed a new company to sell plywood and receive a commission. For the next fifteen-plus years, his partnership sold throughout the Northwest. He was an unbelievable success. His earnings were in excess of $100,000 per year. He proved that the attributes of character, ingenuity, and strong work ethic could make a success of even a lumber industry worker.

However, Bob, unemployed, was on the highway driving from his home in Oregon's logging country. He had heard of a job in a sawmill factory near Redmond. It wasn't a job he could fill, so he turned it down.

As long as he had traveled the one hundred fifty miles, he thought that he would look for other work in and around Redmond. Bob then drove to the Redmond City Hall. He asked about job possibilities around the town. He learned that Redmond had just five thousand residents, but probably more since the count was based on the 1980 census. He was also told that the Eagle Crest Resort west of town was looking for workers.

Bob drove to the resort, which was on the Deschutes River. He was interviewed by the general manager and was hired on the spot. He was told that he was replacing an employee who had been working in the pool and recreation facilities maintenance department. His position would be to monitor the chlorine content of the pool five times a day, fix the pool heaters, and maintain the areas around the spas and pools.

Bob worked diligently and continued in this position. After several years, he became lead man of a five-man crew. He performed this work for eighteen-plus years. At that time, he was nearly sixty-nine and realized that he was coming to a fork in the road of life. It was the third time that he had a job-related major decision to make. Each decision had become a Turning Point in Bob's life, and each involved the Diamond of Life and Bob's personal Traits and Tendencies.

He faced a choice. Should he retire, or should he continue working in a job that he enjoyed doing?

Bob talked it over with his wife and considered the alternatives of continued work, retirement, or looking for a part-time job as he entered his golden years. The choice was his.

Bob knew immediately that a part-time job would not be his cup of tea. He also realized that rest and relaxation in retirement could be dull and boring. He was still healthy, and the couple could spend time seeing parts of the world they had never visited. BUT, did he want to do this for the rest of his life?

The other alternative was for Bob to continue his position as lead man–to work until he was not longer able to perform his duties and then retire. He then would have to face the same dilemma. What to do and how to do it?

His reflection of his past using the Diamond of Life analysis showed that there was no clear-cut decision that could be made at that time in Bob's life.

Although retirement offered new opportunities, it could also become a drag. He was old enough to realize it would be a difficult choice, and that as a Turning Point in his life, the golden years and retirement were made for each other. BUT who knew when?

True to the title of this vignette, Bob became a victim of the fickle finger of fate. At this writing, Bob had not yet made up his mind! *

* On April 1, 2011, Bob died of natural causes. This was his ultimate Turning Point.

# THE ROCK OF 'SLEEPY HOLLOW'

*An Autobiographical Review*

"GET UP! GET OUT of bed, you lazy rascal!" Will rubbed the sleep from his eyes and found himself on the floor of his bedroom. His father had rolled him out of bed. It was the beginning of summer.

The ten-year-old saw his father laughing and saying, "Summertime is time to work first and then to play." His father had arranged to have Will work at the Piggly Wiggly Market restocking the shelves. Later in the week, Will's dad took Will's first paycheck, put half in a bank, and gave Will the other half for him to spend.

His father said, "Someone smarter than me said 'a penny saved is a penny earned.' You'll be a rich man when you grow up." Will never forgot this Turning Point.

Will was six feet, one inch tall in high school—husky for his age. He went out for sports in a big way at his Catholic high school. He was approaching eighteen and had high school experience in both football and basketball. He loved those sports, but as happens so often, he was injured in football and no longer able to play. It was a Turning Point in his life because he was to graduate the following spring, and he would not get the football scholarship he expected from the University of Santa Clara. This injury caused a great disruption in Will's plans. He went to Santa Clara University and took up engineering and mathematics instead of athletics.

By the end of the first year, Will had flunked out of college because of his inability to enter into athletics and because of his choice of subjects. He left school and worked during the summer. This was Will's second Turning Point—a 'downer.' When the fall semester started at Santa Clara, he went to talk to a counselor who happened to be the Dean of the Business School. The result of this discussion was another Turning Point in Will's life. He learned that hard work and diligence in studies toward a profession that he liked was much better than quitting school and getting a job as a worker digging ditches or driving trucks— one he'd end up hating because the upside was so limited.

After he graduated with a BS degree under his belt, Will applied for entrance into the graduate Business School at the University of California. This was at the beginning of the Korean War. Will wanted to enter the armed forces reserve, but he also wanted to get his master's degree in business. This Turning Point in Will's life was monumental. Will chose the reserve, and the reasons were emotional. He liked President Kennedy and voted for him. He liked the fact that they were both Catholic, and he supported him whole-heartedly.

In the army, he was assigned to Fort Ord, near Monterey, California. Will became part of the military police at this army base. He was big, strong, and active. He spent two years as an MP, and while serving, took correspondence courses in subjects that he had not taken at the University of California. He requested that he be appointed as a Commissioned Officer. He became a Second Lieutenant and learned another Turning Point in his young life. It is much easier to be a 'Chief than just a plain Indian.' He also learned the truism, "them that asks, gits."

By that time, the Korean War was over and Will was thirty-one years old. He returned home and was greeted by his parents. His mom said, "Will you are now over thirty. You ought to get married. Find some nice girl, and tie the knot."

Will was a very shy thirty-one. He used to go to the various dances in the Army and he continued to do this. At the San Francisco Hotels, or other dance floors, the girls and boys went without dates, and one asked a girl to dance. At one of these dances, he met a girl that came from Indiana and was of his faith. After going together for a year and a half, Will 'bit the bullet' and asked the young lady to marry him. This was received with an open heart by the young lady and within three months, she was Mrs. Will.

Meanwhile, Will needed a permanent job. Times were tough. He applied for a position at Dean Witter and Company. He was offered a position as a financial analyst at the magnificent sum of $400 per month. With a wife and a baby on the way, Will faced another Turning Point. Should he accept this particular opportunity to get into the financial field, or should he turn it down?

Will reviewed the benefits with his wife. She said, "When times are tough the tough get going." The job was in a field that he liked. It was with a major firm. While it was not at a decent living wage, the alternative he had was to decline the offer and keep looking for work. Will concluded it was his responsibility to his family, and if he worked hard, he could make a go of it. He took the position. This is how 'The Rock' met this Turning Point.

Will was about to face a major Turning Point in his life. In the 1970s, he went on a trip in the fall. It was for his annual deer hunting retreat in northern California. Will received a phone call from the family doctor who said, "We have horrible news to tell you. Your wife was taken to an emergency hospital and is dead. She died from a brain aneurism." Because of his former military service, Will was flown out by the National Guard and attended her funeral.

He was so shaken up by this that he almost had a nervous breakdown. Losing a wife without warning made Will face a life without hope.

During Will's marriage, he had purchased a $40,000 home in Sleepy Hollow, a small, lovely community on the north side of the San Francisco Bay. Even though the house was in disrepair, Will reasoned he would fix it up in his spare time while continuing to work for the Dean Witter Company.

He had one daughter and two sons. He had a modest home in a wonderful North Bay area. He was able to fix his home up and make it a show place. Without a wife and with his children grown, Will felt at times like he should 'hit the bottle' and become irresponsible. That time in his life also was a Turning Point. Should he hit the skids, become a drunk, and go berserk, or should he overcome his sorrow, make his house a thing of beauty, and stand up straight? Will chose a combination of the two. He hit the bottle and he fixed up his house in Sleepy Hollow. Will, 'The Rock' gritted his teeth and faced the future.

He talked to various friends and told them that he wanted to start dating again. He asked if they knew of anybody who would meet his high standards, and if they did, to introduce him to her.

This was the start of a hunt for a second wife. He always checked a potential to see if she was a candidate with his high moral standards. Will wanted his friends to find out if the woman had been married before, was unmarried now, had any children, had been divorced, and anything else they could find out.

During this new partner search, a potential lady, who might be the one, came to light. In terms of age and family status, Will had rigid requirements. She was 'A Okay.' The next Saturday morning, Will was gardening in athletic shorts out in his the backyard. It was hot and muggy and a friend came with a young lady to meet Will. He was very embarrassed because he had shorts on and had inadvertently left his zipper down because it was broken. It was no way to greet someone new. Will beat a hasty retreat, changed his clothes, and went out to meet the young lady. He was pleasantly surprised.

This young lady had three daughters who were eleven, seven, and three. Will found out that she liked the same things he did. She was well-read and quite pretty. They dated for a year and a half and then married. Will had six kids, a new wife, and a song in his heart. This was a major Turning Point in his life. He approached Dean Witter, his employer for many years. He had been promoted from a financial analyst to a stock broker—a 'customer's man.' He had been increasing his income. He went to his boss and told him the situation. He said he wanted to expand his house to accommodate his now enlarged family of eight people.

As a special wedding present to his new wife Patty, Will needed a loan guarantee from Dean Witter to expand his house. He had been working for Dean Witter for almost thirty years. Though it was against company policy, the loan from the bank was guaranteed by Dean Witter. This allowed Will to hire a contractor to expand his home. Will would do a lot of the work himself.

Will was meticulous in his operations at work and at home. He met this Turning Point in his life full square. This was probably the most important decision he made in the past forty-five years, and he was on his way to becoming a very successful broker and a happy man. He had solved all the Turning Points of his life in a positive way. His stock brokerage activity had developed into supervising $100 million worth of stocks.

Will's Diamond of Life Traits and Tendencies were predominately pointing toward success. He did it through his charm, his abilities, and hard work. He was patient, had talent and because of persistence, had become 'The Rock of Sleepy Hollow.' Despite all the trials, tribulations, and many Turning Points, both good and bad, he was like a rock in a river—nothing wore it away. And so it was with Will, 'The Rock of Sleepy Hollow.'

# TOM EDISON—MOVE OVER IN YOUR GRAVE

*Electrical Contractor Revolutionized Housing Industry*

THE E-MAIL CAME FROM the U.S. Patent Office. It read that the "Preliminary Patent Search was Negative." It was signed by a patent examiner. Every century finds at least one industry-wide discovery. Just such an invention was made by Steve, the Electrical Contractor from Portland, Maine.

Steve went to sleep one night thinking about the housing industry. New homes were not selling. Building homes was out of the question. His trade was in bad shape. Steve had very few contracts, and many of them were nearly finished. If he could not get new jobs to complete, it looked like he would have to go bankrupt. Then he woke up. Steve had a new idea. It was a simple invention. If it had not been patented before, and he was granted a patent, it should solve his financial problems. He had a long-term relationship with his local bank. He was positive that he could get a loan and pay off his $25 million debt he had on his books.

Steve's father had started the business fifty years before. Steve had followed in his father's footsteps and continued to build houses. Steve had made quality a key in the contracts he had finished. He added electrical engineering to the firm's activities. All these thoughts passed through his mind as he slept.

Upon waking, Steve had the new building idea on his mind. He quickly put it on paper and rushed down to consult with a lawyer who handled patents. The two of them discussed the best way to get an iron-clad patent. Steve received the e-mail that the preliminary patent search was negative—no other patents were pending. The lawyer explained that

Steve's idea was unique and could be patented if a working model could be presented with the application.

Steve had to develop a model including a material that would adhere to the wooden or metal studs. It was to be the working model. He talked to a friend who had money. His friend was interested about the idea and gave Steve a loan to finish developing his invention.

Six months later, Steve had a working model. He had developed an adhering material. It was a paste that would harden after adhering to the stud. This would simplify the electrical wiring throughout the house. This product and building method would reduce material and labor costs.

His angel friend thought the idea was very interesting and was willing to back the idea provided Steve would partner him into the deal. Steve did this.

Six months after this discussion and contract, Steve had a product that was easy to install. It would cut such costs. His partner lent Steve $500,000 to finance the project and start up costs. Upon the receipt of the patent, Steve and his partner agreed that Steve would accept the $500,000 in return for a 25 percent interest in the new idea. It was up to Steve to promote the patented idea and explain how it would work. Steve was able to disclose to the industry that just such an application of adherent material to the studs would cut twenty percent of the electrical labor costs for the entire house patent. This would be a Turning Point in Steve's life. Steve was ecstatic!

The Diamond of Life analysis demonstrated that this discovery was imaginative and provided leadership in the development of construction practices. It had become a key Turning Point in Steve's life. He was $25 million in the hole. His banker was pressing Steve for repayment of the loan while Steve had $4 million of pending housing jobs in his pocket waiting for the architect to finish the plans. Steve was relieved of the worry of a lifetime. Tom Edison should turn over in his grave and greet a fellow inventor. Steve had joined him—here.

## NAIL-ING IT UP—FOR GOOD

◆

*The King of Lady's Fingernails*

"WOW! HOW LUCKY CAN a guy of sixty be!" thought Robert as he scanned San Francisco Bay from his backyard. It was a sunny day and a great setting for him to review the Turning Points of his life. After all, he was, 'The King of Ladies Fingernails.'

Robert was born in Toone, Tennessee, in 1949. It was a small town of eight hundred people. The town was nestled in the foothills of the Smoky Mountains, about one hundred miles from Nashville.

Robert's teacher, Mr. Taylor, said, "Stand up, Robert." He stood up and bent over. Each stroke of the switch was punctuated by a word. "Do - You - Understand?"

The first Turning Point in Robert's life was 'keep quiet in school or get switched.'

Another Turning Point that stuck in his memory occurred just before Robert's twelfth birthday. His dad summoned him and said, "Son you-all are about twelve, aren't ya? Well, Robert how would you like to earn a little spending money?"

It sounded promising, so Robert said, "Yes, I would."

He was given a job with everybody else in the family— picking cotton in the fields from sunup to sundown. Robert earned two cents per pound. The Turning Point for Robert was discovering that he was no longer a youth. He had become a man doing a man's work.

The next Turning Point was when he was twenty. It came time to make a decision. Continue school or go to work. It was college time. If he wanted to make it in the world, Robert had to go to college. Given the choice, Robert chose the University of Tennessee rather than going to work in Toone.

What about business decisions? When did he decide to go into business? The Turning Point of opening a start up business was caused by hunger! After living on nothing, Robert tried a number of independent ventures in selling for somebody else. One after another, they did not work out for Robert. Selling somebody else's product wasn't the solution he could live with. Basically, he had to open his own company.

It was in the early eighties. The three formed a partnership where Joe, Gary, and Robert would be equal partners. Joe would be Mr. Inside, Gary would be Mr. Outside, and Robert would be Mr. President—an equal partnership. Gary would put up the money, and Joe and Robert would run the business. Joe would be the chief salesman and customer man. Robert would be the organizer, product developer, and everything else other than salesman.

So the deal was struck, and the suntan oil business was off and running. After three years, Robert could see another Turning Point on the horizon. Gary said, "No more money." Every new product Robert developed did not sell well—it was a 'no go.' The three partners gathered up all the money they could and split it three ways. All partners shook hands, said, "Keep in touch," and split. Robert went to Southern California by way of Dallas, Texas.

This trip was also an important Turning Point in Robert's life. While stopping in Dallas, Robert met somebody who was in the cosmetic business who had a new product that he'd tried to develop but had not been successful. This item was an artificial glue-on fingernail product made of plastic. Robert thought this concept had great possibilities. So Robert made a deal to buy a truckload of cosmetic items, including the artificial nails.

Robert continued on to California and settled down in Newport Beach. He opened an office and started setting up a selling organization. Of all the products he bought in Dallas, the ones that really took off like rockets were the artificial nails. Once the artificial nails sales were increasing, Robert sent for ex-partner Joe to come to Newport Beach and join the new company.

The Turning Point of changing the company's product line was a winner! The product line of fingernails made an impact in the market. Once Robert made that decision, his fortune went up, up, up. However, the company had several major problems. One had to do with money and the other had to do with getting a business organization properly established, including its trade name.

Once the product started selling, the business in local southern California beauty parlors and wholesale outlets was booming. A patent had been filed to by Nails Inc. to prevent somebody else from stealing their idea. The lawsuit said that Nails Inc. should receive an injunction to prevent Robert from continuing in business or else work out an arrangement with them so that Nails Inc. would get a commission or royalty. Several years were spent fighting this suit, and it almost broke the company. But a million dollars later Robert was in fat city!

Turning Points regarding expansion when business was at low ebb involved getting investors to buy in, to say the least. Robert got a couple of potential investors to finance this growing new business. These 'money people' came to see the operation and work out a 'money deal.'

During this meeting, Robert sat at his desk facing the office window. As the financing arrangement was being discussed, Robert saw two big burley men come up with a tow truck. They were in the parking lot repossessing his car. Robert gulped a couple of times and asked the gentlemen sitting at his desk with their backs to the window if they would be interested in a cup of coffee. He did this because he had a coffee pot in the warehouse, away from the window to the parking lot. By the time the three finished their coffee, inspected the warehouse, and returned to his office, Robert's car had been repossessed. Robert figured this was the low point in his life—a Turning Point where he either had to get additional financing, get his act together, or get out of business.

A previous Turning Point, and probably the most important, was meeting the girl of his dreams some twenty years before—his wife Jennifer. The couple had two wonderful kids and a true loving partnership.

Now Robert mulled over the situation in the first decade of the 21$^{st}$ century. He had reached a Turning Point, which was to sell his child the startup company. Robert looked into the blue sky where the sun was shining. Although it was the conclusion of a wonderful career, he relished the future. Also, he concluded that it was murky out there in the future. It was always, 'by guess and by gosh,' unpredictable for the most part. He founded a way of life where he has achieved his goals.

Robert felt that he wanted to open a new chapter in his life. He wanted to enjoy the present. To get direction, he consulted the Diamond of Life to select the three most important Traits and Tendencies his psyche contained. Timing (live for today), fairness (treat people the way that he wanted to be treated), and know-how (apply past accomplishments and experience to face the future). This would be the Turning Point of his life. It would be 'nail-ing it up for good.'

## AN ARTISAN BECOMES ARTISTIC

*Making Glass Gorgeous*

WORK OR STARVE WAS a lesson that Arthur learned after he started school. He had been born in a hovel in Guadalajara, Mexico. At the age of five, his family moved to Nuevo Laredo, a city on the Texas border. His father became bed ridden, so Arthur was pulled out of grade school at the age of twelve. Arthur had to go to work. It was go to school or go to work—the first Turning Point in Arthur's life. Little did he know he was making a lifelong decision. He went to work.

This Turning Point was handled well by the desperate young man. The job he found was on the American side of the Rio Grande. Arthur made glass signs to identify the bathrooms in public buildings. It was down and dirty work, but it paid three dollars per day, and Arthur felt himself lucky because of the Great Depression.

After two years, Arthur's dream was going to California because he thought he would be able to find a higher paying job. He went to the Los Angeles area. He needed a job where his not speaking English would not be a problem. He concentrated on the many cemeteries that needed an artisan and the skills he had learned while working in Nuevo Laredo.

Arthur located a cemetery in southeast Los Angeles that needed a worker to personalize headstones. He was successful. He found a job earning fifty cents an hour rather than the three dollars a day he was paid in Texas. There was plenty of work because the Los Angeles area was expanding and so were the cemeteries. Arthur did this tombstone identification until 1954. During this interval, he got married, and a child was on the way. Therefore, he needed more money.

As fate would have it, Arthur was introduced to an artist who had developed a decorating technique using the same methods that Arthur had been using on tombstones. It was etching floral designs on various crystal flower vases made in the United States. This artist had Arthur produce samples. These vases were shown to the gift department buyers for the May Company, Bullocks Wilshire, and Broadway Department Stores.

The artist took the samples to the May Company and came back to the factory with a starting order of the items she had shown to the store's buyers. All three stores were interested in Arthur and purchasing Arthur's products.

One of Arthur's opening orders was for Bullock's Wilshire. Bullocks had special customers—the recently married Clark Gable and Carole Lombard. They had purchased, and were furnishing, their newly built Palm Springs home and needed dinnerware and crystal for the dining room. It resulted in an initial order of several thousand dollars. Bullocks Wilshire placed the order and Arthur had new customers. He used headstone-carving techniques to monogram the glasses designed by Dorothy Thorpe. Doing special gifts and special orders for the movie trade was another change in Arthur's life.

It was at this time that Arthur realized that the theory of the Diamond of Life helped him to be promoted as foreman of production. He had shown the artist that he had leadership capability, a positive attitude, and persistence in his job running the factory decorating crystal glassware for the home. Arthur had a Turning Point to face at this juncture. It was to stay in East Los Angeles and get another job closer to home, or move with the old company to a new facility with expanded duties.

In favor of the move would be a pay raise and new responsibility, a nicer facility to work in, modern equipment, and the prestige that goes with making this move. Against such a move was one hour more travel time, two hours less family togetherness, a distance of about forty miles, and buying a new car to get to work. This decision weighed heavily on Arthur's mind.

His wife left the choice up to him. He had to consider the limited field in which his old employer would become a competitor and a different area in which to live. He had a year to make up his mind. It took six months to build the new facility, and in the meanwhile, Arthur had not made his choice. He finally decided in favor of moving to the new factory with the company he had been working with for twenty-two years.

In retrospect, his choice to move benefited Arthur on balance. Since there had been disturbances in Southeast Los Angeles, the Vietnam War had reared its ugly head, and jobs were difficult to find. The Watts riots in Los Angeles were the topic of discussion. Businesses were not expanding, and positions such as plant foremen, like one Arthur had, indicated to him that the choice of moving with the company that he knew was better than shooting craps with the future in doubt.

Thus, it became possible to be a success even if Arthur was an untrained individual living in Mexico, a country that did not have opportunity for such success. Arthur was able to improve his life. He was able to look to the future with optimism and realize his capabilities. It was a Turning Point for Arthur—an artisan to become artistic for the benefit of all!

# WASP MEETS HIS HONEY B.

*Love and Marriage California Style*

PEGGY WAS EXCITED AS she looked at the new San Diego grade school. It was all hers. This new teaching position was to be a major Turning Point in Peggy's life. She had emigrated from Canada and was to teach second grade in California. It was the career of her dreams.

Peggy was born and bred in Ontario, Canada, and at twenty-two, after graduating from university, she became a teacher in the Quebec area for several years. She was poor. She remembered her Canadian parents would can fruits and vegetables during the summer so that the family could eat them in the wintertime and not go hungry.

This move to America would be a major Turning Point in her life. Leaving Canada and finding her first teaching position in the U.S.A. was her fondest hope. She wanted to teach seven-year-olds how to read and write. Briefly stated, it was stay in Canada where her living condition and future teaching prospects were bad, or immigrate to the United States and teach there.

Peggy was born during the Hoover Presidency. The Great Depression followed. Her parents were poor, but they managed to save enough money out of meager earnings to send Peggy to Wayne University and watch her qualify as a teacher.

Peggy taught in Quebec for seven years and found through the grapevine that there were positions in the San Diego school system that paid far more than she was receiving in Canada. She took a teaching position in San Diego at a new school called Jefferson. There she would teach second grade. It would be a life shaking Turning Point in Peggy's life. She would be earning enough money to support herself as well as send some money back to her parents who needed it.

The next major Turning Point in Peggy's life occurred after her marriage to a young lawyer. She met him on a blind date in the San Diego. He was the son of a judge serving in the California judicial system. This Turning Point involved deciding which of the two would control the money the couple earned.

After the marriage vows, they decided how the couple's income would be saved or spent. This was of primary importance to her husband, Dick, who had his own law practice. She continued teaching. Both earned money.

It was evident to Peggy that Dick wanted to control all of their money. He believed that his money, from any source, was his. Peggy contended the couple shared all the income fifty-fifty. This was a never-ending battle. He was stingy; she had to beg for enough money to run the household. This problem became more and more difficult as the kids grew up. It came to be the foremost obstacle in their marriage.

A final Turning Point came at the time Peggy and Dick needed to move. They had two children and required a larger home. Dick had a client who owned an apartment house in San Diego. The couple decided to move into one of the units. Shortly thereafter, the owner of the apartment house and the couple decided to form a partnership, with each putting up half. It was contingent on Peggy being the on-site manager. The deal was made, and it turned out to be a wonderful opportunity for the two couples.

As with all financial arrangements, Peggy found out the good comes with the bad. This was true even while managing the apartment house. She was always in the position of having to ask Dick for money for the family and their share of the building expenses. This became more and more difficult as time went on. Dick did not want to have his money mixed with their money. This became a major problem in their marriage.

Peggy was faced with a decision. Should she remain in a marriage, or should she split? Are Dick's earnings *his alone*, and her earnings *theirs*?

As the marriage matured, and the apartment house was finally paid off, it meant that Peggy would be teaching until her retirement. Dick wanted to retire as soon as the apartment house was paid off and the income flowed to him. Should she stay married, or should she and Dick go their separate ways?

Peggy related this to the Diamond of Life's Traits. Compatibility and lack-there-of were because of their personalities. Dick had very little ambition. He was satisfied with the status quo. He enjoyed different ways of spending their money and was rigid in his beliefs.

He had two loves in his life—one was money and the other was controlling the marriage using the 'His-Theirs Theory.' Peggy felt inferior to Dick. Her husband controlled the money ,and she had to beg, borrow, or steal to get a share of even her own earnings.

In concluding this snippet of life, it seemed that at eighty, Peggy had reached a crossroads in their marriage. Divorce was out of the question. They would have to have some type of a settlement over the assets of the marriage. The apartment house, which they now owned, was a valuable 'cash cow.' BUT it was Dick's cash cow. For many years, Dick had concealed all their joint property.

Even with total control, Dick was fearful about his financial future. It was a fact that Dick, a WASP (White Anglo Saxton Protestant) had met and married Peggy who became his Honey Bee. The outcome of this major Turning Point—who controlled the money—was still up in the air as of this writing. Only time will tell.

## A CAREER AND THE GAME OF 'SCRABBLE'

*An Autobiographical Presentation*

R AY PICTURED HIMSELF AS a complex character. He had finished high school a year before his age group. He faced a decision brought on by his father. His father had developed an electronics business. His father had expressed himself a number of times. "Ray you are my choice to run the business when I am dead and buried."

Ray did not make a commitment. However, before getting his law degree he told his father, "I don't know yet." He wanted to delay this major Turning Point choice until he had received his B.A. from UCLA.

After six years of additional study, Ray decided to decline his father's generous offer. He decided in favor of working as an attorney for the American Civil Liberties Union, the ACLU. Ray chose this occupation because his next-door neighbor was a member of the ACLU. His neighbor was very liberal, but Ray believed in what the neighbor stood for, and he valued his advice.

Ray believed that Turning Points in his life must provide him room to develop his talents. He planned to use those God-given traits and judgmental tendencies that would point him toward success. He decided he'd either join a law firm or establish his own law practice. Ambition and drive were the traits that would make him successful, and his timing was good. "I will be my own man."

It took eight years of hard work, and he did well. When Ray was in his thirties, he reconsidered his father's request, telling him, "Dad, I will become your heir apparent and learn your business in electronics. However, please don't treat me like a high school kid."

Although he had some difficulty with his father, Ray mastered the business and learned how to deal with customers. It gave him freedom to exercise his own abilities—a personal plus—and still honor his commitment to help his father out. This plan had the downside of working under his father in the family business. In Ray's eyes, his father was temperamental, unstable, and not capable of really operating the business.

Ray realized this, and he often said, "Dad, I know it is part my fault, but the business is yours. If this situation continues to worsen, I will have to get out."

This led to another Turning Point in Ray's life. "Family and family business management don't work well together," as Ray put it. He and his father could not operate together. His father was not stable and the business was suffering. Because of this, Ray tried to ameliorate the situation as best he could. The two of them got a psychologist to try and straighten out his father's life and get everything going in the right direction.

The counseling did not work, and as Ray said, "I was forced to take Dad to court to have an independent person intervene." This decision as to who would own the business and run the show was a major, major Turning Point in Ray's life.

Court action was taken to solve the conflict. Ray was awarded the business to run. His father would receive the financial benefits of Ray's taking over the business.

Ray continued to operate the business independently without interruption. When Ray was a little over sixty, suddenly, without warning, he found his own health failing. He told the family, "My heart is giving me trouble, and I have a decision to make. To sell the business or get a manager in to take over."

But before he could make the decision, Ray had a heart attack, and it took him six months of doing nothing except getting healthy again. "I quit smoking, which had been my bad habit since I was twenty. I exercised, and in general, took life easy and stopped worrying."

Ray's illness meant that the family business would have to be sold or operated by a third party. The family elected to sell the business.

Ray supervised the business sale. Ray also wanted to semi-retire and take life easier than his previous lifestyle would allow. This was done.

In the meantime, Ray renewed the relationship of a high school acquaintance, a woman of Japanese decent called Kuniko. She had returned to the United States. Ray and Kuniko became engaged in the early part of the 21$^{st}$ century. It was a major Turning Point in Ray s life.

Finally, the couple became enamored with 'Service above Self,' the mantra of Rotary Club International. This idea became important, as Ray noted, "After joining it, I formed a singing quartet to raise funds for the Rotary Foundation. This organization is involved in eliminating polio throughout the world, especially in Africa, since polio is very prevalent there." Ray commented, "I am pleased to report that my trip to Africa was successful, as is the Stamp out Polio program."

Ray and his wife-to-be loved to reminisce about their school days together, and they loved to play scrabble. Ray liked to note that the initials of his college, UCLA, were the scrabble word equivalent of the initials of the America Civil Liberties Union, ACLU. Therefore, one of Ray's Turning Points included the unscrambling of the two.

Ray always said, "I love UCLA, the ACLU, and my Scrabble," all of which epitomized Ray—the attorney, the business owner, and the humanitarian.

# 4

# CRIME

S TORIES REPORTED BY INDIVIDUALS who were involved in, or knew of, shady practices are related. Many who told about their lives and careers admitted that crime was a wrong way to go, indicating that they were guilty of having done something criminal. However, some said that such activities were proper as long as they didn't involve widows and orphans.

The victims of criminal activities had a different perspective. In this group of Turning Points are included that of a 'one man gang.' It tells how a young man, not even twenty, bilked a Los Angeles Bank to the tune of $50 million in fake contracts. It was so clever that it caused an insurance claim against the Federal Deposit Insurance Company. This was a case of almost breaking the bank that fell for the scam.

Another crime tells how the 'Mob' operated in the San Fernando Valley by controlling prostitution, illegal drug distribution, and other such crimes. The gang used Sir Sico's restaurant in Sun Valley to meet and enforce gang justice. The story proves that crime, as it is seen by the criminals, has no friends—especially if it looks like someone is trying to steal money from the family. There are eight other Turning Points to be found involving crime and **NO** punishment.

# THE RIGHT ARM RECEIVES A BIG HAND

◆

*Surprise, Surprise!*

THE WASHINGTON, DC OFFICE of the Director of the Federal Bureau of Investigation (FBI) had a new employee—Rosa. She was assigned to the correspondence receiving section. This was a trainee position for Rosa. Although it was in the mailroom of this United States agency, she was told it could be a springboard to a better job. The Director of the FBI had stated that this was the best place in his organization to learn what the agency did for the country. In retrospect, it was to become the Turning Point in Rosa's life.

Rosa graduated from the University of Georgia in Athens and had temporary jobs there. She had heard from a friend of hers who lived in Washington, DC, that jobs were plentiful there. Richard Nixon had been elected President. The United States was in a recession, and she had heard that the Federal Bureau of Investigation was putting on trainees for their office operations.

Rosa hopped on the next plane and went to Washington. She applied at the FBI and was hired. She was to learn the ropes in the mail room. She would be receiving, opening, and distributing the mail. She did not realize how exciting it was going to be. She was going to start as a trainee in that section of the FBI.

On a Monday morning, a year later, Rosa arrived at the FBI building. She went to her section to receive the first of five mail deliveries that had come to her desk. It was a heavy mail day because of the weekend. She started opening the mail and there was a small package that she put aside until last. When she opened it, she removed the bubble pack and received the shock of her life. There was a human hand that had been severed at the wrist!

There was no blood—just a clenched fist holding a hand-written note, the words scrawled in blood, "Surprise Surprise! Have a good day."

Rosa screamed and gently picked up the hand with the bubble pack. She took it to her supervisor. The office was aghast! The supervisor grabbed the hand and rushed it to the director. This was the most exciting thing that happened to Rosa during training.

A year had passed since her hiring. She thought that she was stuck in the mailroom and there was no possibility of a promotion. It was a Turning Point in her life. It caused her to make a decision. She decided to quit the FBI and move on.

Immediately after Rosa quit her job, she began to look for another one. This time it was in the private sector. Rosa was interviewed by J. Paul Galles, who headed the private company that lobbied U.S. Congress. It aided small businesses to get their share of the 'American Pie.' With Rosa's help, this company became the third largest association of the 25 million small businesses in the U.S.A.

Rosa helped the National Small Business Association, a volunteer organization with paid employees, grow in membership. Periodically, the organization testified before Congress for legislation needed for small business. She was employed as the Administrative Department Manager for the nonprofit organization.

The Turning Points in Rosa's life had to do with graduating from college (intelligence), entering the public sector, the FBI, (resourcefulness), and quitting the FBI when she received the shock of her life (courageousness). Rosa continued in her career with the National Small Business Association (adaptability).

Rosa always told people that she started her career because of 'the right arm with the big hand' and finished her career as a big cog in National Business Association. She added that without the shock of her life, she would still be working in the FBI.

# THE JEWELRY STORE SCAM

*An Old Man's Dream*

D ICK WAS CLOSING UP for the day on Friday afternoon. There was a knock on the door, and he opened it. He saw an older man with a beautiful curvaceous young lady on his arm.

Dick said, "We're closing."

The man said with a wink, "I'd just like to show my darling a diamond I'd like to buy for her."

Dick was the heir apparent for Leroy's, a three-store jewelry chain, so he opened the door and let the couple in.

They looked around the store, and the potential customer said, "I'd like to see that diamond ring. It's a little small, but I'll look at it."

Dick got his black velvet display cushion out, laid it on the table, secured the ring, put it on the cushion, and said, "Isn't it gorgeous? Five karats, and it's flawless. Actually, it's one of the best diamonds we have in the store."

The older man said, "No, no, no. I want something much nicer for this young lady."

Dick thought to himself that he had a great potential sale if he handled it right.

Dick was thirty-nine years old. His father owned the Leroy Jewelry Stores, which had branches in San Diego and the San Fernando Valley. The main store was on Main Street near Sixth, and even though it was late on Friday, Dick could not turn down a potential sale.

The older man inspected another ring and was finished when Dick asked, "Do you want me to wrap it up?"

The customer said, "No, no. I want something much nicer than that—something really gorgeous for this beautiful girl."

So Dick went back to the safe, got a diamond necklace, and brought it out for display. The man looked at it and said, "That is more like it. How much?'

"A little over $70 thousand."

The older man turned to the girl, "Do you like that one honey?" He put it around her neck.

She went over to the mirror and said, "My god! That's something I never dreamed of having."

The customer said, "Exactly how much is it? Will you take $70 thousand?'

Dick gulped. "Yes sir. I'll wrap it up."

The older man said, "Let me give you a check. How much is it with tax?"

Dick said, "It will be $74 thousand, including the tax."

Dick went back, wrapped it up, looked at the clock, looked at the check, and told the man, "You know the banks have closed. Have you got any identification that would indicate you're capable of cashing one this big?"

The older man said, "No, but don't you trust me?'

Dick said, "It's not a matter of that; it's a matter of company policy. What I will do is take your check, keep it in the safe with the necklace, and you can come back on Monday morning by ten o'clock. I will have talked to the bank, and you can bring it to the lady on Monday."

The older man said, "That'll be fine. Come on honey. I'll get it for you on Monday."

Monday morning came, and at ten o'clock, the older man came without his honey on his arm. Dick opened the door. He said, "You so and so! I knew it was too good to be true. You gave me a bad check. It's no good. Lucky me. I waited over the weekend till your bank opened. "

The older man said as he picked up his bad check, "Sure. I knew it was no good, but I sure had a wonderful, wonderful weekend!"

This incident and its effect on Dick caused him to change the direction of his career. This actually was a Turning Point in Dick's life. Dick talked to his father about this incident at lunch that day.

He said, "Dad, I made my mind up. I don't like working in the store. It's not challenging enough. I'm going to quit and change my whole life. I want to go back to graduate school here in Los Angeles." He continued, "You know I went to Harvard and got through law school years ago. I need to take a refresher course and try to pass the bar examination again. I am almost forty years old and still unmarried. With or without your help, I'll be able to get along."

His father countered, "I cannot believe this, Dick. You know I have spent my life counting on you, my only son, to take over. I am nearing seventy-five and plan to retire. I will become Chairman of the Board."

Dick looked him straight in the eye and said, "No, Dad. This will be a Turning Point in my life. Why should I not change my occupation if I am willing to devote my time, effort, and money to become a licensed attorney by sitting for the bar?"

This was to be a Turning Point in Dick's life. It was the first time he planned to change course. Dick had given considerable thought to this move. He even weighed the positive traits he had, which could assure his success. Certainly, opportunity was one. His finances, his interests, his intelligence, his education, and his persistence were other strong points. These were countered by his age and timing, the family disapproval of not continuing his career as heir apparent, his ego, and his not having confidence. These were offsetting factors that could lead to misfortune and Dick's failure.

Thus, the Diamond of Life review did not favor Dick making a change. Even after he had taken a refresher course for passing the bar examination, he failed it twice on successive years. Dick was not able to perform under pressure. Dick also did not like the retail business. He told his girlfriend that he was changing jobs. It would be a staff position where he would not have to face deadlines.

For him to secure a position as a researcher at the University of Southern California or a large law firm such as Loeb & Loeb, LLC, in the Los Angeles area, would change his direction; this would abate his negative tendencies.

The Turning Point in his life—namely, failing to become a licensed attorney—would be compensated by his dedication and ambition to be a winner and the traits he had inherited from his parents. In addition, his tenacity in following up a planned course was a positive. The Diamond of Life consultation was done with an eye to the future. His success could be handled with utilization of the traits he had available. His tenacity and intelligence would stand him in good stead. He was persistent in his studies, and even though he was unsuccessful in being qualified as an attorney, he was adaptable in his make-up so that he could utilize his assets as an outstanding student even though he did not pass the bar.

His girlfriend indicated that she would be willing to wait while he was established before they got married. Their relationship had been ongoing for a number of years, and she loved him very much. But she would not tie the knot until she felt his career was on a path to success.

Immediately the plan was told to his father. His father approved it reluctantly, and 'the die was cast.' The Diamond of Life had been helpful in making these decisions possible and in choosing the path that would lead to success. The subsequent years did benefit Dick, his girlfriend, and his family. It shows that persistence and courage could win the day and make success a possible outcome. The fact that Dick was "taken in' by a clever trick made him change his ways and accomplish his aims. Dick often thought the old man's weekend must have been something else, especially when the young lady in question found out after the fact that she was also the victim of a scam.

# BARRY THE 'FLIM-FLAM' MAN

◆

*ZZZZ Best Carpet Repair Insurance Company*
*Was the Scam of the 20$^{th}$ Century*


THE SCAM OF THE 20$^{th}$ Century was perpetrated by Barry, a young dreamer, who created a phantom company doing business as Carpet Repair & Restoration Insurance Company. He practically got away with murder.

The TV screen showed a well-dressed young man standing on a water-stained shag rug with burnt edges. He held a clipboard with a form filled out in his handwriting. He slowly turned to face the camera saying with a smile on his face.

"Hi, I am Barry, president of the largest home restoration insurance company in Southern California." He held up a check made out to CCR & R Insurance Co. from a bank called ANY Bank. "This check is made out to our insurance company to pay us for cleaning and repairing any damage you have in a fire or other causes that are not covered by your homeowners insurance. The people who repair or replace your damaged goods are paid in full. You have your damaged property fixed. ZZZZ Best Carpet Cleaners invoices are paid in full, showing that the damage restoration and replacement invoices have been paid for you by ANY BANK. You can rest easy tonight with nothing more to worry about." The commercial ended with the background music, "Happy Days Are Here Again."

When contacted, Barry reported that his 1985 business was terrific, and his 1986 projections were even better. He said business was never better. He operated on the theory that the insurance plan had a niche for his company. His TV ads were bringing in scads of money. He was able to live luxuriously, drive a new Mercedes convertible, and build and live in a large new home in the San Fernando Valley. It was a Ponzi scheme to end all Ponzi Schemes!

Barry grossed nearly $50 million in the two years after President Reagan was re-elected. 'Hooray for President Reagan and the TV screen.' Then the stock market dropped precipitously, and the optimistic investing public became disenchanted. Barry was still wallowing in dough. He was saved by the bell—the closing bell of the New York Stock Exchange.

An investment banker came to Barry and, after detailed discussions, brought the idea of showing his business acumen and his money machine by allowing new issue specialists to float a $200 million issue of common stock. Barry was told he had a goldmine in the making. The investment banking group explained that it would take about a year because there would be an independent audit of the books, investigation of the company's history, a legitimate purpose for the funds, the appointment of the directors, discussion of his banking connections, and other minor details that they would help Barry solve.

Barry could see a rosy future ahead of him. He had been successful far beyond his fondest dreams.

The Turning Point in Barry's life would be to get $200 million stock issue sold and in the hands of outsiders so he could pay all the banks off, pay the investment bankers off, and continue to control the company.

Between December of 1986 and May of 1987, $50 million worth of stock was sold. In addition, the new issue stockbrokers had commitments from their customers to buy any of the first 100 million tranche that was not sold and paid for. This sum exceeded all the firm debts, including the fraudulent invoices submitted to the bank and funded.

All went well until one of the potential stock buyers of the Barry ZZZZ Carpet Repair and Restoration Company common shares smelled a rat and told the FDIC that it was just pie in the sky. The FDIC quickly took legal action. Barry was apprehended at his home lolling in the pool with the tiled initials B–M imbedded in the bottom. Prosecution followed. The trial required several months, and Barry was found guilty as charged. He was sentenced to twenty-five years in prison. His assets, which were still unspent, were returned to the investors prorate. The beautiful mansion was foreclosed on by the bank and used to offset a small part of its losses due to the fraud.

Seven years later, Barry's sentence was commuted to time served. He was returned to society, a sadder but wiser man. He reviewed his Diamond of Life career that led to his meteoric rise to fame and fortune and then to disaster. Barry had an uncontrollable ego. He was attractive. He was persuasive. He believed that his actions, although wrong for others, were proper for him.

Barry was a 'dreamer and a schemer.' The ZZZZ Best Carpet Repair and Restoration Insurance Company was a sham, but it could not have happened had not its founder been Barry, 'The Flim-Flam Man.'

**Note:** In 2011, Barry was caught violating his parole and returned to prison to serve the rest of his twenty-five year sentence.

# BYE BYE SHAH, HELLO U.S.A.

*Illegal Immigrant to Successful Beautician in America*

S HOULD REZA STAY IN the United States illegally while her husband goes home now that he had finished his degree in government finance, or should Reza and her family return to Iran after the Shah died? The action taken to these related questions would create a major Turning Point in Reza's Life! It was almost a plot that a 'B' moviemaker would relish. The consequences of such a choice would be enormous.

If Reza stayed in the United States illegally, she would be committing a crime. It was punishable with a prison sentence and deportation. Her husband told her that he wanted to return to Iran with or without Reza. He did not want to be a criminal by remaining in the U.S.A.

Reza realized if she stayed, she would need to get a job to supplement her income, look after her infant son, and learn to speak English. If she went home to chaos, no one knew what might happen. This decision to stay in the U.S.A. meant that Reza would leave a substantial family fortune in Iran. Her background read like a bestselling novel.

Reza was born in a small town called Shraz, some four hundred miles from Tehran. She'd been married for ten years and she had one son. She lived an ordinary life in Iran. It was ruled by the Shah. Reza had been raised in a family where her father was an engineer in the sugar beet industry there. He was in middle management and employed to design and establish new plants for one of the larger companies in Iran. Every three to four years, the company would move him on to other areas in Persia to build other factories to process sugar.

Reza grew up in a comfortable but relatively small house. Life had been hectic for her. She got married and went to America while her husband was getting his master's degree at UCLA. He was a government finance manager. She was of Muslim faith, but the family practiced no religion. Her husband's family belonged to the Persian aristocracy, but was politically neutral. The couple had an arranged marriage.

Reza spoke a little English, which she was learning at school. This was interrupted when the Shah was overthrown. Until this happened her plans to go to the United States and return to Iran became problematical. What looked like a rosy future for Reza and her family was not to be!

The family first went to the state of Missouri where Reza's husband attended the university business school. He majored in both government and accounting. He planned to return to Iran, become part of the business aristocracy, and grow with the then expanding oil industry. Through his parents, he knew the Persian Royalty, including the Shah. but he had distance himself from the turbulent times.

In 1980, the Junta took over and Iran was created. There was much turmoil in the streets. Reza was still in the United States. She received the warning from her father that she was not to return until things quieted down in Tehran. She had no idea how long trouble in the Middle East would continue. The new regime took over ownership of the vast amounts of oil and joined the petroleum cartel. This increased the market price of oil from a dollar seventy a barrel to a cartel-controlled price.

Reza made the choice to stay in the United States. She used the Diamond of Life analysis as a tool to consider her abilities and characteristics and to determine her capabilities.

She had concluded that her decisiveness (deciding to stay in America and build a future), her courage (risking prison if she was caught), and her ambition to establish her own livelihood as a beautician in the event her husband went back to Iran.

As an entrepreneur, she was structured (her schedule was exacting). Customers who did not get to her shop on time were warned that if it occurred again, they would be dropped as clients. She was bilingual and verbally social (she talked while she set hair). She was skilled (she was able to please her customers with her talents).

Becoming a success as a beautician was an important Turning Point in Reza's life. Since her family told her that a return to Iran was impossible, she found a friend who 'baby sat' while she learned her trade and Reza continued working as beautician in the San Fernando Valley. She was resourceful. (Reza needed to work near her home in Canoga Par).

Having only one car, Reza was able to begin working in beauty shops within walking distance of her house. She quickly established a clientele who loved the way she was able to do their hair the way they wanted. And she was always ready to converse with them so that she could learn better English as she did their hair.

Within a year, her English improved so much that she could have a conversation with little or no accent. She developed a business primarily with women fifty or older who wanted to have their hair done every week. She was efficient and quickly accomplished the necessary beauty techniques. Within two years, she was making a reasonable living.

All in all, Reza exhibited decisive action as she met and solved the Turning Points in her career. Literally, Reza faced a life that was fraught with new challenges but met them with a head that was held high and a spirit that was indomitable. She became an American citizen.

Successful in a chosen occupation as a beautician, Reza became an example of success in the twenty-first century. Reza proved that becoming a naturalized citizen and saying the "Pledge of Allegiance" solved her crime.

## 'THE FAMILY' TAKES CARE OF ITS OWN

*Organized Crime in a Los Angeles Suburb*

B EING RUBBED OUT BY the mob affected the future of Frank. Why? He was the only one left of three brothers who was a straight arrow. The other two, Fred and Joe, were killed by the mob named the Dragma Family.

Frank went straight because he was a small town boy. He had borrowed money from the other two brothers who had stolen it from the gang's victims. These people were gamblers, prostitutes, pimps, 'enforcers,' and the like. The loot had been stolen in Las Vegas and in Southern California.

Joe promoted and took care of illegal activities for the mob. Fred was the enforcer for the mob. He took over when the victims did not play the game! He saw to it that a potential mark played ball or was found face down in the desert. The mob felt that once a deal was made with 'the family' and an individual did not keep his word, it was bye bye baby—he did not deserve to live. He was rubbed out.

Frank, the straight brother, lived in the Sun Valley area of Los Angeles. He had purchased a grocery store and proceeded to remodel it into a restaurant. This restaurant, called Sir Sico's Restaurant, which still exists, was owned by Frank and his wife, Goldie. The dinner house was rebuilt with funds borrowed from the Dragma Family. This loan to refurbish the restaurant was not a good thing for Frank and his wife.

This loan was used to pay for the cost of updating restaurant reconstruction. It was mob money. The loan repayment became a Turning Point in the life of Frank and Goldie.

Why? The 'family' looked at a loan in a different way. No matter what the money being borrowed was used for or what the documents said, it is the mob's money, and it must be paid back. The money had to be returned to 'the family' with interest—no ifs, ands, or buts. The money still belonged to the mob!

Sir Sico's restaurant business had flourished during the Korean War. There was not a cloud on the horizon until the Dragma Family, represented by the mobsters, Mickey Cohen and Bugsey Segil, moved from Los Angeles to Las Vegas in order to start the construction of the famous Flamingo Hotel.

This move was also an important major Turning Point in Frank and Goldie's lives. Should the owners of Sir Sico's restaurant sell the operation, building, and all, and escape to a different environment? Or should they tell the Dragma Family to move its operations from Sir Sico's into a new location and be prepared for retaliation from the mob?

Frank and Goldie did neither. They left things alone during the construction of the Las Vegas Flamingo Hotel.

During the building of the resort, the Dragma Family used Sir Sico's as its headquarters. The gang's Southern California operations were moved to Sun Valley and became the nerve center for Mickey Cohen and Bugsey Segil to handle the mob and supervise the hotel's construction in Las Vegas.

The Flamingo was to be a ninety-three-room hotel. It was going to be the last word in new major hotels throughout the world. It was completed in the post war era of WWII. It was reported to cost over $6 million when completed. It was luxurious. It had major gambling rooms, dance floors, dining rooms, and fancy shops. Women could buy clothes, and men who accompanied them would buy them jewelry and other fancies, like fur coats. It was a dream palace run by the Dragma Family.

The Flamingo was a success from the start. It became the talk of California and the rest of the nation. It was the darling of the Dragma Family. The hotel opened in the forties prior to the Korean War. The war did not have much effect on the illegal operations in Los Angeles run by the Family. It just made Joe and Fred busier than ever by expanding all of their gangster activities.

In the meantime, Frank, the non-member of the gang, had purchased a home in Sun Valley and had his family move there. Everything was running smoothly until one of the brothers 'stubbed his toe' and was caught smuggling furs, tequila, and other valuable items into the United States. Both Joe and Fred were caught, tried, and sentenced to ten years in federal prison.

In the meantime, Frank continued to run Sir Sico's. The fact was that Lockheed's executives could not entertain as much as during WWII. Also, there were no food shortages, and rationing had been eliminated. All of these negative factors affected the operation of Sir Sico's Restaurant.

There were other clouds on the horizon. One of these, gambling in Gardena, south of the city of Los Angeles, started, and the Dragma Family was involved. In Las Vegas, new hotels were being built to compete with the Flamingo and were cutting into the Flamingo's operations.

The Los Angeles area gambling aficionados were going to Vegas, where they not only could find all types of gambling, but also many other activities which would appeal to all. These included both the legal and illegal operations in Vegas, which were mostly Mafia run. All these Las Vegas doings certainly affected Frank's restaurant and pocketbook.

Joe was released from prison. He turned over a new leaf. Having served his term, he moved back to the Sun Valley area with his wife. Joe had learned his lesson. He found that crime did not pay. He had saved enough money from his illegal operations to maintain his modest lifestyle for the rest of his natural years.

When all is said and done, the Turning Points of the three, Joe, Fred, and Frank were quite unique. All were born in the San Fernando Valley. One had a successful ordinary life, another had a major change in his life after serving time in a penal institution, and the third, met a gangster's end, face down in the Las Vegas dessert.

Heredity could not be the cause since the three had the same parents. It was not environment since they reached maturity while living at home in Sun Valley California. As gamblers often say, "It is the luck of the draw."

The Diamond of Life review showed that luck, both good and bad, came into play, but one thing was certain: reviewing the history of Frank, Fred, and Joe attested to the fact that the expression "the Dragma Family takes care of its own" meant what it said.

## SUCCESS IS JUST A BOWL OF CHERRIES

*But Not in a Prison Cell*

THE JUDGE GRIMLY SAID, "Mr. Ronson you showed a serious flaw in your character when you broke into the liquor store. You are a three-time loser. I sentence you to seven to twenty-five years in prison in Atlanta, Georgia. Next Case."

It was a tough sentence. It was not the first time Freddie had been caught, but it was the first time he was apprehended for a felony. He was shaking in his shoes as he was taken back to his cell. At twenty-two, unemployed, and a drug user, Freddie faced reality. This was a Turning Point in his life. He must change his ways, serve his sentence, and earn as much time off as he could, or he would spend much of his life in the pen.

Freddie's early years were a jumbled memory. He was born in Atlanta, Georgia, and lived there for seven years. His earliest recollection was driving to Kansas City, Missouri, in the back of an old truck with his six brothers and sister. There his dad deserted the family, and his mom ended up on welfare.

Everyone was hungry, and Freddie roamed the streets, pitching pennies and stealing when he was penniless. He ditched school, and in his teens, he was busted after joining a gang. He received a fifteen-year sentence and served ten years before being paroled.

The Major Turning Point in Freddie's life involved his criminal career and cleaning up his act. It was right then or never! He had spent a number of years as a convict. They were lost years. After his release in Kansas, he was apprehended in the act of committing a break-in. It was a jewelry store at night. He was one of three robbers, and he was sentenced this time for five years.

After getting out of jail, he rejoined his gang. The gang operating in Kansas City was very powerful, and once someone joined, he was a member for life. The gang did thievery, stickups, break-ins, and anything imaginable. Freddie participated in these acts during a five-year period. Freddie did not elaborate about the Kansas City gang for fear of retaliation.

During his twenty-five-year criminal career, he had difficulty getting a job of any importance because of his criminal record. It was a revolving door—committing crimes, getting caught, and serving time.

In his late forties and on parole, Freddie became a pimp in the truest sense of the word. He would get girls for any gentleman who would pay the price. He arranged to house the working girls and promote their lives as prostitutes. He provided drugs for their drug habits. He found out that most prostitutes used drugs. It was Freddie's opinion that pimps would not be able to operate as they do currently in the United States. Prostitution could be eliminated if and when illegal drugs were controlled.

Freddie was arrested for pimping, and every time he would get arrested, he would move to a different city and establish a relationship with the prostitutes to represent them in plying their trade. After several such moves, Freddie ended his career in the Northern California area.

At the age of fifty-two, and at the spur of the moment, he went to a revival meeting. He met a counselor and actually got religious. He realized the error of his ways and studied under the guidance of this religious leader. Freddie took up spiritual activities. And this is how he earned his living. He saw success when he began to use TV and the internet to counsel religious-minded individuals, many of them reformed criminals.

With his experience in the life of crime, Freddie began a very interesting and successful life. Still unmarried at the age of sixty-three, he admitted that he used dope during his career, but remained clean, as they call it, for fifteen years. He has had a number of converts and continued to give spiritual advice. He used all available methods as a way of contacting people.

Freddie appeared reasonably prosperous. He wore the national uniform of the United States, which is not the Army or Navy uniform, but blue jeans with a sport shirt to match. He had graying hair, was of slight of build, and was about six feet tall. He drove a 2000 Buick. He spoke without accent and actually was self-educated and quite knowledgeable.

As a spiritual advisor, he had a flock of several hundred. He continued to utilize the TV medium as a method to contact his followers. Asked which of his Turning Points in his life he considered the most vital, he said, "Number one was my becoming a spiritual advisor and spreading the word of a higher being."

Asked if he had it all to do over again, would he have gone through his life as he did, Freddie answered, "Probably. I was a victim of my environment and managed to see the light. Success came to me. God showed me that I have many more years of a great life ahead."

## LEARNING TO LIVE A LIE

*A Con Man with a Typewriter*

T O A TWELVE-YEAR-OLD, everything is real. He saw a neatly dressed, fifty-year-old man sitting at the dinner table. It was summertime, and the man would gaze out the window, wistfully pick up a cigarette, light it, and let it hang loosely from the side of his mouth as he puffed away. He would then start typing. He'd type several sentences, and then stop to look at the blue sky. He seemed to be busily at work.

Robert, the twelve-year-old, being brash and gutsy, approached the man saying, "Hi, I'm Robert. What are you doing?"

The man smiled, turned around, and said, "Hi there, I'm George. I'm typing a story, making it up as I go along."

The young man asked, "What are you going to do with the story? Can I read it?"

Slowly, the man answered, "No. When I'm done, I'll let you read it."

Given such a curt reply, Robert went outside to play.

Robert was with his mother on a two-week vacation in northern Utah. Robert had hay fever, an allergy caused by pollen from flowers found at lower altitudes. Mother and son were staying at the Hot Pots, a small resort hotel that catered to summer vacationers. The guests spent their time soaking in the hot pool's natural waters or relaxing in the big lobby.

The hot water came from springs heated through a fissure in the earth's crust. This was a popular attraction to be enjoyed by all visitors going to northern Utah. The reason the young man was there was to get away from flowers that caused his breathing difficulties. Here Robert had no hay fever to bother his breathing. It was a great relief for the twelve-year-old to live where he could breathe again.

After a morning swim, Robert and all the guests would come to eat. Usually, they found George W. at the typewriter. The guests assembled at the dinner table, sat down, and waited for the food to be served. The man at the typewriter put out his cigarette, went upstairs to wash his hands, came back down, and sat at the dinner table.

He addressed everybody with a hearty, "Hello, I'm George Weston."

Everyone replied in succession. "Hello George, I'm Hazel, I'm Dale, I'm Jim, and the young twelve-year-old said, Hi, I'm Robert—you remember me, and I'm pleased to meet you."

Robert's mother said, "I've noticed you are busily typing away all the time. What are you doing?"

George said, "I write stories for the Saturday Evening Post, and I'm up here to get more background for local stories. I want to write about the Hot Pots, Holiday, Salt Lake City, and the West with a little bit of history added. I've been talking to the locals in this small town, and I will be here for another week."

The week went by and George Weston got to know the other guests, including Robert's mother. Robert's mother had read the Saturday Evening Post and knew of George Weston, the writer, but obviously had never met him. She talked to him for a while in between his stints at the typewriter.

At the end of the week, she said, "I am going back to my home in Salt Lake City, and if you would like to spend a day or two there, we would love to have you."

George Weston said, "Well, I don't know whether I can do that, but I'll check my schedule and see if the following weekend is okay."

George Weston came back downstairs and said, "Great news, I've checked my schedule, and I will have the next two weeks available. Any part or all of it would work for me. I'm willing to stay in Salt Lake City as I can get background information and do my work there."

Robert's mother was ecstatic. She was talking to a real live writer from the Saturday Evening Post, and he was going to stay a few days at her home. She had a weekly bridge club who would love to meet

George Weston. Robert's father played golf at the country club every Saturday morning. Robert's mother was sure her husband would invite him to play with his foursome.

This charade, Saturday Evening Post writer George Weston's stay at the Hot Pots, went on for the remainder of the week. Robert's mother noticed that when George Weston left the Hot Pots Hotel, he did not pay and did not thank the proprietor. He left with a wave to her.

Robert spent the next two weeks in Salt Lake City watching his mother and father entertain Mr. George Weston nonstop—except for the brief interludes where he would be heard typing away at his 'background stories.' George Weston was wined, dined, and entertained for the two weeks that he 'had available.'

At the end of that time, George Weston went down to the Union Pacific Station in Salt Lake City, hopped on the train, waved goodbye to Robert's parents, and left the scene. Of course, this should have been the end of the story, but it wasn't.

In the mid-thirties, Salt Lake City was in the midst of The Great Depression. People were desperate. They couldn't find work. Robert's parents were in a small manufacturing business. It was family owned, and though times were tough, the candy that the company made was salt-water taffy using salt water from the Great Salt Lake itself. The boxed taffy was distributed throughout western America. It sold as Sweet's Salt Water Taffy.

The fact that George Weston, the featured writer for the Saturday Evening Post, was an imposter was discovered several months after his stay in Salt Lake City. This fraud was discovered several months after the fake George Weston left for greener pastures. Each week when the issue of The Saturday Evening Post came out, Robert's parents would skim the contents to see if there was a story by George Weston.

Finally, after six weeks, there was a story by the real George Weston. The Post had shown a small photograph of the writer along with a brief description of his background information. It seemed that the real George Weston had written more than a hundred western stories during the last ten or twelve years just for the Saturday Evening Post. However, the picture that was shown at the end of the article was not the George Weston that Robert and his mother had met while at the Hot Pots Hotel.

It was obvious that Robert's parents had been duped, the victims of a scheme that supported a way of life for Mr. George Weston, the fake.

The Turning Points are obvious. Meeting an affable stranger can make even a hard working businessman, his loving wife, and his twelve-year-old son victims of a swindle. George Weston, the fake, was a skilled charlatan. He led people astray with a good story, a winning way, and a good 'prop,' the trusty typewriter. He made a pleasant living doing so. George was never sued or prosecuted by The Saturday Evening Post, the real George Weston, or any of those suckers who fell for his charade.

The Diamond of Life shows that to tell a lie can offer temporary success but leads to failure in the end. The judgment and the gullibility factors based on appearances led Robert's parents and their friends to believe the unbelievable—to be taken in by a con man who earned his living by living a lie!

**Note:** "We Wuz Robbed." Yogi Berra, former catcher of the New York Yankee baseball team could not be reached, but he has been quoted so much the author assumed it was permissible to use it!

# WE WAS ROBBED, TOO

*A Constant Worry of a Druggist*

IT WAS 7:00 P.M. when Louis left his pharmacy. He walked quickly to his car, which was parked next to the medical building. He had the day's receipts in a brown paper bag. He was about to enter his car when he felt someone stick a gun against his back.

The man grunted, "Gimme the money."

Louis said, "Yes sir. Can I turn around and get it from under my coat?"

The young man holding the gun stepped back about three feet and said, "Turn around slowly with your hands in the air."

Louis was quaking in his boots but did as he was told. The robber patted Louis down to see that he had no gun and snarled, "Turn around and let's go back inside your pharmacy. Just don't try any funny stuff."

It was evident to Louis that this man had been checking out his store and waiting for him to close.

The two men entered the store. The holdup man said to Louis, "Lie face down, head toward the door. Put your hands behind your back and shut up."

Louis replied, "Yes sir," in a very forceful manner. He closed his eyes and waited for the inevitable.

This was a Turning Point in Louis's life. Louis contemplated his future. If I make it through this, should I continue my independent career as a pharmacist, or should I get a job with a national drugstore chain? He began to decide between slaving away until retirement or enjoying his golden years. Louis was middle aged, unmarried, and fancy-free.

The holdup man interrupted Louis's thoughts, and said, "Where are the drugs, and I mean all of them?"

Louis replied, "They are actually in a small safe that I have in the back of the store."

The holdup man said, "I'm going to drag you over to the safe, stand you up facing the safe, and untie your wrists so you can unlock it. Remember— I still have my gun pointed at your head. One false move and you're history."

Louis said, "Yes sir," and continued to lie face down on the floor. The holdup man did what he said and Louis opened the safe.

Louis took a step backward and said, "You'll have to help me get back on the floor because you retied my hands behind my back."

The holdup man said, "Here ya are; get face down."

The holdup man proceeded to sweep everything from the safe into an empty garbage bag. He threw in the paper bag with the day's receipts. He then said to Louis, "Keep on the floor for ten minutes. Hope you're not late for dinner." With that, the robber grabbed two packs of gum, threw a dollar bill on the floor, and said, "Here's for the gum. Bye bye."

Louis heard the door close as the holdup man left. This heist hadn't taken more than fifteen minutes to occur, and Louis thought, "What do I do? Do I go through this again, or do I find a job? I think that I can sell the store with my lease on it, and be a relaxed guy and know I'll be alive when I reach sixty-five. Do I want to continue a dangerous occupation as a pharmacist? I've been employed and made a reasonable living. I'm making enough money for my retirement. Or do I retire and enjoy the fruits of my labor in another area of California like Palm Springs, Palm Desert, or in San Diego?"

Louis took several days to decide. He chose to keep on going in the occupation and profession he loved. He would take other steps to prevent such holdups again, but other than that, he would live life as best he could and use work as a way of reaching his 'Golden Years.' This was a decision where being safe (working for a chain) lost out to being an entrepreneur. He continued being a small businessperson (pride and independency). This was a 'non-Turning Point. It was 'straight ahead and let the robbers be damned!' Bully for Louis!

# TOO MUCH ON FRANK'S PLATE

*An Electroplater's Dilemma*

"HELLO, POLICE DEPARTMENT? I want to report a break in. I was robbed. My name is Frank and I own AAA Plating Company, 905 Thompson, in Burbank, California."

Fifteen minutes after this reported robbery, a black and white police car with two officers entered Frank's parking lot. Drawing their revolvers from their holsters, the two entered and checked for intruders. Finding none, one said, "We came as quickly as possible. What happened?"

Frank ushered the two policemen into his office and said, "Sit down officer, I'll tell you what happened. I came to open my plant at seven this morning. I was early. Our regular hours start at eight, and we usually operate our plating operation five days a week, twenty-four hours a day. We coat all different types of items from Lockheed Aircraft parts to silver and gold jewelry items. We've been in business for twenty years, and I have been the owner since we started after the Second World War.

"I've lived in Burbank all of my life. Went to Burbank High School, was in the army during the Second World War, came back, started my plating factory, and have operated it ever since.

"This is not the first time I have been broken into. As we are next to the railroad tracks, we have vagrants and bums walking the tracks. The hobos sleep overnight in the lumberyard next door. However, based on this latest episode, I think that this robbery was committed by a former employee, as he knew exactly what to take. He stole our plating electrodes, which are solid silver and gold. This is all I can tell you about this. I am concerned that it will happen again. Can you help us?"

The officers stood up to begin their report, and one of them said, "We'd like to see what damage was done and where your precious metals are kept."

The two officers followed Frank into the back of the factory. The structure was eight thousand square feet with a receiving dock and a series of eight-by-four-by-four tanks, each of which had an electric plating solution connected to the power supply. "This is the finishing department where the plated objects are cleaned for delivery to the customer." The officer noted that some of the wires to the tanks had been cut, and that the employees were standing around observing what had happened.

The officer said; "This is a bummer. Tell me how you became an electroplater?"

Frank said that he had been in business since he got out of the army after the Second World War. He was born, brought up, and schooled in Burbank. Except for the three years when he was fighting in Europe, he had been lived in Burbank.

After the war was over, Frank opened the plating business located. He pursued Lockheed and other manufacturers in the San Fernando Valley to use his chrome plating facilities. He had gotten the local jewelry stores to use his services. He developed, and capably managed, a profitable business, which became locally known. He had a foreman to run the facility, and his wife came in to do the books and act as his part-time secretary while he managed the plant using operators.

Frank had made his life bearable, but he had complaints about the city employees and the city government. Burbank had a city council that met once a week. The members were elected to pass city laws and to govern the more than fifty thousand citizens of Burbank, one of the major cities in the San Fernando Valley.

The City of Burbank was an independent community, and Frank had had problems with the city's Building and Safety when he established his business. The city would make periodic inspections for compliance with the building code. Frank appealed some of the changes required by these inspections. He felt that such regulations were unfairly placed and should have been grandfathered in since they referred to areas supervised by a previous building owner and had been approved by Burbank.

In fact, Frank had intended to file for election as one of the five city council people. The election was going to be in March, and he intended to get elected so that as one of the members he could clean up the community laws.

Now with this unsolved break in, Frank felt it was a former employee who had known where the precious metals were stored, where the small safe was kept, and where there were various other items of value. The police concluded that it was an inside job by a former employee. The police developed no leads for several months.

Frank made up his mind to run for political office in the March election. This would be a Turning Point in Frank's life. If elected, Frank would run for office every five years as one of the five city council members. He felt that he could run his business as before and also guide the community to greater heights.

His platform while running for office was simple and concise. It was to interface with public employees and the businesses in Burbank. While a member of his Chamber of Commerce, he had noted that its members had objected to the inactivity of the public employees that worked for the city. He also felt that improvements could make the city safer and less vulnerable to break-ins, such as he had suffered several times.

Thus, the Turning Point in Frank's life would be to add public service to an already successful career and become a member of Burbank's city council at the next election. Such duty would be a great achievement! The down side was that it could also be too much on Frank's plate. What a dilemma!

5

# EMPLOYMENT

FOR THE INDIVIDUAL WORKER, the job is most likely to provide life's Turning Points. The employment picture frequently supplies tales that are unbelievable. Crimes created while being employed can change a person's life forever. Illegal incidents are frequently unreported since the vast majority of Americans work honestly and don't want to borrow trouble. Becoming employed, changing a job, and being fired are major employment actions exposed to the light of day. These are life altering Turning Points.

## THE MOVE TO NEW ORLEANS

◆

*It Goes with the Territory*

BOB LOOKED BACK AT his career. He lived in and loved New York City. He had slaved as a salesman for nearly ten years while he pioneered distribution of office machines. He had worked as a salesman in a developing computer industry in Manhattan. He had done a bang-up job and was excited about the future. And what a future he would have!

Then came the Turning Point. Bob had to decide whether to quit his sales position or allow his sales area to be divided. Bob had to decide what to do! He sensed that if he said, "Yes" to a proposal once, it would be bad. If he allowed it to happen again he would be out of his mind! Putting it another way, allowing it the first time was habit forming!

It was the early seventies, and change in the business world was in the air. This change would be from top to bottom. It would include many elements of the office machine industry. It would involve the Comptometer Company and its machines, the products that Bob sold.

It should be remembered that the personal computer (PC) had not been perfected, but rumors were floating around that it was expected soon. When it happened, Bob's experience told him that its use would sweep the U.S.A. Rumors about the PC were rampant about how it was a coming challenge to salesmen.

An important development occurred that caused a Turning Point in the life of Bob. It involved his sales activity. The two partners of the company summoned Bob to their executive office. He was told his sales record was exemplary, but he had done such a great job that the company wanted to help him out by putting another salesman in Manhattan. They told him that the new salesman would help service all their accounts in Manhattan.

Bob was stunned. He said, "Do I put the man or men in my territory?"

The partners excused themselves from the room saying they had not considered that alternative. Bob waited while his future was at stake.

Bob realized that if the company divided Manhattan, and he did not receive the commission for every Comptometer sold in Manhattan, he would not be bringing home as much bacon as he had earned the previous year. It was a horrible thought.

Before this meeting, Bob's future looked rosy. But he sensed that it all depended on what was currently happening! This would be decision-making time for Bob.

On the partners' return, one partner said, "Bob, frankly we hadn't thought about you hiring the new salesman and you paying him. We need to control the territory. We will pay the new man for his sales. We will pay you for your sales. Please let us know your choice."

The meeting had been turbulent and hectic, but now the future looked lousy. Bob sensed that it was all over. Bob looked at the other partner for help. Even knowing that Bob was the firm's top salesman, the other partner shook his head negatively.

A crestfallen Bob looked shaken by the news. He slowly said, "I didn't think this could happen. I'll clean out my desk and pick up my things along with my final commission check on Friday." He exited and, without further ado, he left the office and took the elevator down.

That evening Bob told his wife of fifteen years the happenings of the day. He said that the partners made it clear that it was their way or no way. He said that he wanted to talk to Comptometer Corporation about getting his own territory. He wanted to talk to key customers, to important suppliers, to a landlord for office space, and to the bank about how much money he would need and when he would need it. He wanted to talk to his four teenaged kids as well, but most of all, he wanted to go over it with his wife.

Bob discussed this Turning Point with his wife—about how it would affect not only his career, but also their marriage. He said that the partners must have planned this sales change for a long time. They wanted to split his sales territory and thus reduce his earning power since his earnings were based on his sales volume. He told her that since he was paid on a commission basis, he would earn less immediately if he accepted their proposal. He said the worst part of their proposal was it could and would probably happen again, even though during the ten-year period, he had been a tireless employee.

Bob said that he was shocked and disheartened at the prospect of what amounted to starting over and what it could do to their marriage and the family. He added that it meant that the two of them would have to face this Turning Point of their lives!

This was a split in the road—whether to stay or to start over in a new venture. The latter would be in his own business or working as an agent for a different company. He reasoned to stay meant he would be working as a slave to the system, with no permanent benefit from his efforts.

Bob's wife said that if it meant leaving the New York City area, she was against it. She said that if his new career was the same as the last ten years he had worked so hard, she couldn't stand it. To move out of New York would end their marriage. It would mean separation.

Bob spent the next two weeks planning his life. He talked to his wife again several times, and each time she said she had too many roots in the ground to make a drastic move. Bob again contemplated the prospects of success if he opened his own sales agency.

Bob had heard of the Diamond of Life analysis. He looked at his new start probability and the prospects for success. Of the forty-eight Traits and Tendencies in the chart, five were found that were very important and favored the move. They were ambition (Bob had a ton of that), attitude (facing the change bravely and positively), intelligence (learning and earning his position quickly and well), leadership (never failing to be a leader), and planning (a talent he had plenty of). The negatives of such a drastic move were many, cast in stone, and almost impossible to face. It looked as if his the marriage was doomed. His wife did not want him to change companies.

Bob talked to the major office machine and computer companies, including Comptometer. Most of them were very interested in having Bob carry their lines. He asked what territories were available. They offered him the Philadelphia area, the state of Illinois, except Chicago, and any state or group of states in the Southeast except Atlanta, Georgia.

Bob had been to Chicago and Philadelphia. He did not like the prospect of either one. With that, Bob thought he should make a clean break, and so he chose the Southeast territory. He decided to make New Orleans his home.

Bob had been to New Orleans several times as a youngster and young adult. Bob felt in his bones that he would do well in Louisiana and the other states in the southeast territory.

Bob then revisited the city of New Orleans. He went to the Chamber of Commerce and talked to the major wholesale firms in that city. In other words, Bob did his homework.

This Turning Point, especially its requiring separation from his wife and family, was almost impossible for him to make, but make it he did. This basic choice proved to be a wise decision, and the rest is history. Bob's company flourished, being one of the most successful personal computer sales and service organizations in the Southeast. He met a southern belle and married her. Bob's career was a great example of persistence, planning, and the work ethic!

For nearly thirty years after experiencing this Turning Point, Bob was pleased with himself. He met a major challenge and chose the right path to success. This move was a major one. A life's Turning Point.

# AND THE WINNER IS GEORGE

◆

*A Dream Come True—A Trip to the NFL Pro Game*

THE PRESIDENT OF BLUE Chip Trading Stamp Company reached in the bowl and pulled out a ticket. He said, "The winner is George."

George couldn't believe his good luck. George sensed that this surprise, a bit of luck, would change his whole life. It would be a Turning Point in his everyday existence.

A look at George's resume showed he had a tough life. He was uneducated and had the rolling stone syndrome. George had a number of jobs that he didn't like or they didn't like him. He finally signed on with the Blue Chip Trading Stamp Company as an independent salesman. It was over three years before.

At thirty-three, George thought it was about time his luck changed. He had been born and had grown up in East Los Angeles, which was the wrong side of town. George had gone to public school instead of parochial school as many of his other friends had. He was an Irish Catholic of medium height—a roly-poly man with blue eyes and an Irish brogue. He realized that the years of schooling had not provided him a profession. He had not gone to college. He had worked in high school on Saturdays, Sundays, and after school. His jobs were menial and boring. George felt that life had dealt him a bad hand. He went from one job to another and ended up as a salesman at the Blue Chip Trading Stamp Company.

The Blue Chip Stamp Company was one of the two largest in the world They sold trading stamps to supermarkets. These stamps were blue in color. They were given to customers with every purchase to stimulate retail business. This was what the Chinese called 'Kumshaw,' that little bit extra given by the merchant as a gesture of goodwill. The people purchased food at the supermarket saved the stamps. Once the books were full, they could be traded for merchandise at the Blue Chip trading stamp store.

For many years, trading stamps like Blue Chip were cool in California. The retailers loved the program because using them brought customers into their stores. The customers loved it because it was free. And the trading stamp companies loved it because it was a new and profitable channel of distribution.

As a commission-paid salesman, George had not been successful. Even after three years of selling, George was barely able to keep food on the table. Fortunately for George, he was not married and could live very economically while he learned a new trade. The employment change George had in mind was to be a Turning Point in his life.

Should he, or should he not, quit and get another job?

George could not understand why he was having difficulty selling the supermarket chain stores the trading stamp program. One reason might be the field was very competitive—there being several other trading stamp companies in the market.

While Blue Chip was among the leading companies, it was not countrywide. The size of S&H Green Trading Stamp Company in Minnesota was enormous. S&H was the biggest company in the business. George had not been able compete successfully for the trading stamp business.

A second reason was that George had grown up as disadvantaged. His family was poor. He had not gone to parochial school as many other Irish Catholics had. The third was George's lack of what the Diamond of life called ambition to succeed.

George had made up his mind, He was going to quit because he wanted to look for a new job. He wanted to see the pro-bowl football game held in Ohio. He planned to look for a position involving professional sports. He would tie the two goals together. The trip to Ohio was an opportunity to make contacts for his new position.

George entered the Blue Chip Stamp's general offices and went to the room where the meeting was in progress. His timing was immaculate. The last item was the annual drawing to give two tickets to the Pro-Bowl Football Championship game. George, down on his luck, was just waiting for the meeting to end so he could say his goodbyes to the company president.

The President pulled the ticket from the bowl and said, "And the winner is George."

It was awesome. George walked up to the front of the room in a daze. He took the tickets amid the applause and envy of every member in the room.

The question remained. Did George use this instant of success in front of the crowd as the time to announce he was quitting or did he change his mind?

George thanked the Blue Chip president, took the tickets, and said, "For once in my life I won." Then he said, "I'm quitting while I'm ahead of the game," and he left the meeting!

# RENE THE FIX-IT MAN

◆

*A Good Man Is Hard to Find*

"**D**AMN, DAMN, DAMN," THE voice from the kitchen screamed. "Call Mr. Fix-it, and tell him our sink is plugged up again."

Rene, Mr. Fix-it, answered to his first name and also to his nickname. He answered the anxious call with, "I'll be right over," and he went.

Mr. Fix-it lived in a suburb near a large city. He was facing a dilemma in his life—should he continue on with his university education to receive a master of science degree, or continue to ply his trade as a fix-it man?

Rene could repair anything. The choice between the two courses of action would be a Turning Point in any young man's life. His being twenty-five, a college graduate, and a diligent job hunter in the midst of a depression, did not bode well for Rene. What should Rene do?

The fix-it call woke Rene out of a deep sleep. It was an emergency and happened in the middle of the night. Rene had answered the phone and had talked to a customer wanting to use his services. He let the woman know that it would be at 9 o'clock the next morning before he could be there, and he thanked her for thinking of him. This was a typical night for him during the past year.

Rene had a wonderful education, lived at home with his parents, and had a knack for being able to fix anything. Thus, the title that he had heard from customers and friends was Mr. Fix-it.

It was in the midst of the 2008 recession. It was troublesome to find any kind of a job. Starting and continuing to run a small business also was very difficult. The choice of Rene's going back to school, graduating, and becoming a CPA was a challenging one.

If Rene was to become a certified public accountant (CPA) he would have to go back to graduate school, major in accounting, and get a job as a junior accountant in an accounting office near his home. It would take him three additional years of schooling.

He realized that being Mr. Fixit had the advantage of continuing doing what he was doing and making a career of it. Rene had the ability and aptitude to repair anything and everything, but he depended on word of mouth to get new customers and needed more experience. Rene's living expenses were low. He had been living at home. He enjoyed taking a high school friend out to a movie and an occasional dinner. Even this was tough to do when one did not have a regular job.

This type of choice was very prevalent in the first decade of the 21$^{st}$ century. Rene knew it was one tough time to select accountancy as a profession. It required more schooling, which was expensive, but the future after getting his degree appeared to be much better. The timing was better. He would be getting his advanced degree, and he hoped the 2008 recession would be over by the time he did. He would be with a smaller group of contemporaries looking for a firm where he could get the experience needed to sit for the CPA exam of the state of California.

There were negatives of returning to school. Only one out of four passed the CPA examination on the first try. Rene's family was not in a position to support him for several years. They would have to supplement his salary as he gained experience for a CPA license.

This Turning Point in Rene's life was a mammoth one. It was unlikely he would have another opportunity until he finished his graduate degree. His girlfriend wanted to get married—if not to Rene then it would be to her college sweetheart. Rene did not have somebody else to romance.

Thus, Rene was hard-pressed to choose between being self-employed immediately or working for someone else after becoming a CPA. What did Rene choose? He chose getting an education rather than starting a small business and having it grow. Only time would tell whether his choice of more education was the right one, or if growing the Mr. Fix-it as a startup business would have been the better choice. Such Turning Points were difficult to predict. If this were not true, success in life would be a certainty. In today's business world, who can tell?

## BEN AND JENNIFER MAKE SPARKS FLY

*A Fairbanks Alaska Traveler's Tale*

B EN WAS FLYING TO Fairbanks, Alaska, a city on top of the world. The flight was ten hours, portal to portal. It was in July of 2009. Most of Alaska was a 'basket case' because business conditions were so depressed. All of the service industries throughout the state were complaining bitterly because their incomes had faltered from the lack of tourism, the delayed stimulus package promised by President Obama, and the reduction of military personnel stationed in Alaska. All of these had provided the money in the state of Alaska for the public to spend. Public spending had been declining.

The plane soared on as Ben, an electrician, told his tale. It was a story about him and his wife, both members of the International Brotherhood of Electrical Workers (IBEW). His wife had joined the same union, which did electrical work for the federal government. Sometimes the married electricians worked on the same project. This meant the two were with each other 24//7.

The couple lived in Red Lodge, Montana, which is located near the north entrance to Yellowstone National Park. They had lived in Red Lodge for years, were very happy there, and had a wonderful marriage. Their children were adults and had moved to other states.

The Diamond of Life theory pertained to the couple's ability to ignore plying their trade in a dangerous occupation. The two were doing contract electrical work. This work took courage and made 'safety first and always" their motto. The two would go anywhere and work with electricity. This trait alone had contributed directly to their being successful. Both the husband and wife had the courage to go to a far-away job and face bad weather and suffer loneliness to do so. Secondly, they were resourceful by discovering where there was work, even though it meant leaving Jennifer at home. Finally, Ben was optimistic about his future, despite the gloom and doom found in Alaska. Truly, the traits that Ben displayed assured success despite all odds.

Ben explained why Jennifer, a licensed electrician, was left at home, although either could contract as electricians separately or together as the case might be. They could move anywhere in the United States and be qualified under the IBEW banner to do work for private contractors or for the U.S. Government.

Ben being fifty-three and still vital, was interested in perhaps retiring from the contracting work. Ben was contemplating starting his own contracting firm with his wife. One of the drawbacks in doing it alone was that business conditions throughout the country were deplorable. The housing market had been overbuilt. The builders had inventory that they had been unable to sell. As a result, the various contractors and speculative home builders had no jobs for electricians.

The slowdown of building affected a number of other businesses, such as carpeting, home furnishings, and landscaping. It had a multiplier effect, which actually resulted in an increase in the unemployment figures from six to ten percent.

This brought the couple face to face with Turning Points in their lives. At fifty-three and forty-nine, the two had accumulated enough money in their pension funds to allow them to retire and draw on the money to set up a bed and breakfast. The two could use their home in Red Lodge to do so. It meant taking in tourists both in winter and in summer when Yellowstone National Park was open. On the other hand, winter sports enthusiasts thought that snowmobiling and skiing were 'to die for,' and the need for electricians would increase.

This potential occupational change was a dilemma. What to do— to retire and start a new venture, or continue in the electric contracting field?

The decision would affect the rest of their lives. They said they were leaning toward early retirement and utilizing the money to finance their bed and breakfast operation in Red Lodge, Montana.

This decision was influenced by there being fewer jobs for the electrical workers throughout the country. The need for such contract workers could not increase. Thus, early retirement might be the better alternative.

It was a difficult decision. This Turning Point had required careful thought. This trip to Alaska would postpone the decision for a few months at best. Retiring young on a good pension had its appeal—travel, no money worries, and familiarity. Then there was the downside—no inflation protection, no travel cost coverage, and the social need for making business contacts.

The bed and breakfast alternative seemed riskier. The couple did not know the business. And they didn't like the idea of being stuck in one place all year round.

The couple could not make the choice so Ben continued travelling to Fairbanks and leaving his wife at home. This avoided the negative aspects of retiring, selling their house, and spending their lives together in relative peace and quiet. The choice would be the ultimate Turning Point. This decision of their lifetime allowed Ben and Jennifer to face the future and watch the electrical sparks continue to fly for the foreseeable future.

# A BOSTONIAN BECOMES A CHAMELEON

◆

*The Story of a U.S Rangerette*

"**N**ECESSITY IS THE MOTHER of invention." This often-quoted saying hung on the wall of the Boston, Massachusetts, downtown office of the U.S. Department of the Interior. The customer waited patiently in front of sign and thought, "How apropos."

A customer service officer turned to provide information. Seeing it was a woman, the customer gulped and said, "Hello, I was surprised to see a woman in a park ranger's uniform. Come to think of it, the antidiscrimination laws make being a ranger not restricted to men only." The customer continued, "Hello, ranger, can I get some help please?"

A uniformed ranger turned to face the counter. She appeared to be in her forties. She looked vivacious and interesting. She was one of the nicest U.S. Forrest Rangers in downtown Boston, Massachusetts. These employees were on duty all day, serving the many New England visitors.

It was a strange location for such an office, but when asked about the location, the ranger said, "My name is Dorie. I decided to be a 'rangerette' just last year. I don't know the reason."

\* \* \*

*Dorie:* "It was last winter after being unemployed about six months. I had a job as an archivist for the Gillette Company that I truly enjoyed. However, because of the recession, my job was eliminated. A colleague and I maintained the archives for the company. Unfortunately, my contract ended when Gillette decided to cut all costs it could.

*Visitor:* "Then what did you do?"

*Dorie:* "I looked at the Society of American Archivists website and found that there weren't many jobs out there for archiving. So on a whim last winter, I applied to become a U.S Forest Ranger. I'm a historian by trade, and I have a master's degree in early American history concentrating in Boston and surrounding career. It was only recently in April that the Manager of this unit called me and said they wanted me to be a Park Ranger"

*Visitor:* "And?"

*Dorie:* "I said to myself, 'I need cash,' so that was when I decided to become a Park Ranger. When you showed me the Diamond of Life, I know I had made the right decision. I felt I had the opportunity and judgment to become successful so I took the offer."

*Visitor:* "Seems it has been a good move. What now?"

*Dorie:* "I am married. I have two kids that are grown up. They live at home, but they are immature so they need me to say, 'No' They don't need me for other advice. They are twenty-two and twenty-five. They do their own cooking and cleaning. My one daughter's starting graduate school, so she's staying with us since the school is nearby."

*Dorie:* "My son just finished college and he is back at home. At least he's self-employed as a Computer Designer. If this works, he'll be home for a little while. Computer game design seems to be the only growth field in America, so he's lucky, unlike his parents. You know as mentioned earlier, I'm a certified history teacher and have a degree in American history. I have a second masters in library science with a concentration in archival studies, and I am now doing this."

*Visitor:* "What made you decide to become a ranger?"

*Dorie:* "About finding a program within the National Park Service? The answer is I like meeting the public! But other than meeting people like you, it has been difficult."

*Visitor* "I am writing a book on Turning Points in people's lives. You've told me a bit—getting laid off. Name two more good reasons."

*Dorie:* "I caught my husband cheating, He said, 'Okay, let's see a marriage counselor.' We rediscovered each other. Thank God ! We did."

*Visitor:* "Your associate is high-signing you. Thanks for our little talk."

* * *

The Turning Point in Dorie's life showed that she had persistence in looking for a new career. She had capability in adapting to a new job. The attitudes exhibited by Dorie shows that necessity was the mother of invention, even when it comes to becoming a forest ranger. She was forgiving. She also was just like a chameleon, which changes color to save its life. She changed her employment to save her life and marriage.

# EAST IS EAST AND WEST IS WEST

*A True Love Story*

COINCIDENCE IS FOUND AT the beginning of many romances and so it was with Tom and Vivian. They lived a world apart until they met in California on a blind date. This chance encounter would become a Turning Point in both their lives. It was to decide whether or not the two who came from different backgrounds should get married and move to the Silicon Valley, or say to each other, "Thanks for a wonderful week and goodbye."

Tom, who originally came from India, had received a scholarship to attend Stanford University. His acceptance into Stanford was dependent on his taking the entrance exam and being in the upper ten percent. Tom scraped together all the money he could. His family mortgaged its soul to get money for a ticket to the United States. Tom took the exam and passed it with flying colors. He would enroll in the class of 1961. He was majoring in Mechanical Engineering, and he was ecstatic in having such a bright future.

Vivian, on the other hand, wanted to get her teaching certificate for the Salt Lake school system. She graduated from West High School in 1959 and attended the University of Utah for three years. She decided to take a vacation during spring break and go to San Francisco where her Salt Lake boyfriend was working. Vivian looked forward to this trip. She took the Union Pacific train to meet her friend in the city. The week went by, and the vacation was dreamy—not because of her old boy friend but because she met Tom.

Tom was enrolled in Stanford, and as luck would have it, Vivian's girlfriend was dating a student at Stanford who was rooming with Tom. The three went to a dance held at Stanford. The blind date for Vivian was Tom. Both Tom and Vivian danced their feet off and had a couple more dates. Both wanted to see each other again. Vivian went back to the University of Utah, and Tom continued his engineering studies at Stanford.

In the summer, Tom decided to get a job in Salt Lake and asked Vivian if her dad, who worked in the Utah Copper Mine, could get Tom a job. Vivian's father talked to the employment office at the Utah copper mine, and they agreed to have him spend the summer working out at the mine itself.

The summer was a great one for Tom and Vivian, at the end of which Tom wanted to go steady with Vivian and did so. This happened even though they were separated by a thousand miles.

The letters were fast and furious. By the end of Tom's freshman year, they talked to each other and decided that when Tom graduated, he would go to Salt Lake and work as an engineer at the Utah Copper Mine.

A year and a half after meeting, the most unlikely situation occurred. The two, being in love, decided to get married as soon as possible. In order to do this, Vivian had to quit college and get a job as a secretary in a law office in Salt Lake City. She would be the bread winner of the newlyweds.

On the other hand Tom, could continue his last year at Stanford and graduate as a mechanical engineer. Tom had told Vivian that he wanted to try his hand elsewhere rather than working at the copper mine. He had applied at IBM in Silicon Valley for an engineering job. He got the job. The couple were happily engaged to marry. The rest is history.

Tom and Vivian had to change wedding plans because of the slump in the economy. IBM 'surplused" some of their workers. Tom was among those chosen. He immediately told Vivian that she must continue to work as a secretary. He would go back to Stanford and get his MSN and MBA degrees. This would improve his ability to climb up the ladder of success by getting a better job than he had before. Vivian agreed that Tom should and he did graduate. They moved to the Los Angeles area. They both got good jobs! The two truly enjoyed Los Angeles and being madly in love with each other.

Reviewing the two in the light of the Diamond of Life, Tom was brave to leave India and go to Stanford. Vivian was lucky to meet Tom during the short vacation the two had. They demonstrated patience to finish their education and get married. They complemented each other like sugar and cream. They had so much in common that they disproved the Rudyard Kipling's saying, "East is east and west is west and never the twain shall meet."

Their Turning Point of meeting on a blind date became a major event in each of their lives. They had so much in common that they disproved the Rudyard Kipling's saying, "East is east and west is west and never the twain shall meet." Their meeting was one of east and west. The Turning Point in each of their lives contradicted Kipling's poem—the twain did meet and fall in love. They have been together for nearly thirty years. It was a major Turning Point—the two meeting on a blind date, marrying, and never looking back.

# GIVE 'EM, THE AXE, THE AXE, THE AXE

◆

*The Stanford Mantra for Eric*

THE YEAR WAS 1978, and Eric was looking for his first job. Eric had a M.S. degree from Stanford, and a B.S. degree from MIT. He received them in 1958 when he was twenty-three years old. He was looking for his first position. Eric had graduated from one of the most prestigious universities in the world. He was confident that even though there was the Cuban missile crisis, he could get a position.

Among several interviews with the German firm, Siemens, Eric joined the firm as an engineer. He helped design turbines for use in electrical generation plants as well as in the nuclear industry. Although this was a German firm, Eric was kept at the American facility while he was trained. He worked in design for eight years.

Eric then quit the job with Siemens for a better offer from a firm who manufactured frames for eyeglasses. He was to report directly to the president and owner of that Company. Eric was asked to design a new device by the owner. It would custom-fit the patient with frames by measuring the width of the nose bridge, the location of the eyes, and the width of the distance between the ears. The eyeglasses then could be made for an individual using his own dimensions. At the end of the year Eric had met the president's request and had designed such a device.

The owner was a chemical engineer who had developed the plastic formula used for the frames he planned to produce and market. On the other hand, Eric was a mechanical engineer. His design worked well, but in 1985, the Company he worked for was sold to a plastic manufacturer who did not plan to make eye glass frames. Eric's job was eliminated and so was Eric!

In 1985, the National Economy was in the doldrums. As is so often true, the device that Eric had perfected was not marketed and the international company Bausch and Lomb purchased the patent rights from the former owner of the company. Thus, Eric was out of a job during difficult economic conditions.

This was Eric's Turning Point. It was a difficult one. Eric had to decide how to find a job in a hurry. What could he do and now! He had an offer from a firm that he felt had no future in the Los Angeles area. Eric turned it down.

After six months of looking, Eric decided to enter into the industrial real estate field locating and selling plant sites. He also analyzed the building requirements for various types of industries. This occupational change became a difficult Turning Point in Eric's life. He was thirty-four years old and had very little experience in any field, except large machinery design, and no experience selling real estate. He had only been involved in one occupation a design project for eyeglass frames.

Eric was married. He had two youngsters and no job. This was certainly a Turning Point in his life, and he did not like his prospects.

Having entered a new field as a real estate salesman of industrial plant locations, while it was a very competitive one, he had a large territory in which he could work. It was the eastern half of the San Fernando Valley. Eric was 'cold calling' on industrial companies to find a client who had outgrown its facilities. He found such a firm,

It was headquartered in Burbank, had five facilities, and was ready to expand. Eric asked to see the facilities manager. The receptionist had been talking to Coldwell Banker's Glendale Office and was setting up an appointment for a real estate agent to talk to the president about a new facility for their main plant. Eric couldn't believe his ears. He knew it was a lead that was priceless!

He left the office quickly and drove to a property that was on San Fernando Road. It was several acres in size, a couple miles north of the current location. It had ten sheet-metal buildings on it. His research showed that they were available for sale. It was near the Burbank airport and a great location for Eric's potential buyer. It was a manufacturing company using metal and selling supplies.

Eric called on the president of the firm and told him he had a wonderful industrial site in mind because he had noticed how overcrowded the building his firm was occupying Eric added that he had a location that should meet the company's needs, The president of the potential buyer, made an appointment with Eric to look at the property.

The showing was made and the president was impressed by the presentation. He talked at length to Eric, learning about his abilities as an engineer and his experience with Siemens. The president felt that his firm needed just such a man who would report directly to him.

The deal was struck, and Eric started a new career that would last twenty-three years. This Turning Point of changing employment when he was over thirty was crowned by success beyond both parties' expectations.

Thus, Eric had turned adversity into success. He had secured employment in a new field, a new staff position and had showed that imagination, necessity, and versatility could win the day. Such traits of character made Eric the success for which he had strived.

It was the Turning Point of Eric's life—one that he would remember as his family matured and he approached his retirement years. Yes, it was after 'getting the axe, the axe, the axe,' (Stanford University's Mantra) that Eric discovered that his life can be beautiful. Getting fired can and did lead to a dream job, a golden opportunity.

# JACK BE NIMBLE, JACK BE QUICK

◆

*Jack Can't Jump over the Candlestick*

A NINETY-THREE-YEAR-OLD man sat in the kitchen of an "assisted living home'. He got up from his chair and motioned to his guest to sit at the table. The oldster was sprightly and appeared very alert as he greeted the interviewer.

Jack said, "Hi, I am Jack. I got your questionnaire. There were a couple of things that I didn't know about or that I wasn't sure about... so you want to know about my life for a book you're writing called Turning Points. I've had many of them. These days they are all bad ones."

With that, Jack started a soliloquy.

"The first thing I remembered was playing in the upstairs office of our family-owned hardware store. My dad gave me nuts and bolts. I put them together, and when I finished, he came in and gave me a nickel. I bought an ice cream cone. Guess you'd say I got paid for doing work I loved. My pay was an ice cream cone!"

"My next excitement of note was when I was playing baseball in the park next to 'Poly High'...I was a catcher and after the game, a young lady, about my same age, came and said, 'I'm Pauline and noticed you.' I asked her for a date."

"After I finished going to UCLA, I married Pauline. It was then that I got my college business degrees. Even though, we had two kids, I was drafted for the infantry in World War II.

"I was about twenty-four when I entered the army as a 'grunt'...yeah I was a private in the infantry. I probably could have gotten a deferment, but ...no, I wanted to go fight the Nazis. I got some basic training in northern California at Fort Ord and then 'shipped out' going to France."

Jack smiled as he said, "In Europe I served as a private in the infantry. Advancing toward Germany, I was hit by a mortar shell. The guy next to me was killed, but I was only wounded. I woke up to some shoulder pain. After that, I remember the Doc saying, 'You'll be O.K. soldier … in six weeks to two months you will probably be ready to go back to the States.' I came back home to Sun Valley. Yeah, Pauline was glad to see me. It was good to be home."

Jack eyes got misty as he continued. He said, "But now to get back to cases. I was in my eighties and alone. Pauline had died. It was tough to live alone, but I did. Soon I couldn't hack it living by myself. My sons didn't want their old man around. Then came, as you say, a Turning Point…it was major to me.

"My hardware store, Roscoe Hardware, burned to the ground. My folks had opened it almost a hundred years ago. I had enough insurance, but my two sons did not want to run the store, not even a brand new one. So I called it quits… I came here to be with other old folks. It is assisted living. I can get around pretty good, though I'm not as spry and quick as I used to be. That's about all. I'm tired out now…so bye-bye and thanks for letting me remember."

Thus were the Turning Points in the relatively placid life of Jack. There were not many, but they were catastrophic. Jack was wounded in World War II. His two sons did not want to take over the family business, and Jack, a widower, was lonely.

Consulting the Diamond of Life in Jack's case showed him to have Traits and Tendencies to be Lucky (wounded but not debilitated), to be Healthy (at ninety-three, nimble, though not quick and certainly not able to jump over the candlestick). All in all, a conundrum but a wonderful life.

## TAKING THE HEAT AND LOVING IT

◆

*How to Make a Success in Life*

MILLIONS OF FOREIGNERS DREAM of emigrating to the United States of America from their country. It is said to be the land of milk and honey. It is quite the opposite unless one is willing to pay the price. This price is in 'blood, sweat, and tears.' It is taking jobs that no one in the United States wants. And so it was with David.

David came from Tlaquepaque, Jalisco, Mexico. He was twenty-five years old, and had trained to be a matador since he was fourteen. He was daring and talented but so was the bull. During one of the Sunday bullfights, David was gored by the angered bull. After a month in the hospital and a partial recovery, the doctor said David would never fight the bull again.

The Diamond of Life's prediction of disaster for David. He had bad luck in getting gored and having to start a new career were major drawbacks. Such difficulties were offset by David's agility, determination, and drive (wonderful natural talents).

Leaving the hospital, a disappointed David returned to his hometown of Tlaquepaque, a few miles south of Guadalajara. He got a job in the community's major type of business— pottery making. This little town produces plain pottery with an orange brown surface glaze. Its surface is both decorative and permanent. This type of earthenware is sold for use in both the dining room and kitchen. This pottery is used in the Western Hemisphere. It supports the city's economic needs.

Being employed by these potteries was a Turning Point in David's life. He tended the ovens, became the manager, and learned a new trade. David did this for several years. He was the lead man for the pottery. If anything went wrong, David was responsible. David liked his new responsibility, but he wanted new fields to conquer.

After spending five years in the pottery business, David showed how adventurous he was and how courageous he could be. He decided to emigrate to the United States and seek his fortune there.

He made his way to Tijuana, which is on the southern border of the United States. Hundreds of people were waiting to pass through the gate, and the line was long.

David's English was passable. He was dressed in Levis and a tee shirt and was feeling lucky. The immigration officer asked David what he wanted to do in the states, where he was from, and what he had in the duffle bag. As luck would have it, and good luck it was, the interviewer was a Mexican who was also from Tlaquepasque. The agent knew the pottery and where David had worked. After a few dollars changed hands, the agent aided David by talking to the man in charge. David felt that this passage was the Turning Point of his life!

Migrating to Glendale, California, and based on his experience as a potter in Mexico, David got a job at Franciscan Pottery. The employment interviewer decided to give him a temporary job on the graveyard shift. David was concerned because he was an 'illegal.' Once again, the Diamond of Life smiled as President Reagan declared 'Amnesty,' and David's deportation worries were over!

David remembered his father's advice that hard work, a little bit of sweat, and a lot of dedication would be the key to his Success. Nearly twenty years later, David realized how true it was. David knew instinctively what the Diamond of Life stood for. He had worked hard, and he had mastered many different positions. He had drive and ambition 'to boot' as he remembered what his father told him long ago.

After twenty years, David was still employed in the same factory. He had worked in all the departments and had learned every function. He had great employer relationships. He was notified that he would be given a job as Production Manager and that his salary would be doubled.

It was a major Turning Point that David never expected. He had met a wonderful woman and married her and had two young daughters to show for it. He believed that he had had a successful life. Wherever he had worked 'come hell or high water,' David had always taken the heat and loved the challenge. Not only was his life a success, it was Awesome!

6

# FAMILY

INANIMATE OBJECTS ARE CALLED a family when gathered together by use of a common feature. Humans think of the word family as a group of related people. These short stories are about family members, friends, and neighbors. Such Turning Points involve life altering relationships. These incidents pertain to events reported by individuals during their lives and notable enough to be remembered.

A typical example tells about two people meeting while working, find common ground, and are united purportedly forever. *As* a result, the partners form a family unit that faces an unknown future. The family so created changes its plans from time to time. Among these are where they want to live, when and if to have children, and how to make a living.

One of the snapshots of family life shows what a man would do "to not be the top dog of the family business." There are twelve other tales in which family choices. are presented. These Turning Points appear to have a life all their own.

# WHAT DOES A DESIGNER DO TO PLEASE HIS WIFE?

*A Designer's Dilemma Extraordinaire*

B OB, A LEADING DESIGNER of items used in a home, had received an ultimatum from his wife. She said, "Either you get rid of your artwork and old samples cluttering up our house or get rid of me!"

After receiving this threat, Bob thought to himself, "Connie is not kidding. I better clean house and do it real soon. I must do it and fast!"

Bob ruminated about his problem overnight, and he came up with a solution to this vexing situation that could destroy his married life. But let the details show what happened as Bob tried to meet his wife's request. Her ultimatum was choose between his precious samples or her!

Bob spent the next Saturday cleaning up his art studio, the basement mess and loading his SUV. It was stuff he'd kept around for years such as his artwork, his design samples and his client's items that they had left with him but failed to pick up.

Before Bob was finished, his van was filled to the brim. He knew there was a big swap meet the first Sunday of every month. It was famous and well attended. The month of December was the biggest swap meet of the year because of Christmas.

It was at the Rose Bowl in Pasadena. It was held in the parking lot. The swap meet charged each vendor fifty dollars for displaying their wares and making sales.

On Sunday morning, Bob got up at 5 o'clock. He jumped into his SUV that he loaded the night before. He drove to the Rose Bowl via the Pasadena Freeway. He lined up waiting for the gates to open. He waited in the dark so he could be one of the first to put his 'goodies' on display. It was freezing cold as Bob waited. It took fifteen minutes to get in. Bob paid his entrance fee. He had one hour to set up and get ready for his customers to show.

Bob found a place to display his samples, his artwork, and the rest of his obsolete items. The spot he had been able to find was far from the entrance gate but it was the closest one he saw. Bob forgot to bring tables or racks to display what he had for sale. What a mistake! He saw others using tables or racks to show their merchandise. Bob had neither, so he looked for somebody who had an extra tables to sell.

After looking for ten minutes, he found a vendor who rented display tables. The rental cost was twenty-five dollars each, with a ten-dollar refundable deposit in case the table was not returned. Bob rented two tables, each eight feet long and four feet wide. Bob placed the two tables together in the center of his display.

He proceeded to unload his car and park the SUV behind his display. The sun had not come up yet. He was freezing, and he bought a steaming cup of coffee to warm up. He shivered as put the artwork on an easel that he had brought with him. He took all the samples and either put them on top of the table or piled them underneath so that he could replenish any "goodie" immediately after it sold.

Bob's items were unique designs. Some of the artwork were sketches that he had made. He had clamped the sketches to the top of the easel so that a buyer would be able to turn the sketches one at a time and remove the one he wanted to buy.

Bob had made some cardboard signs that read, "Artist original sketches $5 to $55."

He brought all of the designer samples that he had and priced each of them from two to twenty dollars. Bob looked at his setup and felt it was going to be an awesome clearance sale. He knew instinctively that nothing was to come back from the swap meet, except Bob himself—and money.

Bob was set up for the swap meet by 7:30 am. The sun still was not up. He stood around and shivered in the early morning cold. It was a damp, bone-chilling cold. After fifteen minutes standing around waiting for the swap meet gates to open, Bob said to himself, "I cannot stand the cold anymore. There must be somebody here selling sweaters, coats, or something that I can put on. I will find out if I can borrow one. If not, I'll just have to buy it."

Bob started walking around the Rose Bowl, and finally, after ten minutes, he found a vendor who had army overcoats for sale. They were those olive drab full-length trench coats that were matted material and evidently very warm. Bob looked at the coats, tried one on, and asked the vendor, "How much? I am selling my stuff on the other side. I am colder than hell. Please give me a good deal."

The vendor looked at him and said, "That you should have known. Always it is cold in Pasadena in the early morning and on your side of the Rose Bowl parking lot, there is no sun until 10 or 11 o'clock. It's twenty-nine dollars. Buy it or get lost."

Bob reluctantly pulled his wallet out, found the cash, gave it to the vendor, and said, "I'll see you later. Maybe you will buy it back from me because I have no need of this after today."

The vendor smiled and said, "How am I going to make a living by giving you your money back?" Bob realized that it was useless, paid the $29 , wore the overcoat, and went back to his display on the other side of the Rose Bowl parking lot.

The gates opened at 8 o'clock, and Bob waited for the crowds to swarm in. He knew this was a very famous swap meet. It was only open every fourth Sunday, and besides, Christmas was just three weeks away so people would be buying their Christmas gifts at the swap meet.

The crowds did start to come in after 8:30, and they walked around the parking lot and walked right by Bob's display. He thought his samples were unique, but he had priced everything on the basis of what unique samples by a famous designer and artist, such as himself, would bring. He figured that he always could negotiate, and that once the people had looked at his items, they would be falling all over themselves to buy them.

After 9 am, Bob realized that with the prices at five to thirty dollars, he would probably have to bargain and meet any offer he received with a counter offer. He started to yell "Come on! Come on! Come over- Christmas Specials Marked Down a lot!"

As the day wore on, Bob realized he had made a major error in judgment. He should have figured another way of merchandising his beautiful designs, original samples, and miscellaneous items.

By noon Bob was desperate. He was acting like a barker at the circus saying, "Come on, come on, come over! Original samples half price. Original artwork, Christmas specials. You tell me what you'll pay me." He kept shouting trying to get the people wandering through the parking lot to look at his stuff.

By one o'clock, with the end of the show at two, Bob had sold thirty-eight dollars worth. His voice was so hoarse from shouting that he could barely talk. He went to several of the miscellaneous sellers and tried to get them to come over and give him a 'job lot' bid for his entire stock. It was to no avail; his decision to meet his wife's demand, and do it by selling it himself at the Rose Bowl, was a big mistake.

Bob had a major decision to make since this was a Turning Point in his marriage and his life itself. It was having an empty SUV when he came back home , or he would never hear the end of his stupidity.

Bob went to several nearby vendors and tried to get them to leave their display and come to his to give him a closeout bid. At each stop, he realized that it was hopeless. He was rejected by everyone he talked to, and he figured that he had better find another way to dispose of his stuff.

Bob went to the swap meet office area and told them his problem, gave them his space number, and asked them what he should do. They smiled and said, "Well, how much have you got?" Bob told them he had half a van full of merchandise and artwork. Bob said, "Come look at it, or just give me an offer."

The man said, "I'll take anything you got if you pay me twenty-five dollars because anything that we can't use or sell, we have to take to the dump, and they will charge us at least that to throw it away."

Bob thought for a minute, gave the man twenty-five dollars, proceeded back to his car, as he realized that it was a Turning Point in his life. It had saved his marriage and taught him a good lesson, which was, 'don't think you are smarter than anybody else. Most of the time you will be surprised that you aren't as smart as you thought. Furthermore, and it will cost you an arm and a leg to learn the truth.'

Bob thought to himself as he came back to the SUV, "I have to tell my wife this sad story and take the verbal whipping I am sure she will give me for my doing it the wrong way. It is a Turning Point in my life, but not a good one. It sure cost me money to find it out."

As The Diamond of Life points out—experience, judgment, and luck are traits that lead to success. Bad luck, poor planning, and lack of foresight certainly portend failure. In Bob's case, it was 'get rid of the samples or never hear the end of it.' It was a true dilemma. What do you do with obsolete samples and artwork to please your wife? Give it away if you can or pay somebody to junk it! In any event, you must come home clean as a hound's tooth!

# MARLENE BE MINE

*It's the Principal of High School Having an Alaskan Romance*

A LASKA HAS AN ATMOSPHERE of its own. That's the reason the Turning Points related by Alaskans are so unusual and special. This vignette concerns a high school principal in Stewart, Alaska. This tiny city is located on the Kenai River, approximately one hundred miles south of Anchorage, Alaska. This fact leads to a dichotomy between the two sexes. It is the story of Marlene and Roger, citizens of the state of Alaska, and how they found each other. This discovery was the Turning Point of their lives.

In 1990s, the Stewart High School principal, Marlene, was helping out her school. This high school was crammed with students and was short of discretionary funds. The principal was unmarried at that time. She was very well thought of by the students and parents.

In this case, the high school needed funds to help the student body participate in certain non-curricular activities. Marlene and her subordinate teachers went out into the area to contact people who could make contributions for the use of the students.

Marlene called upon various business people in and around her high school— people who were capable of making donations, no matter how big or how small. Marlene called upon people who had homes and lived on the banks of the Kenai River, where the rich and the salmon fishermen live.

Marlene was in her car and going on the back roads. She wanted to make her pitch regarding the high school and its needs to all those she knew. Her character traits shown in the Diamond of Life cannot be ignored in the case of Marlene.

She was a good-organizer (ran community events well), intelligent (school principal of Stewart High School), smart appearance (always nicely garbed), and imaginative (unique raising funds for charity).

As it happened, Marlene discovered Roger's Angler's Lodge, a beautiful big house on the grass-covered riverbank. Marlene did not know its owner. She parked her car in front of the fence, got out, opened the gate, returned to her car, and pulled into the driveway. She parked facing the Kenai River.

There was a man standing at the edge of the river with a fishing pole in his hand. The man was dressed in coveralls.

Marlene hailed him saying, "Are you the owner of this lodge?"

The man turned around and said, "Yes'um, I am."

She said, "I am from the high school, and I'd like to talk to you."

The man reeled in his line and walked toward her car holding his fishing pole, leaned it against the side of the house, came over, and said, "What can I do for you lady?"

Marlene said, "Well, I'm the principal of Stewart High School. I came to talk to you about making a donation for the high school students so that they can to go to a dramatic production in Anchorage next month. It is "King Lear" by Shakespeare."

Roger said, "Hmm. I am supportive of education. In fact, I was in the computer business up in Anchorage until I moved down here. I changed my occupation, purchased this place, and now I run this fishing lodge."

The principal said, "Well, that's interesting. Will you make a contribution for the students of Stewart High School?"

He answered her with an, "Mmm," turned around, looked up at the sky, pondered a minute, and said, "I think I can do that. Who do I make the check out to?"

She replied, "Make it out to the Stewart High School, Senior Class of this year."

Then they walked into the house together. Marlene looked around, and saw that it was definitely a man's paradise— evidently no women in the place. There was a Native American housekeeper who cooked for the guests and, of course, the owner, Roger himself.

Roger sat down at the dinner table, which he used as his desk. He wrote out a check for one thousand dollars.

She looked at him and said, "My goodness, that's a lot of money, considering you've never been to our high school, didn't attend it, you're not an alumnus, and we barely know each other."

Roger smiled. "I'll come down and visit the high school in the next week or two, and you can show me around. Since you've seen my place, I'd love to see yours."

She looked at him and looked at his coveralls. She saw that his red beard was down to the middle of his chest. Marlene said, "Well, when you come be sure you are dressed properly for your visit."

He said, "What does that mean?"

She answered, "That means, you shave your beard, or at least trim it, and wear something besides dirty coveralls, which evidently are part of your business operation."

He said, "Ma'am, do I have to call you before I come, or do I just stray down there any day of the week?"

She said, "Call me first. We'll meet for a cup of coffee, and I will see if you pass muster as a guest and contributor to the high school."

This was the beginning of a romance intended to end all romances. The statistics for marriages in Alaska are something else. There are four men for every eligible woman. The divorce rate is the highest in the United States. Alaska has a total population of six hundred thousand people while being the largest land areas of any state in the union. It's the eighth wonder of the world that anybody who lives there for any length of time gets married, stays married, or doesn't leave the state of Alaska.

At the appointed time, Roger went down to the local coffee shop and met Marlene. He looked like a different person. She hardly recognized him. He was in a business suit, wore an open shirt with no tie, and his beard was gone. He was what woman call a 'vision of masculinity.' Well, this was a Turning Point in both their lives. They went outside together and they toured the entire campus.

Roger said, "How about another date? They are having a dance downtown, and I'd love to take ya Friday night."

She said, "Well, that would be wonderful."

And this was an epic romance in the state of Alaska. After a few dates, Roger popped the question, and they eloped. I am glad to say both Roger and his wife Marlene have been happy ever since.

She still is very fond of Stewart High School and her years there as principal, but now, as Mrs. Roger, she assists with the fishing guide and recreation service. Roger guides and hunts for a living. She does the cooking, which all guests appreciate. The guests enjoy the unbelievable story about her torrid romance.

Marlene's Turning Point has improved her life. This chance meeting is a treasure to both Marlene and Roger. It will be inspiration that means as much to the man as it does to the woman.

This is especially true in Alaska since good women are hard to find. Strangely enough, the homonym of principal and principle is true. The principal of an Alaskan school—Marlene, and the principles that Roger uses to make Angler's Lodge the best salmon fishing in Alaska. It provides all the local residents a great story of 'Marlene be mine.'

# THE HOUSE THAT TALKED

◆

*A Judge's Life and His Home That Talked*

IN THE SPRING OF 1928, a California colonial house was built using white clapboard and green shutters. The solid oak front door was painted green to match the trim. It was located in a fashionable area named Westwood, adjacent to Beverly Hills.

Built on a pie-shaped lot, the house was surrounded by a lush lawn, a beautiful garden, and a winding concrete pathway stretching from the street to the front door. The house was completed just before the stock market crash in the fall of 1929. It was the 'home of homes.'

It was built by a developer/builder who was well known throughout Southern California. He had a reputation of 'Building Your Dream House.' The builder had picked a good location. The area chosen had expensive homes and amenities, such as UCLA, a famous university in nearby Westwood.

After the house was completed in 1929, it did not sell because of the Great Depression, so its builder moved into it himself. Such self-financing was frowned upon by the banks during the hard times in the country. But the builder got away with doing it.

## ITS BIRTH

The first Turning Point in this house's life was its construction and sale by the builder. It was on the market for three and a half years before an attorney, Manny, 'stole it.' He purchased it when he found that his law practice in Los Angeles had grown to the point that driving fifteen miles to his office did not bother him. His clients came from miles around. He wanted to entertain in style. Manny wanted to own a wonderful house in a wonderful area, so he bought it.

## GROWING UP

On its third birthday, the house found its owner. Attorney Manny made the house a home. According to the Diamond of Life, imagination (its architectural design) and persistence (the builder keeping it until it sold) led to success. This success included the house being featured in the "Home Section" of the Los Angeles Times. Thus, the Turning Point of this house was the date of its acquisition by Manny, the new owner.

Certain features of the house were especially important to Manny and his family. The home had been designed in such a way that all members could do their own thing. All the rooms were utilized for special purposes. Manny had a radio room for worldwide communicating. His wife had a reading room. The youngsters had a playroom. There was a party room overlooking the exquisite gardens. The Turning Point in this instance showed foresight, good planning, and creativity—all pointing to a successful house.

## ORDINARY LIFE

Several years passed, and a Turning Point in Manny's life also affected his family and his home. It was during the summer of 1946, and polio was a frightful disease. At that time, the youngest of Manny's children, Ellen, contracted polio, and was dead within six weeks. It was his only daughter. Sadness, gloom, and doom made the house dreary and woebegone. The shutters were closed and the curtains drawn.

Polio was a blow that neither parent could face. Manny had a nervous breakdown, and his wife used alcohol to make her loss bearable. Such tragedy resulted in the couple destroying themselves. The practical result was that Manny and family had to convert one of the bedrooms and bath for use by a series of incompetent live-in nurses. The house suffered through this disaster. It was maintained as before.

The Diamond of Life scenario was reflected by Traits and Tendencies of the owner's mental attitude. It also showed that such analysis resulted in the deterioration of the home's appearance. All of these negatives, including misfortune, pointed to failure.

## REVIVAL

After several years of mourning, the next Turning Point was one of hope and joy. For the house, it was reflected by a complete renewal of the house's interior and repainting of the outside. It looked like it did when it was new.

Coincidentally, its owner, Manny, received a phone call from the Governor of California, Ronald Reagan, appointing him to the bench. He would be a Municipal Court Judge for the City of Los Angeles. The swearing-in ceremony was to be at the house on Bonaire Road. It would be held outside in the luscious backyard. The house was ecstatic.

Without hesitation, the wheels of progress were put into motion. Inside and out, the house and yard were updated. The appointment of Manny took place, his title became Judge Manny, and he was added to the municipal court bench.

## THE TARNISHED YEARS

The calendar moved ahead, and Mrs. Manny had a stroke. After being confined to living in her bedroom for a number of years, Mrs. Manny died. The Judge was alone, but he continued to live in the house, single and lonely. The house suffered through these trying years.

Though only seventy, Judge Manny was an eligible bachelor, and became even more so after he was appointed to the bench with lifetime tenure. His home in Westwood was free and clear. Judge Manny was set for life. The new judge sensed that, in keeping with his judicial career, he should keep his home in immaculate condition, and this he did. This was a Turning Point of the house's life. Such changes would add twenty years of extra use to the home. The Diamond of Life showed that the qualities of proper planning and timing could and would lead to success.

## THE DECLINING AND TERMINAL YEARS

Driving from his house to his downtown courtroom, Judge Manny suffered a mild stroke. His doctor told him that he would be confined to bed at home for several months. This illness resulted in the judge employing a caretaker who would also maintain the house. His new caretaker, May, was from the Philippines and twenty-five years younger than the judge. She became what the judge called 'his chief cook and bottle washer'. She could drive, maintain the home, and attend to all his bodily needs. The happenings of the next year became the major Turning Point of the house on Bonaire Road.

The structure was forty-three years old. At that time, Judge Manny was in his seventies. His health had been excellent before the stroke. His recovery was normal, but Judge Manny decided to retire from the bench and marry his nurse, May.

This became the final period in the lives of Judge Manny, May, and the home. The house on Bonaire Road suffered from neglect. May was now half owner and mistress of the House that Talked. Many Filipinos were allowed to live in the house, and the little regard they gave to proper maintenance led to its decline. Judge Manny went to his maker. Unfortunately, the house did not go to its maker.

## CONCLUSION

The ultimate Turning Point for Judge Manny occurred when he became ill. As with all people who become ill, they pass into the great beyond. But this was not before he married his caretaker who became the sole owner of the house and all of the other assets the judge had. The effect of his passing was a disaster.

The condition of the house, the yard, and the rubbish found inside the Bonaire Road home was a crime. The mess was detrimental to the entire community. The other property owners of Westwood turned the matter over to the city council. It was evident that, if Mrs. Judge Manny continued to occupy the house, it would only get worse.

## THE POST MORTEM

Mrs. Judge Manny's residence continued to be in disrepair. The neighbors were up in arms. The guests from the Philippines did a few repairs, but the future surely did not look promising. The home would be condemned and die. This, the final Turning Point, would be the most disastrous one of all.

It showed that if a house was not given the proper care and maintenance, the best of structures, both beautiful and well built, would become a physical wreck. Despite having a great life and being over eighty years old, the House That Talked had become an eyesore. If the house still could talk, it must be saying, "Help me, help me, I'm Dying."

## SIXTY FOUR YEARS OF FUN AND GAMES

◆

*The Last Half of the 20<sup>th</sup> Century*

"WINDING DOWN IS DIFFICULT for anyone who has retired." So said senior citizen David when asked to name a major change in his life. The following speaks for itself.

The main Turning Point was altering David's single status— meeting his wife and marrying her.

The year was 1946. David was in his first year of postgraduate study at Stanford. His roommate, Bill, lived near San Francisco and had suggested the two of them go to his uncle's house over a weekend. They went to the city and entered the uncle's community apartment.

This apartment was an entire floor of a building on top of Russian Hill. It was the ultimate in San Francisco living. The living room had a picture window with a baby grand piano framed by it. The view from the window was unbelievable—an unobstructed view of San Francisco Bay, Alcatraz Prison, and the Bay Bridge.

In the center of the bay window was the grand piano. On top of it was a picture of David's wife to be. She was a raving beauty. Seeing her in this setting caused David to ask Bill, "Who is that? She IS gorgeous. I will marry her. How can I meet her?" It turned out that she was Bill's cousin.

Two months after seeing the photograph of the lady in the window, Bill sent David a clipping from the society section of the San Francisco Chronicle. It was of the same girl, but in a different setting. She was in a wheelchair at the Debutante's Ball. She had broken her leg. There was a swarm of males around her. The clipping title was "Debutante Attends Ball in Wheel Chair."

After an orchestrated courtship of nine months, she became David's wife. Sixty-four years of wedded bliss—a fruitful marriage, four exceptional daughters, no in-law problems, and great solutions to marital rifts before they became painful.

Bliss has followed this courtship. David attributed it to having a wonderful wife.

The Diamond of Life provides a reason the couple has stayed together for eons. This analysis demonstrated clearly that humor (being able to ignore errors of the partner with a smile) was important. Friendship was another. Their good attitudes made their marriage work. Each had a few very close friends, but one was the other's best friend. David's fun-and-games marriage of over sixty-four years proved that marriage after the Second World War was a blessing.

## AHOY MATES, LOBSTER BOATS:
## REPAIRING AND REPLACEMENT

*A Question and Answer Session*

JUSTINA TURNED TO FACE the author and said, "My dad and my husband are not here. They are out on the dock working. This is part of a family business that has been handed down for several generations. We've been known as Ahoy Mates-Lobster Boats for ages."

"My statistics? I am thirty-two and have been married for nine years. I have two boys who are in grade school and are watched by their grandmother. I work in the office of Ahoy Mates as a girl Friday. I do everything from buying supplies to answering the telephone and keeping the records straight. I have been doing this for years, and I love my work."

The author asked, "What did you do before?"

Justina answered, "My background before I came to Portland, Maine? I wanted to get away from city life. Everybody comes here to spend what summer vacation they can afford. The town, as you can see, is jammed with visitors."

She babbled on. "I graduated from the University of Florida and was a beauty queen at the university in my senior year. When I graduated, I found a job working for a cosmetic company who needed a 'detailer' who was attractive enough to sell their products. I did this for several years."

The author asked, "And....?"

Justina said, "I visited Portland during my vacation time. I met my husband at the boat show. We met while I was looking at his display. I saw beautiful lobster and pleasure boats. I wanted to see his place of business. As you can tell by our title, the company repairs and replaces boats. The shop has been in business for almost a century, and it has occupied this space on the dock for many, many years.

"After we are done, we can look around the dock and see where John, his father, and crew are working. You will find out what boat repair is all about. Portland, Maine, the Bay of Casco, and the Fore River make an ideal harbor for any type of boating, especially lobstering.

Justina went on."Even before I met John, I had a major decision to make. Since I had a wonderful life being a former beauty queen, I wondered whether or not I should stay in Florida.

"The ball was in my court. My choice was made more difficult because I had several guys on the string. These Don Juans added to my difficulty. I hoped to get married one time and live happily ever after. I was in a quandary. Should I go to another location in the U.S. where I would meet somebody, fall in love, and get married?"

The author said, "Yes, go on...."

Justina said, "I realized that I was at the stage in life where I would have to decide what to do with the rest of my life, including where I should live. This would be an important choice in my life, and I couldn't afford to make a mistake."

Then the phone rang. Justina answered it briefly and continued. "As you can tell, I decided to move from Florida and relocate here in Maine. I met John at the boat show where the company was one of the exhibitors. We had dates while I was in town. Each of us made several trips to see each other during the following year, and we became engaged, got married, and have been happy ever since."

The author thought Justina had found a Turning Point in her life by going to Portland, Maine, going to the boat show, meeting John, an eligible man, and falling in love. This became a magical instant in their lives. It led to marriage and togetherness.

This scenario demonstrates how the Diamond of Life Traits and Tendencies, namely the proper attitude, a convenient opportunity, and a dollop of luck, put John and Justina, the Ahoy Mates couple, on the road to paradise. "Lobster Boat Heaven."

# IS DIVORCE THE ANSWER?

*A Wife with Three Kids Wants to Know*

WILLIAM, A SERVICEMAN FOR American Telephone and Telegraph (AT&T), rang the doorbell of a customer in a suburban area of Los Angles. It was in the summer of 2007. Betty answered the door, and the serviceman told her that he would be working on the TV line for thirty to forty minutes. When he was done, he would come back and notify her if he had been able to fix the problem. Betty, a housewife, said okay and continued her duties.

An hour later, William rang the doorbell and Betty answered it. The serviceman said, "Your TV line should be okay now. Turn the TV on and check the picture and let me know if it is okay."

She did so while he waited on the doorstep. In a couple of minutes, Betty came back to the front door and said, "Thanks very much. It is working now."

As he turned to leave, William said, "Ma'am, could you get me a glass of cold water? It's a very hot up on the telephone pole."

She said, "Yes, of course," and went to get the water.

William thought to himself, "I have to get some advice from somebody. I just don't know what to do." Something was puzzling William, and he needed to run it by somebody else.

When Betty returned with a cold glass of water, he drank it and said, "Thank you very much. I have solved your problem. I know this is very gutsy of me, but will you listen to me? I need some advice."

She answered "Why would you ask me, an ordinary housewife, to give you advice?"

He said, "I am so upset. I want to talk to anyone who might give me some idea of what to do."

She said, "I will, but you must realize you're asking an unqualified person to give you personal advice."

William said, "I am thinking of getting a divorce."

She answered, "What about your kids? How many have you got?"

He said, "Well, I have three kids—two boys and one girl. One is twelve, one is eight, and the youngest is three." He added, "I have been married for thirteen years. We live in a house in Pasadena. I have been working at my job with AT&T for about twenty years.

Betty said, "Well, what's happened that has caused you to want a divorce? This is certainly a Turning Point in your life. Have you really decided that divorce is the only answer?"

William looked away and said, "During the last three years, my problem has been my wife and her drinking booze almost every afternoon. I have talked to her a number of times, and she has promised to clean up her act so we can resume our happy marriage."

Betty said, "Well, that sounds promising, but have you still decided that divorce is the only way to go?"

William said, "I just can't take it anymore. I go to work five to six days a week, put in a full day doing my job for the phone company, and when I come home, my wife is plastered. She is lying on her bed. She cries when I ask her what she has done all day."

Without waiting for her answer, he continued, "Her drinking will ruin our family, and it will destroy me. What should I do in your opinion?"

Betty thought a moment and said, "If it were me and my husband, I would certainly see a professional person with my husband to find out what happened after thirteen years and three kids."

William said, "I've tried everything you mentioned and the result is my wife is on the wagon for a month or so and then again the same damn thing. This has happened for the last three years, and it is getting so difficult that I have been considering divorce. Again, I ask you as a stranger and somebody independent to tell me—is divorce the way to go? What else can I do?"

Betty thought for a minute and said, "Try counseling again, and do it where you attend part of the sessions together and part of the sessions where she is with the counselor alone."

The serviceman, William, looked at her and said, "Is that the best you can do?"

Betty said, "Based on the brief amount of information that you have given me, yes. I repeat, find a professional and visit him with your wife and without your wife. Don't do anything hasty because divorce is the last thing a family should do."

Again, William thanked her and said, "I appreciate your taking your time. I know it is crazy that I did something like this, but I am at my wits end. This is a Turning Point in our marriage and for my family."

With that, William turned and went back to his truck and sped off into the summer afternoon. He still was not sure of what he should do, but he felt a little better having met a sympathetic soul and unloading his problem on her. He thought to himself, "What I have got to lose by following her advice? My wife and my kids are still so important to me that it is worth the try."

Deciding to wait to get professional advice fit William's personality and patience, attitudes found in his Diamond of Life. Certainly his wife, the kids, and a marriage that has gone sour deserve a second chance. In one sentence—divorce was the last answer to William's question!

# "OUT, OUT DAMN SPOT"

◆

*William Shakespeare*

"CHEERS TO THE BRIDE and groom, Sam and Ruth," said Louie as he held his glass of champagne high. Louie added, "Long may they live."

This toast was in honor of two San Franciscans as each celebrated their second marriage. This event was held in the home of Sam, the groom. After their nuptials, they lived and loved in his home. Sam had a young boy and Ruth had a little girl from previous marriages. Sam had owned his home for nearly fifteen years. Sam and Ruth each had a dog. The two families merged and started what was supposed to be a marriage made in heaven.

And so it was for a couple of years. Sam and Ruth were ecstatic. This paradise included the two children and Spot and Macbeth, the two dogs—all of whom got along famously. The dogs ate together, took romps together, and really enjoyed each other. The two children did the same. The togetherness seemed to be a great merger. The two families clicked for the first two years.

The flies in the ointment were Fred and Marion, the boy and his stepsister. Fred was ten and Marion was seven. The two children vied for the attention and approval of their parents and soon it became a problem for Sam and Ruth. The children squabbled all day long except at school. When Fred's grandmother came to visit, Fred and Marion fought for her attention as well, and the family situation became impossible.

Sam and Ruth went to a marriage counselor to see what could be done to save their marriage. After a number of sessions, the couple and the marriage counselor agreed that a divorce was the only solution.

Sam and Ruth decided that they would use a settlement mediator to help divide the community property. These arrangements took nearly a year. During this period, the two parents met with the arbiter to work out the division of property and solve any other problems that might arise.

At the final settlement meeting, Sam and Ruth met at the office of the arbiter. It was in downtown San Francisco. Both arrived separately having lived apart for several months. The arbitration was discussed and the ins and outs of who got what were decided quite amicably. All community property was listed and decided by the arbiter. The division of property went along beautifully. It was accepted by both Sam and Ruth. And both agreed to sell their home and divide the proceeds.

Obviously, the two children, Fred and Marion, went with each parent. The last item to discuss was the dogs, Spot and Lady Macbeth.

The arbiter was told that from the first day they moved into the Walnut Street home the dogs had been constantly together. The dogs got along famously. They went on walks together, they went to the vet together, they played together, they ate together, and they even slept together. And it was apparent that to divide them would be one of the cruelest acts either Sam or Ruth could imagine.

"I want the dogs," said Sam.

Ruth interrupted and said, "No, I get the dogs."

Each of the two supported claiming the dogs with excellent reasons for requesting custody.

And so it went for the first four or five minutes. The arbiter excused himself, and as he left, he told the two almost divorced persons, "You two better decide who gets the dogs or I will make the decision to split the dogs." The arbiter left the room.

Sam and Ruth argued back and forth and finally Sam said, "I give up. Ruth. I want the divorce as much, or even more, than you do. I know you don't read very much, Ruth. But remember this…I'll give both dogs to you, but as I do, I am quoting from Shakespeare's Macbeth when Lady Macbeth says, 'Out, out damn Spot.'… You take the dogs Ruth, and I'll say it again—'out, out damn spot,' and take Lady Macbeth with you!"

# DINING AT DIMION'S

◆

*The Old Guard Blows the Family Whistle*

AN AGE-OLD PROBLEM reared its ugly head. It was the 'old guard' families versus the 'newbees.' It was two groups in a small community Chamber of Commerce battling for control. It was a conflict between the old-time family members versus Mike and Eleni, the newest family in town, who wanted to start a new restaurant.

The new dining facility was to replace an older establishment frequented by the old guard.

The old-timers did not like the idea of change. They cited that the existing operators of Mr. C's had served the community for over thirty years. The restaurant had been opened during the middle of the 20th century. The structure was built by the tenants on a location owned by the past president of Sun Valley California Chamber. It was lease-renewal time, and Mike and Eleni had moved to the San Fernando Valley.

The couple was from Greece in the eastern Mediterranean. They wanted to open a Greek, full-service restaurant complete with a cocktail bar. This would be new construction. In question was a site on the Golden State Freeway bordering the Hollywood Burbank Airport. The new restaurant required tearing down two old buildings and building a beautiful new structure that could seat two hundred guests.

The bone of contention involved the size and type of restaurant it would be. The old guard members felt that the north eastern San Fernando Valley had enough big new restaurants. They objected to adding another, much larger, upscale restaurant to the business mix. It was the same old problem: "Don't rock the boat, it will tip over. We like it the way it is NOW!"

This Turning Point affected three groups. It affected the city itself. It affected the new chamber members buying the property, and it affected the Chamber of Commerce. The new members had sold a previous restaurant operation having this growth goal in sight. If the existing members succeeded in blocking the project, Mike and Eleni would have to go back to square one and locate in another area of the San Fernando Valley. Such a delay would cause loss of income to all three groups. The new owners had sold their old restaurant operation to raise capitol so that they could start this new family type restaurant. They wanted to have their son own and operate it after they passed on, They had drawn plans, met with a number of professional people to review the site, and continued to develop their concept.

The city of Los Angeles was looking forward to increased income from an expanded business and the taxes that it would bring in. It also wanted to have the city grow so that other people would move to the city. In this way, new business would be welcomed in the San Fernando Valley, and the city would cooperate.

If the old guard had its way, each of the three groups would have to go back and start over. This new restaurant concept and resulting Turning Point for the community was dependant on favorable action on the part of the city of Los Angeles. In addition, the other old members of the Chamber of Commerce would have to withdraw their objection to this economic expansion.

The Turning Point for Mike and Eleni was whether to continue their fight to open the new restaurant after they had become members of the Chamber and had purchased the site or cancel and move their new business operation to another site outside the city. The case for the Chamber of Commerce was, "No more eating-places with bars. We don't need a new family to tip over the apple cart. Even though it is family owned, family run. Why change the good thing we have now?"

Such a decision was a major Turning Point for the president of the Chamber of Commerce and the old guard. This item would be placed on the agenda as the first item to be considered by the board of directors. After a thorough debate, a vote would be taken as to what to do. Should they approve a new family business and improve the community, or keep the status quo?

The following month, the consideration of the matter was taken up by the Chamber of Commerce as the first item of business. Both positions were represented at that time. The vote for or against was held at the end of the meeting by written ballot. The ballots were opened and the votes counted.

The Diamond of Life analysis predicted success for the new family-type restaurant being allowed to go ahead. Mike and Eleni had done their planning well. Their honesty in doing it right and their willingness to meet the entire objections paid off handsomely. Rather than being unyielding in wanting it all their way, Mike and Eleni had paved the road for moderation on the part of the old guard and it resulted in success. The small suburb in the San Fernando Valley could add a new restaurant to the two thousand two hundred other businesses in the area.

The result was a mixed bag. The Turning Point in the new venture, to be called Dimion's, was that Mike and Eleni had faced an uphill fight for expansion. As new members, they were welcomed into the community. So was Dimion's Restaurant and Bar, but with restrictions as to hours of operation. Needless to say, the old guard was not happy, but they accepted the new restaurant because, as new members of the chamber, the community as a whole would benefit from this decision.

The outcome was positive. A year later, dining at Dimion's was enjoyed by chamber members and non-members alike. This was a great accomplishment due to the efforts of a pro-restaurant group. That meant that the chamber and the community had welcomed Dimion's for dining after the fight was over and the smoke had cleared. It was a success for all three groups. Dining at Dimion's was awesome.

# THE ETERNAL TRIANGLE

*Businessman Faces the Future with Dedication*

"THE THIRD TIME'S GOT to be a charm." This thought crossed Mason's mind as he left his home. He was on his way to join his bride-to-be at the synagogue. He had divorced his first wife while living in the Midwest. He had buried his second wife after she committed suicide. Now he was about to marry Shiela and adopt her three children. Mason laughed as he thought, "No delivery room for me."

Mason had adopted a philosophy that his life would be the Eternal Triangle with three equal sides, the base of which was his Religion. He was an orthodox Jew and lived by the tenets of the Torah (Hebrew Bible). The second side was Business (work hard and be financial secure). Lastly was the Personal side (have a happy and fruitful family life).

The upcoming event was to be a major Turning Point in his life. He remembered when his adopted daughter, Marsha, had told him that she felt abandoned and all alone in the world after her mother died. Her birth mother was dead; she had committed suicide. Mason, Marsha's stepfather, had married her new mother even though both had been single for just one year. The third marriage would be it.

Minneapolis was Mason's birthplace and where he had spent his first twenty-five years. He had gone to the University of Minnesota and graduated in business administration. He was a product of the Second World War. His business career started in 1953. He made a pilgrimage to Arcata, California, a town in northern California and in the center of timber country.

The reason for Mason's going to Arcata was simple. A distant relative had started Arcata Plywood Company at the end of the Second World War when the housing boom blossomed in California. Plywood was needed to build houses. Mason wanted to take advantage of this building boom, and Abe Rochlin, a relative and plywood maker, would give him credit to start a new lumber business.

After making his deal with Arcata, Mason returned to the Los Angeles area and set up a lumber and plywood-distributing firm. His younger brother, Joe, was able to join the venture and the Mason-Joe Plywood Company was opened. Special pricing and delayed repayment made this Turning Point a major success.

The Diamond of Life characteristics showed that ingenuity, attention to detail, and contacts made the plywood distributorship a viable business. With a business operation in place and running well, Mason faced his personal problems, which he attributed to the Eternal Triangle of Life. Simply stated, his two marriages had failed. One was by divorce and the other by suicide.

He analyzed his life as to why the marriages failed. According to the Diamond of life theory, his first marriage failed due to immaturity of the two partners. Both were young, straight out of college, and without money— not a good recipe for success. His second venture into marriage was terminated by tragedy. Mason thought it had been a happy union despite not having any offspring. He was startled by Meg drowning herself.

Mason's wife's suicide, and his desire to marry for the third time, were major Turning Points for Mason. The destruction of his family so suddenly was tragic. Mason felt that he could have avoided it if he had not been so dedicated to his business.

Mason's closest friend introduced the two. Shiela was Jewish and a divorcee with two children. She was devoted to Judaism and seemed to be a great choice. She might make Mason's life whole. She could complete Mason's existence, the Eternal Triangle of Life. After a courtship of two years, Irwin and his soon-to-be wife got together. Mason realized that the third time must be the charm.

Twice married and twice separated, Mason showed that life's Turning Points can be faced if he had the courage to face adversity for yet another time. Experience influenced Mason's future life. The completion of the Eternal Triangle's base—having a fruitful family experience—was Mason's goal. He was about to marry for the third time. He hoped that the tempering of unfortunate events would turn tragedy into happiness. And so it was with Mason, Shiela, and their Eternal Triangle of Life. Business, family, and religion were united. The major Turning Point in Mason's life had arrived.

## WHAT CAN A CREATIVE WRITER'S WIFE DO WHILE HE IS CREATING?

◆

*Cry a lot!*

AN ELDERLY COUPLE FACED a Turning Point in both their lives after the husband retired. The wife of sixty-two years had been extremely happy until her husband hung up his necktie and retreated to an office in their home. Prior to the changed event, his wife always kissed her husband goodbye at 8 o'clock in the morning and greeted him warmly at 5 o'clock in the afternoon when he returned. Now it was different.

He had rented his office in downtown Redmond, Oregon, to a local merchant. His wife was upset because it changed their lifestyle. Her husband was concerned because he had nothing to do until he started writing a book called *Life's Turning Points.*

The Turning Point in the lives of the couple was whether or not the wife's loss of freedom, after so many years, would cause a breach in their marriage.

The husband had told his wife that he would dedicate this epic to her. He said that the warmth of what he would say about her in his dedication would be determined by her behavior while he was writing the book.

She responded by saying that their house was small, and that when he took over the great room, the living room, the dining room, and the kitchen in order to have peace and quiet, she had become a prisoner in the bedroom.

His explanation was, "If I am to complete my book, I will need silence, peace, harmony, good food, and a Diamond of Life analysis."

### THE DIAMOND OF LIFE REVIEW FOR THE HUSBAND

Following his request, she was permitted in the kitchen for a limited time, such as from four to six p.m. for cooking and preparing dinner. Of course, such privileges could be suspended by either marriage partner. She was thrilled she could go down in literary history with the world's finest dedication. She also was happy to be able to go to the Redmond City Library during its open hours. There, her husband, the writer, could peruse the many books to get background information regarding Turning Points of the ordinary people he had met during the past sixty-two years. This research involved using the library's computers and GOOOGLE.

This meant that the computer that they had at home had to be used by him exclusively to supplement the ones he used in the library. This led to a Turning Point. Would the restriction of freedom of his wife of sixty-two years destroy this marriage of many years? Only time would tell!

**Editor's note:** The party of the first part was given the right to review the above but not given permission to edit it. She told the party of the first part that, while true, it does not represent the whole story, and she will prepare an answer.

7

# HEALTH

H EALTH IS ONE OF life's necessities. Without it, living is deadly according to the GET WITH IT theory. The other three—intelligence, hard work, and timing—while vital, may be postponed on the road to reach success. Health and intelligence are personal attributes. Wealth can be acquired by hard work, and timing is a matter of circumstance.

Many philosophers have reasoned that without one's health, failure is a probability. This chapter highlights the Turning Points of eleven individuals where age, illness, vision, sexual orientation, habits, and physical condition impacted decisions.

These individuals faced Turning Points head-on—some successfully, others to no avail. Once a decision was made, it was often irreversible. The past became history, and the future became murky. These stories relate how health affected individual lives and what could or could not have been changed.

# A MOVIE SCENE IS PROPERLY SET

*Frank Furnishes ER for TV*

FRANK SMILED WISTFULLY AS he remembered how happy he had been. He was not joyful now! His wife had just died. Frank's wife had spent sixteen years working with him. Without her at his side, it would be lonely. She had made it a fulfilling marriage. Frank had sired four daughters and had built a unique type of business for the motion picture industry. It didn't involve handling movie stars or supplies or people things.

His company rented everything used on a set to produce a movie or a TV show. It was based on personal contacts. It was not about *what* you knew; it was *whom* you knew.

Frank had provided everything from operating tables to aspirin that were used in making the weekly episodes of "ER" ("Emergency Room"). However, Frank was lonely and missed his wife dearly.

His reverie ended when his cell phone rang. as Frank was standing on the second floor balcony of his warehouse. He had been gazing at three acres of the paraphernalia used in the business. After looking at some hospital emergency equipment, he began contemplating his success.

He had become the top dog in a niche market renting all sorts of props for TV programs and making movies. One of Frank's major customers was ER, a TV show that rented all the props needed to film the weekly show.

But why would TV production companies rent the same equipment week after week for more than a year or two? The answer is availability, reliability, and long-term relationships, even though it cost those who produce the program more to rent than to buy!

The reason for this oddity can best be shown by looking at Frank's background.

Frank was born in Connecticut. When Frank was in the ninth grade, his father died of cancer. The family was up against it, and it was bad economic times. Frank eventually went to California to make his fortune. As expected, this move became a Turning Point in his life.

Three years of taking any and all jobs he could get in the L.A. area, he ended up working as a gopher in a company that serviced the movie industry. He became a buyer of all of the items used in making movies—from safety pins to movie sets.

Frank eventually was promoted and became a sales representative. This new job turned out to a Turning Point. This promotion required Frank to go into the field where the action was.

In the early eighties, Frank called on the trade. During a sales call, he heard a rumor that a new show was to start up. It was to be staged as a hospital—an emergency room drama.

Frank thought, "This new company will need loads of props to be rented from somebody. Why not me?"

Frank would be facing an important change in the economic aspects of his life! It meant going from sales into managing. It meant forming a new business. It meant shouldering all the responsibilities of being an employer and not an employee. It was a staggering thought, and certainly, by all standards, a major Turning Point in his life!

He talked it over with his wife. By then he had four kids and very little money. Even if all went well, it would be tough sledding for a long time. But they both wanted to give it a go. And go it they did. They started small, and because of Frank's reputation, the business grew rapidly. Frank knew they would need more capital.

This was yet another Turning Point. Frank took in a partner—a woman who had the money for expansion but wanted to work only as a financial partner.

Ten years later, Frank and company were successful to the degree that led to the two major Turning Points in his life—one good and one bad.

In the first decade of the 21st century, through hard work and good timing, Frank's company flourished. He purchased a one-hundred thousand square-foot facility on three acres of land near the studios. This in itself is a Turning Point of great magnitude. A two and a half acre warehouse was no laughing matter. He worked very hard and so did his wife until she was stricken with cancer.

A year after the onset, Frank's life was blighted by the death of his wife of over twenty-five years. She died from pancreatic cancer. This Turning Point put a cloud over Frank's existence.

Frank looked to the future by forming a foundation in memory of his wife. Its purpose was to help cure this deadly disease that took the light of Frank's life. Frank often thought, "My life would be complete if she could be here now." This tragedy remained the major Turning Point of his life.

## A Vow Taken in Haste
## Is Repented at Leisure

*Polio and a Living Death in an Iron Lung*

TRUDY'S HEART WAS POUNDING as she looked at her husband Peter. His six-foot frame was racked with waves of shaking and involuntary twitching. He was asking for water, but he could not swallow it.

Trudy thought that most young adults have the happy life. In her case, she had married quite young, had an infant son, and thought little about the future. The Turning Points that Peter and Trudy had were few and far between. The couple loved each other madly. They tried to keep each other interested, satisfied, and happy.

The doctor Trudy called came from L.A. County Hospital. He arrived, and after examining Peter, said, "Looks like polio, but I will take a blood sample to confirm my diagnosis. You better keep your son out of here until we find out for sure."

As he left, Trudy started to sob, "What will happen to us now?"

Peter and Trudy had met in college. Peter was an engineer, trying to get his master's degree. Trudy was a young teaching student. Their marriage took place in the late forties. This illness was a shocker out of the blue. It struck without warning. It was a health problem that presented itself and would affect the couple's lives forever.

Peter and Trudy had taken their marriage vows implicitly because they were Catholic. Little did they know that their vow to be together forever would be tested so soon.

The morning after the doctor had sent Peter to county hospital, he called Trudy and said that the tests show that Peter was a very sick man. He has the disease called polio. Trudy was stunned. They had been happily married for a few years and so Trudy became unglued. It was a "Catch 22" situation.

Peter developed all the crippling effects of polio. It affected him from his neck down—his breathing and his arm and leg muscles. Peter seemed destined to spend the rest of his life surround by an iron lung. All his bodily functions would require help from others. It was not only a horrible existence for Peter, but also horrible for Trudy and their young son, David.

Peter was consigned to the County of Los Angeles Hospital called Rancho Los Amigos. He was to receive care twenty-four hours a day, seven days a week, until he died. It was like being buried alive.

Peter's arrival at the Ranchos Amigo Hospital was typical. Peter was put in isolation and became more acutely ill as his stay in the hospital lengthened. He lost his ability to move his arms and his legs. He had quadriplegic polio and the attending physician said his iron lung would extend his life for many years. This machine kept Peter breathing.

The doctor talked to Trudy and said they would not know the extent of the physical problems that Peter had until thirty-five days elapsed. The doctor said that each case he had treated varied as to the effect it had and the ability of the patient to rehabilitate himself. He assured her that Peter was getting the best of care, and that she should come to see him as much as she wanted.

Trudy left the hospital in a daze.

During the six-week isolation period, Peter was incapacitated. He had difficulty breathing, was paralyzed from the neck down, and, according to the doctor, would have difficulty ever leaving the breathing apparatus. The fact that Peter had polio was certainly a life altering Turning Point in the life of the family.

Peter was incapacitated. Trudy would return to teaching her classes. David, their son, would never get to know his father. It was a Turning Point of great magnitude.

Three years passed, and Peter was still in the polio ward. Trudy was still telling David about his father. The children in the neighborhood avoided David even though neither Trudy nor David ever contracted polio. Both had taken the Salk vaccine.

Then Trudy faced another major Turning Point in her life. It was the marriage vow she had taken during the marriage ceremony. The couple had pledged to stay together through sickness and in health till death separated them.

Being a Catholic, she faced a major decision. Should she live her life in the way she had during the previous three years with Peter as a virtual dead man? Or should she break her vow and the sanctity of her church, get a divorce, and raise David as a normal child?

This Turning Point decision was constantly on Trudy's mind.

The Diamond of Life review made Trudy step back and consider her plight. Persistence (keep your marriage vows at all cost), religion (illness is no excuse for divorce), and development (giving David, her son, a normal life as he grew up).

Trudy's values favoring divorce and a new life were two-fold— common sense and fairness.

After mental turmoil, Trudy chose divorce as opposed to a life with no future. She had not taken the marriage vows lightly, nor did she have to repent in leisure. She had given Peter ten years of her life. The vow taken when she was a young adult she had kept. There was no number two waiting in the wings. She did nothing to violate her commitment to Peter. She finally decided on divorce. It had become Trudy's turn to live again!

# MAKING HAY WHILE THE SUN SHINES

*Health, Wealth, and Happiness Are the Keys to Success*

THE DOCTOR TOLD GORDY, "You have esophageal cancer. You will lose your voice. The treatment is very painful, and the cure is problematic."

Gordon's face paled as he asked the doctor what could be done to give him the best chance to survive. He then asked when his treatment should begin. The doctor said it should be started immediately, and the opportunity to survive would depend on how well the treatment helped.

The next few months provided an important Turning Point in Gordon's life. The choices he had were taking the cure or toughing it out. The doctor Gordon had consulted had been a member of the Sun Valley Rotary Club for years. He was a personal friend. He advised Gordon to get a second opinion. The second opinion confirmed the cancer and the procedure.

Gordon decided to be treated. It was a six-month period of radiation and chemotherapy. But whether the cancer would return would not be known for five years.

Shortly after his bout with cancer, another Turning Point occurred in Gordon's life. It was the day his business building burned to the ground. It was about 8:00 o'clock in the evening when Gordon got a call. The local fire chief told him that his building on Sunland Boulevard was ablaze. The chief said that it looked like the building would be a total loss. He added that Gordy should come down immediately.

After phoning his insurance agent with the news, he went to look at the fire damage. Only the walls were standing. It was a building that he had occupied for many years. The building itself was a brick structure with a high roof and a dirt floor because it was used for hay and grain storage.

The horses, owned by local farmers in the surrounding Sun Valley area, ate the hay and were shod at Gordy's location.

Gordon contemplated his financial loss on the way down to see the damage. As he approached the burning building, he saw that the roof was gone. The timbers were still falling and the rest of the structure was in shambles. It was completely destroyed.

He had a choice to make—one that would influence the remainder of his life. Should he rebuild or move his business to a new location?

Gordy knew that money would be no problem since his wife, Nancy, had just paid the renewal premium within the last month, and the insurance money would be available for either choice. The decision that he must make would depend on the engineering reports.

If the building walls were not damaged, Gordon had to decide if he would rebuild in the present location or move to a better location on Glenoaks Boulevard. He considered the old saying, "When deciding where to buy real estate, there are three things to consider— location, location, and location!"

The cost of replacing a roof and the other equipment would be far less than having to prepare a new site, to have plans made, to get the plans approved, and construct the building. In addition, it would take over a year to build new; whereas, staying with the present location would take six months. That was the Turning Point decision that Gordon faced. It was to rebuild or move to a new location!

Gordon was able to make such a decision because the Diamond of Life demonstrated that he had the right attitude in responding to this casualty loss problem. He had the ability to get his good customers to postpone purchasing while he replaced his inventory of hay, grain, and feed. He had the finances from his insurance to make the replacement, and he had the time to draw everything together for a successful conclusion. He chose to build a new building at a more desirable location.

At the end of a year, Gordon had a new facility on Glenoaks Boulevard with available hay and feed for sale. He was able to re-establish his business, and it exceeded his hopes.

However , health problems faced his son. Cancer often occurs in other members of one's family, and so it was with his forty-year-old son. His annual physical determined he had cancer, too. This devastated Nancy, Gordon's wife.

All three incidents were Turning Points for Gordon—the building fire and esophageal cancer of both father and son. These can be explained by the Diamond of Life. Gordon was haunted by bad luck. His Traits and Tendencies reflect a good attitude, even when bad things happened. He had strength of spirit in facing an early death, and he had good judgment in considering alternatives when misfortune decreased his chances.

The change of the building location was a success, but Gordon's health problem was not. His esophageal cancer examination and discovery had occurred in the late seventies. As it happened, the major Turning Point in Gordon's life was meeting the grim reaper. His bout with cancer lasted a year and a half. Gordon's family was not only depressed, but also, to make matters worse, his son, who was only in the early forties, had similar symptoms as Gordon.

The diagnosis from the doctor was that the father and son both had esophageal cancer. Gordon died at sixty-nine and his son at forty-five. These were Turning Points in the life of Gordon's wife. To lose two of her dearest family members, one at the age of fifty, were Turning Points of tremendous proportions. Thus, the truism 'making hay while the sun shines' was vital to those Gordon left behind!

# YOU'VE HAD TOO MUCH TO DRINK - PLEASE LEAVE

*An Alcoholic's Lament*

"YOU'RE DRUNK KELLY. I'LL see you another time. Don't call on me again unless you are sober. I will never see you when you are bombed!" These words were said by Harold Christensen, a buyer for Marshall Field and Company, one of the finest department stores in the United States. He ushered a wobbly Kelly from his office. It was the beginning of the end for Kelly. It was also a Turning Point in his life—one he would never forget.

This was not the first time Kelly was drunk when he called on a good customer. Drinking too much was a habit that Kelly could not shake. The only reason he kept his job as sales manager for a small, but very famous, china, glass, and gift company was that his parents owned the business.

During World War II, Kelly worked in a defense industry so he was deferred from serving in the army. After the war ended, Kelly reactivated his career by reentering the small company his parents owned. He was a good salesman and quite successful.

He travelled the country, going to major cities to call on the trade and write up orders. He bought a car to travel to retail stores like Marshall Fields. He visited Chicago to call on the buyer of the key stores in the Midwest.

While waiting for his luncheon appointment, Kelly had a few manhattans and became drunk. He went up to Harold Christensen's office to apologize being late, but he was thrown out of Christensen's office.

Kelly was thirty-one years old and had been working for his parents' company for several years. He was a good-looking, single man and had a smile that wouldn't quit. He was a great salesman and a good sales manager. His road to ruin was alcohol. His alcohol problem developed very early in high school. Eventually, his drinking habit resulted in his alienating the buyer of the largest and most important customer in the United States. This was a Turning Point in Kelly's life.

Kelly had been working for the family-owned business for eight years, ever since his father had a heart attack. At the start of the war, Kelly had been unable to enlist because he had a heart condition of his own.

This lost opportunity was caused by demon rum and Kelly committing the ultimate sin—not treating a major customer with due respect.

Kelly had a number of alternatives. He could go back to the Glendale Company, beg forgiveness, and promise he would never do it again. He could look for another job in a similar field and start over as a sales representative. He could open his own retail china, glass, and gift store in Southern California. This was a business he understood.

Still in an alcoholic haze and uncertain of his next step, Kelly decide to sleep it off. Awaking in the middle of the night, he arose, dressed, and headed to Kansas City, Missouri. Kelly had another major account there—Hall's China, Glass, and Gift. Kelly thought that he would stop by there, talk to the buyer, whom he knew very well, and ask her advice.

At this impromptu meeting, the Hall's buyer said that if she were Kelly, she would open a retail operation in Southern California. The buyer added, "Kelly, be sure you have enough money to finance your store and that you stay off booze."

Following this conversation, Kelly chose to open an exclusive china, glass, and gift salon in a posh area near Newport Beach, California. He knew becoming a retail store owner could be a new start.

Kelly went over his entire life during the twenty-four hour trip to his home in California. He decided that his opportunities would be limited. He had sold the company car. His revolving door incidents of sobering up for a few months and having just one drink were well known. It would take time and money to clean himself up. Kelly concluded that his operating a retail store of his own was the best choice he could make.

Kelly had spent time selecting a good location for a retail store. He chose Newport Beach, a seashore town south of Glendale. Then he called his parents and told them he needed money to open up a retail store. He gave them details about what he intended to do and told them he felt confident he could be successful. He promised to dry himself out and told his parents so.

Kelly said that if he did not stay away from alcohol, they could terminate the deal. They could liquidate all his assets and pay themselves back the money he had used to set up the business in Newport Beach.

After a week passed by, Kelly called and asked them if they had come to a decision. They said that they were getting legal documents drawn up, and that he should be able to get started soon. Kelly jumped at this opportunity. He had been without alcohol for several weeks and felt he could continue to stay dried out for the rest of his life.

The lease was prepared for the Newport Beach location. The merchandise was ordered, and the store opened within six months of this decision. The operation continued for the next year, and it looked like Kelly had a new career. He had quit drinking and had started a retail business. But his changing from being the sales manager for somebody else to owning his own store was not to be.

To quote Robert Burns' famous saying, "The best laid plans of mice and men often go astray," was so true in Kelly's case. This Turning Point in Kelly's life was not successful. He went out of business in eighteen months. He was bankrupt within two years. He was dead in five years. It was an unfortunate Turning Point in Kelly's life.

Kelly had not studied his Diamond of Life characteristics. Too little willpower, too much optimism, and no perseverance led to his downfall. Kelly, still indulging, and swearing as he did so, said, "I'll never have another drink until the cocktail glass touches my lips."

This was the Alcoholics Lament! In Kelly's case, rightfully so.

# TWO MEDICAL DOCTORS –
# LIKE FATHER, LIKE SON?

*Two Careers in the 21ˢᵗ Century*

A FATHER AND SON, both in the medical profession with a forty-year difference in age, provided an interesting tale. In the case of these two doctors, heredity played a great part in their careers as to similarities as well as differences.

Dr. Smythe Sr., the father, and Dr. Smythe Jr., the son, never practiced together. Each went to different medical schools, and each had different careers, but both practiced in the San Fernando Valley, California. One of them practiced through four decades— from the fifties to the eighties, and the other practiced through three—from the eighties to the twenty-first century. Each had their own practice.

Dr. Smythe Sr. entered the Navy as an officer during the Second World War. Upon his discharge in California, he spent forty years doctoring in the San Fernando Valley. Dr. Smythe Sr. came to California after his service in the Navy. Even though he had spent his youth in New York, he wanted to live in California. In 1950, he purchased a practice from Dr. Wells, a Sun Valley general practitioner.

Dr. Smythe Sr. continued to provide medicine to the San Fernando Valley's small community of Sun Valley. His office was located immediately north of Lockheed Aircraft manufacturing facilities in Burbank, California. Dr. Smythe Sr.'s patients came from the eastern part of the Valley and included many Lockheed employees and their families.

Dr. Smythe Sr. was six feet tall, of slight build, and athletically inclined. He was intelligent and a well respected medical doctor. Dr.

Smythe Sr. had a wife, Esther, and a family including a son, Dr. Smythe Jr.

Dr. Smythe Sr. ran for trustee in the Community College district in the year 1951. He won the election and proceeded to serve as a trustee of this local community school district. He devoted his time to that service while he continued his medical practice.

Dr. Smythe Sr. was a Democrat and was appointed by California Governor, Earl Warren, to serve on the newly formed Community College Board of Trustees, which made educational decisions for the Junior College District. He was elected in 1952 to the Board of Trustees. In the 1956 re-election of Republican President Eisenhower, Democrat Dr. Smythe Sr. lost his bid for re-election.

Dr. Smythe Sr.'s son, Dr. Smythe Jr., also became a medical doctor by first going to Davis University, a California State educational institution. He graduated in the seventies and decided to practice in the city of Winnetka, part of the north central San Fernando Valley. Dr. Smythe Jr. was also a general practitioner. He also joined the Sun Valley Rotary Club and became part of the Republican political organizations located in the valley.

In the year 2000, Dr. Smythe Jr. was elected to the California State Assembly. He was re-elected assemblyman twice. In the year 2006, he decided to run for State of California Treasurer, a statewide office, which controlled the financial interests of the state. Dr. Smythe Jr.'s campaign for the California State Treasurer was not successful.

Dr. Smythe Sr. and Dr. Smythe Jr. had varied careers in many respects. They had different Turning Points and made different decisions which affected them. The old saying applies to the father and son, 'The fruit does not fall far from the tree.' In many respects, this applied. However, there were dissimilarities, especially when it came to Turning Points in each of their lives.

The choice of location to set up a practice, the area in which they decided to practice, and their choice of running for public office when serving their community, was 'like father like son' as the two followed a similar path to taste the fruits of success. Glory!

Note: Doctor Dr. Smythe Jr. died in 2010 of brain cancer.

# TO SEE OR NOT TO SEE-THAT IS THE QUESTION

*Dr. Lee-The Ophthalmologist's Day in the Sun*

THE WAITING ROOM OF Dr. Lee was full and overflowing. The impatient patient, Arthur, was contemplating his navel. It was decision time. Dr. Lee, a young-looking doctor, gave Arthur a choice. It was either 'yes or no' to undergoing delicate eyelid muscle surgery during which a drooping eyelid would be raised. This operation would eliminate any restriction of his view. Dr. Lee told the anxious patient that without the procedure, he would become progressively worse. After surgery, his vision would be improved. This was final.

A Turning Point for the eighty-eight year-old in relatively good health depended on a prompt decision by the patient. Aside from some blurred vision in one eye, Arthur was having little trouble reading or seeing at close distance. He would have this procedure because of personal vanity. He felt that an oldster with a drooping eyelid looked gross. The doctor had an eye operation batting average of ninety-seven percent for some improvement. For complete recovery, it was fifty-fifty.

The choice would be a Turning Point in both the doctor's and the patient's lives. Doctor Lee wanted to do the surgery now! Arthur wanted to wait. Who would prevail?

Leaving the doctor's office with his wife, Arthur knew that it concerned not only him but also his wife of sixty-three years, who had gone through thick and thin together. They had four children, his wife had suffered polio, and Arthur had experienced blurred vision in one eye for over a year.

Dr. Lee had studied at Harvard Medical School, came well recommended, and belonged to a famous group of eye specialists in the

San Fernando Valley. They were renowned for eye surgery. Dr. Lee spent a year and a half training in Chicago, Illinois. He had wanted to be a medical doctor for years. He thought that cardiology would be his specialty, but after a year and a half of general medicine, he changed his goal and wanted to become an ophthalmologist. Harvard Medical School provided his internship and his final years of training. Fortune smiled on the then thirty-year-old. He got a position with Dr. Colvard. This in itself was a Turning Point that would start the doctor on the path to success.

The Diamond of Life analyses were outstanding for Doctor Lee. He was intelligent and precise. He made sound choices when it came to education, setting up his practice, and choosing his associates. He joined prestigious organizations, such as the American Academy of Ophthalmology in Chicago, Illinois. Dr. Lee got on the staff of a famous eye doctor by answering an advertisement. Subsequent response to Dr. Lee resulted in his getting the opportunity of a lifetime.

All signs in his Diamond of Life—ambition, timing, and skill—were favorable. Little wonder that patient Arthur decided to do as Dr. Lee advocated.

To paraphrase William Shakespeare's quotation from *Macbeth,* "To be or not to be, that is the question." We find that Dr. Lee in his practice answers this question, "To see or not to see, that is my question."

Dr. Lee told his patient, "I can make you see better ninety-seven percent of the time." Even Babe Ruth couldn't bat nearly that well!

# THE FIRST 100 YEARS ARE THE HARDEST

◆

*Living It Up and Loving It*

BEAMING AS HE CUT his cake made especially for his one hundredth year, Robert coyly tried to pinch the waitress's behind. Typical for a centurion? Who could say? He found that life's drama was cool!

Robert was a young man from Scotland who traveled the world. He moved from Scotland to the United States in 1926. This move to the states was an awesome change.

Then, settling in the Midwest, Robert met, courted, and married Sadie. As his wife, she stayed at home and worked part time. She served as a housekeeper for an elderly couple. Robert and Sadie had two children. The family of four lived near Chicago. After the kids were born, Robert went to sea as a merchant seaman. He sailed the seven seas, from Canada to Constantinople. He was a world traveler, sailing on merchant ships and luxury liners.

During his lengthy travels, his wife stayed home. Sadie's death became a Turning Point in Robert s life. Both were ninety-five at the turn of the 21$^{st}$ century.

The Diamond of Life cautioned that life was a matter of one's skills, attitude, opportunity, and luck. These factors determined whether or not you would achieve success. In the case of Robert, he lived to be over one hundred and was still living it up and loving it. That was the peak of success!

The major Turning Point ended his career on a high note. Few people live to be one hundred, and those who aren't healthy, wish they were pushing up daisies. As of this writing, Robert was under the care of an assisted living facility. Robert's daughter mused, "Dad is as happy as a bird dog and as healthy as a horse."

If asked how his day went and what he did, Robert would smile and reply, "I don't know how my day went, but I sure know one thing—I had fun doing it."

# A STROKE OF LUCK IN EVERY WAY

*It Is Better to Be Lucky Than Smart*

"CALL THE AMBULANCE!" WAS the cry.

Stuart lay flat on the pavement twitching. He tried to get up on his feet, but the fact that he weighed almost three hundred pounds did not help. It was a stroke of luck that this incident happened a block away from the San Fernando City Hospital and that Stuart had been on his way there for a semi-annual physical.

The start of the 21st century was when it happened. Stuart met Ida at the hospital. She was a nurse in the ward where he was admitted for rehabilitation therapy. He was flat on his back when he heard the doctors say, "Nurse Ida, this is our rehab patient. I told him that we would not know the extent of his physical impairment for several weeks. In the meantime, make him as comfortable as you can. I'll return tomorrow for a look-see. Any questions?"

Nurse Ida told Stuart that strokes are serious. This evaluation would not take place until after a month of rehabilitation. Stuart was seriously overweight. He must lose weight. Recovery would take six months to a year.

Stuart worked hard at getting well. Ida was by his side in the hospital taking care of all his needs. She was Stuart's nurse. Some nine months later, she became his emotional provider, too. This resulted in Stuart and Ida getting married after the recovery period ended.

This stroke and marriage was a Major Turning Point in the lives of both Ida and Stuart.

It was the first marriage for Stuart and the second for Ida. Ida came from the Philippines and entered nursing in the United States. She had been married before and had two children from her previous marriage. One was twenty-nine, and the other was twenty-three. Ida had left her children back in the Philippines since both were married.

Some nine years later, when the couple decided to improve the economics of their existence, Stuart retired from the Edison Company at sixty-seven with full retirement benefits. The couple received checks from the IBEW and the Edison Company.

Ida was happy to quit her nursing occupation and enter a new business with Stuart. It was back to school for both. The couple entered the L.A. school district real estate course, and after some months, passed the California Real Estate exam. They became licensees.

This was a complete change for both. Stuart had managed to purchase a property on the beach in Ventura, California. It had greatly appreciated in value. This property was a long way from their home since the couple had moved to the City of San Fernando in Los Angeles County. These properties were a home and apartment adjacent to each other.

Two years later, after much work and dedication, these properties had become much more valuable than when they purchased them. This was called sweat equity. The couple worked hard getting it ready for sale. It took them almost a year to do the revitalization work.

Stuart and Ida thought that they could sell it themselves. The couple proceeded to put it on the market. It sold in two months. It sold pending the finding of a replacement property of greater value. This search for a property to trade up became a Turning Point in both their lives.

Stuart and Ida, although complete novices in real estate, sold their own income property. They bought a property in Chatsworth, one of the prime areas of living in Los Angeles! Through attention to detail, careful planning, and their own sweat equity, the two reconstructed this home and made it a show place!

Stuart and Ida, two of the most unlikely prospects for marriage and from opposite sides of the world, were joined together. As a joint venture, the two liquidated their savings to purchase a property in the city of San Fernando, rehabilitated the property, and sold it for over two million dollars.

Stuart and Ida used that equity to trade into a Chatsworth, California, four-thousand-square-foot home in one of the best areas in the city of Los Angeles and San Fernando Valley. What a stroke of luck!

It was a lesson to all who marveled at ingenuity and effort. This snippet of life showed how hard work, a stroke of luck, and a successful marriage, could offset being a stroke victim and in ill health. Proximity and tender loving care could turn one's life around. This was true for Stuart and Ida, an unlikely couple who made it big!

# A LOVED ONE DIES...NOT MY SON

◆

*A Tragedy*

THERE WAS A PHONE call in the middle of the night, and a strange voice said, "Mrs. H. this is the California Highway Patrol. Your son has had a fatal accident. It happened after midnight. It was a head-on collision caused by a drunken driver on the wrong side of the road. Please accept condolences from all of us at the CHP."

She dropped the phone to the floor and screamed, waking her husband of twenty years. Mr. H. rushed down to find his wife sobbing on the floor. Their two daughters came rushing in. It was a special Turning Point in all of their lives. Death is always met with sorrow.

Mrs. H. came from Washington State near Spokane. She had met her husband while in Southern California. They both were attending dental school at the University of Southern California. After a short courtship, they were married, and the couple returned to northern California. Mrs. H. became Dr. H.'s dental hygienist in Kent, California.

This tragic accident and Turning Point in Mrs. H.'s life interrupted a relatively placid existence. Her family consisted of a loving husband of twenty-nine years, two other children, both daughters, and a very satisfactory career in a profession she loved.

Being a dental hygienist was not her career choice when she was a college undergraduate. Before her marriage, she wanted to become a social worker. The job market was terrible during President Carter's regime. It was the wrong time to become a social worker. Her timing was wrong, and Los Angeles was not the place to look.

Being an intelligent woman, Mrs. H. decided to take a postgraduate course at USC (University of Southern California), a well-known and respected graduate school, especially in dentistry. During the two years she spent becoming a licensed, well-trained dental professional, she met her husband, and they decided that they wanted to be in Northern California after graduation and marriage. The two liked the climatic conditions in the bay area—much like that of Washington State.

The move to Kent, California, an upscale town of just two thousand five hundred people, was an important Turning Point in their lives. The newlyweds established a practice in Kent, California, just north of San Francisco Bay. She had been very happy while working, having two children, and living the good life.

She and her husband remained together. One daughter is married with grandchildren, and the other daughter is finishing college.

Looking back on her life, Mrs. H. feels that she has had an ideal existence after the major Turning Point of her life—the death of her son at eighteen in a accident. However, the Diamond of Life indicated that being optimistic and having good judgment had served her well. A loving husband helped ease the tragic loss of their son, and time healed all wounds.

# A MIRROR IMAGE

*How a Couple Keeps Hope Alive*

THE CROWD ROARED AS it milled around in the Castro District of San Francisco awaiting the start of the Gay Parade. It was in late November 1982, and the parade was to commemorate the Harvey Milk assassination of 1978. Even after four years, everyone remembered this horrible event. In a word, the street scene was bedlam!

Thousands of marchers were about to stream down to the San Francisco city hall area. Two people in this raucous crowd of humanity bumped into each other. They simultaneously smiled and said, "I'm sorry." It was Terri and Mary. Terri came from back east where she was finishing med school. Mary was a worker in the Cesar Chavez farm workers movement located in Fresno, the heart of California's central valley. It was the instant of finding each other.

Both women were born in the early fifties. They found each other at the parade and lived together during the ensuing years. Mary attended California State University of Fresno from which she received her BA degree. Terri had gone to school in the East. She had majored in social studies and health. Terri continued her education, studying to become a medical doctor. Terri received her BA at Amherst Massachusetts and her MD degree at the University of New York in Sunny Brooke, New York.

While Terri was getting her education back east, Mary was involved in several different occupations. She wrote a book pertaining to electric cars. She was also involved in writing music. She wrote a libretto and began working on another one. To support herself, Mary worked for Cesar Chavez in his organization of the United Farm Workers.

The two women bought a home together and soon thereafter disaster struck. That event became a major Turning Point in Terri's life because the illness she incurred affected her lower back. It involved the degeneration of the disks of the spine and was very painful. This illness became another life-altering Turning Point, and it happened to a trained and licensed physician.

It was a progressive disease. The ensuing years were sheer torture for Terri as her back hurt all the time. Such a condition deferred her major goals of life, and she was anxious to recover from this debilitating disease. The two women became vitally interested in President Obama's healthcare program.

Despite her infirmity, Terri began attempting to get social justice initiated throughout the U.S.A. and the rest of the world. Terri was doing this as she tried to recover from her painful trauma. Terri kept a stiff upper lip as the medical doctors searched for a way to cure her back. Spinal operations did not improve Terri's condition.

Mary, on the other hand, was involved with social justice issues for a number of years. She continued her involvement in music by writing a libretto to follow her first musical work and getting it published. Finally, she planned to teach the cool new technology about electric automobiles that did not run on gasoline. They were recharged every night by plugging them into ordinary home electric outlets. Both women owned and drove these cars.

All in all, Terri's deteriorating health was certainly the most important Turning Point in her life, and without a doubt, affected both Mary as well. The Diamond of Life portrayed Terri as being stalked by misfortune. Poor health and a physical disability tended to block her road to success. Mary achieved good progress in protecting the environment with the hybrid electric car. She owned four electric vehicles after the turn of the 21st century. Mary changed the direction of both women's lives by shying away from the farm workers union and its belligerence. Mary's positive attitude directed her efforts in imaginative ways. With a modicum of good luck, Mary and Terri would have success. The two represented a mirror image in that their lives reflected each other.

# 8

# HAPPENSTANCE

CURRENT CONVERSATION OF THE young is replete with new words and phrasing, such as *cool, awesome,* and *get with it.* And so it is with *happenstance.* The translation of the word happenstance in the 'King's English' is dumb luck.

In this chapter, there are life's Turning Point episodes that involve happenstance. These incidents can be attributed to being in the right place at the right time. The snippets in this chapter include a route salesman who, while servicing an ice cream machine in a Los Angeles neighborhood restaurant, invented and patented a device that helped the bartender make mixed drinks. He became a multi-millionaire as the item was used worldwide. The reader can find nine other stories that 'just happened' as each person traveled toward eternity.

# MOVIE STARS MEET A SODA JERK

*A Filming in Yellowstone National Park*

A LINE OF SIX touring cars pulled up to the gas pumps at Old Faithful Lodge in Yellowstone National Park. It was a rest stop on the way to a motion picture location. It was hot and dusty that July afternoon in 1936. Twelve people jumped out of the cars and headed into the Mini-Mart behind the filling station. They were a group of filmmakers from a Hollywood motion picture studio. Half of the group rushed up to the soda fountain, sat on the stools in front of the counter, and began to order cold drinks and coffee.

The entourage was filming a movie called *Yellowstone*. It was to be a full- length feature film starring Ann Rutherford as a shy teenager. The male lead was to be Wallace Beery. The film was to be shot off-location, with the studio using the national park as its background. The group of cameramen, directors, and bit players were there to assist the two stars while they worked in Yellowstone Park.

The filming group had traveled into the park in six rented touring cars. The Hollywood director also wanted to film scenery so that the viewing audience would find out what the park really looked like.

The cars and the equipment stopped at the Old Faithful Hotel. They parked at the Hamilton Stores Gas Station and General Store. The hotel was one-quarter of a mile from the most famous geyser in the world—Old Faithful, which spews a stream of extremely hot water one hundred feet straight up into the air. This spectacle occurred every hour and continued for five to ten minutes.

In addition to this outdoor show, there were many more hot pools to add to the production. One was the Morning Glory Pool with the flower's sky blue color. The Fire Hole River running by the hotel added to the unique scenery.

The movie director stopped the line of cars and said, "Take a rest here, get 'petrol' and then register at the Old Faithful Hotel." The group included the two movie stars, eight or ten extras, and a few other locals who would make up the cast. He planned to shoot the movie scenes using local attractions for background to the storyline. The director said that he anticipated it would take a couple of weeks to get this part of the film completed before the cast and crew returned to Hollywood.

While they were gassing up, the two stars, Ann Rutherford and Wallace Beery, went into the store located behind the gas station. Both were tired and thirsty. They walked to the soda fountain near the rear of the store. The two stars sat on the stools in front of the fountain, ordered their drinks, and watched Ronald, the soda jerk, operate.

Ronny, as he was called, was spending his summer vacation helping Tom Hamilton, the owner, by 'jerking sodas' for customers ordering ice cream, milk shakes, or Coca-Colas during the hot Yellowstone summer.

This noon break at Hamilton Stores was ending. The star, "Wally" Beery was well known. He had made many pictures during the 1930s. He usually played a rough and tumble lead who took no nonsense from anyone in the film. He was very heavy set and middle aged. Ann Rutherford, on the other hand, was a budding young actress, not even eighteen years old. Her part in the film was the ingénue.

As she sat at the counter, she saw the soda jerk Ronny. She smiled and said, "Could you hurry my chocolate soda? And please bring me a glass of water, too. I need them fast so I can spend a few minutes shopping in the rest of the store."

Ronny answered, "Yes ma'am. You look like somebody that I met someplace else."

Ann Rutherford said, "Well, I don't think so, but we are making a movie here, and I have been in other movies playing a young teenager's part."

As he delivered her chocolate soda, he said, "Now I know you. How long are you up here for?"

She answered, "I think the director told me two weeks, but it may be a little bit longer. Why?"

Ronny said, "Please to meet ya, Ann. Here is your soda and water. What are you doing Friday night?"

She replied. "I don't know yet, but why do you ask?"

Ronny answered, "They are having a dance at The Lodge, and a bunch of us workers are going over there. Maybe you can come over. If you do, I'll ask you for a dance. I think you will have a lot of fun with the western dancing we do up here."

Ann said, "If we're not still shooting the film. Sometimes we work until midnight, but if I can make it, I will."

After the crew left the Hamilton Stores, Ronny went to the registration desk at the hotel and saw that Ann had signed in and that Hollywood was her home. Ron thought to himself, "I hope she can come. It would be fun to dance with a movie star and write home to mom about my dumb luck."

That Friday night, Ronny went to his room over the general store and dressed up for the dance. He put on the buckskin shirt, cowboy boots, and Levi's that he wore on Sundays or when he went to any dress-up affair.

He thought to himself as he stood looking in the mirror, "Not bad for a young guy. I sure hope she shows up tonight. In case she does, I'll ask her to dance, and what a Turning Point in my life this will be. If she dances with me, I'll ask her for her autograph and a signed photograph so that I can show them to the gang after the summer is over."

An hour later, Ronny arrived at the lodge for the dance. In came some of the movie cast. Ann Rutherford was part of this group. She was not looking like she did at the store. Ann was dressed in a western style dress. She carried a fan and had her hair done up on top of her head. She looked like a real movie star should.

Ronny hurried over to greet her and said, "Remember me. I'm the soda jerk that made your chocolate soda."

"Oh, yes," she said. "I remember you, and I am sure you remember me because you told me about the dance tonight."

Ronny asked, "Save me a dance?" Not waiting for an answer, he took her coat over to the coat rack and hung it up for her.

The band came in and started playing western music. Everybody started to dance and one of the main dances was the Virginia Reel, a favorite with the locals at Yellowstone Park.

In this dance, the men are in one circle and the woman are in another and they change partners periodically so that everybody gets a chance to dance with each other. When Ronny came to Ann Rutherford, he said, "Let's go and get a cold drink. I'm usually serving them, but this time I get a chance to have one. I'd love to have one with you."

Ann said, "Me too."

With this, the two got soft drinks. Then they went to the bar area, sat down, and started talking. Ronny asked Ann a little bit about her life, and how she got into movies. She asked him what he was doing jerking sodas, where he lived, and other questions about his life. By the time all the niceties were completed, the only thing that Ronny remembered he wanted to do was ask Ann for a photograph with her autograph.

The next day Ann brought her photograph to the soda fountain. As she was signing it, she looked up and asked, "Do you spell Ronny with a 'y' or an 'ie'?

He said, "I'm Ronny with a 'y.' You can just put, 'To Ronny, with love.' "

The dream was almost over. Ronny had a Turning Point in his life. He had become a man working in Yellowstone. He met and danced with a real live movie starlet who had come all the way from Hollywood, California. She was making a real movie, and she had danced with him.

The Diamond of Life portrays success as putting it all together by having the proper attitude and most of all, having the drive to make it happen. This event in a soda jerk's life gave him a tale to tell as long as forever.

This became a Turning Point in Ronny's life. He found out that Hollywood people are just the same as those they entertain. He felt he had finally grown up and become an adult. Such Turning Points in one's life are remembered forever and always. They can even happen in Yellowstone National Park when a movie star meets a soda jerk named Ronny, and he has an autograph to prove it.

# V - E DAY SHENANIGANS

*Two 2ⁿᵈ Lieutenants Play Hooky*

DENVER, COLORADO, MAY 8, 1945. "Attention...Attention...," the radio announcer said in an excited voice. "The Germans have capitulated, and the European war is over!"

This was a major Turning Point in World War II. Jeff and David, Second Lieutenants, were in flight training for the U.S. Army Air Force. The two pilots were being checked out to fly B-29s. They were stationed at Lowry field near Denver, Colorado.

Just the day before, they had been told by their squadron commander, "You flyboys are about to go bomb the Japanese." He added with a smile, "Don't send any of your laundry out to be washed!"

President Truman had given a speech to the nation. It was an exciting time, and, of course, the commandant of the Air Force base put out the word, "We still have the Japanese to worry about even though Germany surrendered! I want all personnel stationed at Lowry Air Force Base to return to the base immediately. I repeat return to Lowry immediately."

The base commander used all types of media possible—loudspeaker, telephone, and radio. He notified the military that all passes were cancelled, and everyone would be confined to the base until after the weekend. It was the Turning Point caused by peace being declared.

The two officers in question knew that they had been ordered to return and that the war was partially won. BUT they figured it would be an opportunity to plan what to do when the Japanese war was over. Jeff, the older of the two, said that he was going to return to Michigan, the state from which he came, while David indicated he would go back to Stanford University and finish his degree.

Then the question came up of what to do over the three-day weekend created by President Roosevelt's declaration of 'VE Day.' It did not take them long to decide their fate for this special weekend. They reasoned that they had two options. One was to go to downtown Denver, find a local bar, and wait until the MPs instructed them to report back to Lowry field and be confined to the air base for the weekend.

The other option was to head for the hills to a little town called Golden, Colorado. It was a one-horse town with a small hotel, a bar, and several retail stores. The most important benefit it had was that it was the home of Coors Brewery. The two Second Lieutenants decided to go to Golden just thirty miles from downtown Denver. They had chosen to ignore the commandant's declaration. The fairy tale excuse they would use was that they had been hiking in the mountains. and did not learn of the order to return to Lowry immediately. The other alternative was to obey the radio command.

The decision was, "No problem—on to Golden, and let the devil be damned!" The two bought enough gas to drive to Golden for the weekend using Jeff's last ration stamps. It took the two second lieutenants about an hour to get to Golden, which was west of Denver, high in the Rocky Mountains.

The car wended its way slowly up the narrow mountain road. During the drive, they took care not to be stopped by the police or have an accident. They expected to have a fun time off base with the personal leave they had granted themselves. It took about an hour and a half to reach Golden because the people who lived in the Golden area had jammed the road driving to Denver to be with the crowds who were celebrating.

After arriving in Golden, the two officers went into the Golden Hotel. They asked the clerk if he had a room and if they could stay there for the weekend. Getting the affirmative answer, they went upstairs and hid out until 5:00 o'clock. They were AWOL—absent without leave. They had no idea whether or not the military police would be looking for those missing men who had been confined to quarters.

"But we were up in the Rocky Mountains hiking and knew nothing about the order to return to the air base," would be their story and excuse.

After five p.m., they went to the little café, called the Golden Nugget, and had, of all things, a spaghetti dinner. It was delicious, and when coupled with glasses of wine, it was a wonderful way to celebrate the end of the European conflict.

The next morning they got up and realized that if they were caught they would be court marshaled, and it would be a Turning Point in each of their lives. But being young, daring, and a little bit stupid, they decided to spend the whole weekend in Golden. And what a weekend it was.

As the first order of business, they visited the Coors Brewery, which had a light beer that was supposed to be the best in the nation. It was a way to pass the time. The two had bought 'civvies' so they were dressed like ordinary visitors from Kokomo, Indiana. They took the tour through the brewery. It was enlightening to see Coors Light brewed.

As an added feature, the tour ended up in the tasting room. Of course, being out of uniform, the people on the tour wanted to know what they did, where they were from, what was going on, and wasn't it wonderful about VE Day now that Hitler was history.

After finishing the tour, the two decided they had better get an alibi based on truth, so they went on a hike in the Rockies. Being in civvies was also strictly a no-no, but these brash officers decided that their story was at least plausible.

At about five in the afternoon, the spring sunset made a wonderful ending to a great afternoon, and their first day away from Lowry Field. Then it was bar time and the duo went back to the bar and hoisted two more Coors beers before having dinner and going to bed.

Sunday came up bright and early with no clouds and the temperature in the forties There were services in small country Episcopalian Church in the town. The two officers put on their uniforms and went to church. It was the first time since the beginning of the conflict of Pearl Harbor that either of them had gone to a religious ceremony. Upon completion of this, the two went back to the bar, which opened late on Sunday, and continued their lost weekend.

After some discussion, they decided that they should return to their post at Lowry Field and check in before they were reported AWOL. Their story would be that they were back from hiking in the Rockies and ready for duty.

The Turning Point in this story was the two pilots had knowingly violated orders and could have been court marshaled. It led to both young men to return from WWII, go to university, and finish their education, rather than making the U.S. Air Force their career.

In later years, when Jeff and Dave met, they remembered how they had violated Air Force regulations and were lucky enough to get away with it. The two had shown imagination, cleverness, and good luck in not getting caught. These are all Traits and Tendencies in the Diamond of Life, showing that such factors can lead to success.

However, the lack of sound judgment could have led to disgrace, misfortune, and failure if they had been apprehended. It was a Turning Point that neither of the two men would ever forget. VE Day shenanigans—a weekend Jeff and David would treasure the rest of their days!

# OH MY GOD! THAT IS A BEAUTY

*A Switch in Time Doesn't Save My Sailfish*

"COME ON IN, ART," Bruce yelled to his friend. "I have to show you something beautiful."

After striding into Bruce's private office, Art stopped in front of Bruce's desk and saw the mounted sailfish hanging on the wall. "That's cool...outstanding! It makes your office look perfect Bruce." The office staff clapped in appreciation.

It was a great day for Bruce and a Turning Point in his life. It validated his being a member of the select society—the *I Caught a Sailfish Club*.

The story behind the story is that in 1994, Bruce and Art were in the Florida Keys waiting while the *Chelsea I* pulled up to the dock. It was six o'clock in the morning. Bruce had never caught a sailfish, but Art had. As the two anglers got ready for the fishing experience of their lifetime, the captain told them that the fishing had been good the day before.

Bruce was in his early fifties and his fishing pal, Art, was ten years older. Their wives dropped them off at the Los Angeles Airport and told them to bring home the bacon—their catch. This fishing trip would be expensive. However, it was catch fish no matter what it cost!

The *Chelsea I* crew waited for the two anglers to jump aboard. In less than an hour, they arrived in the area where sailfish were caught the previous day. The fishing boat started trawling back and forth with the fishing lines dragging baited hooks from the rear of the boat.

The fishing was lousy. No luck. It wasn't until late in the day when Bruce's line began to sing. The captain hollered, "You got a sailfish on your line...count to ten and set the hook hard."

Twenty minutes later, Bruce gave Art the thumbs up sign as the deck hand hauled the fish on board. The sailfish flopped around the deck. The captain said that the fish should weigh around one hundred pounds. Bruce was ecstatic.

The fishing lines were baited and let out again. Just before fishing was done for the day, another fish was caught on Art's line. This time it took Art twenty-five minutes to get the sailfish onto the boat. It was a beautiful catch. The fish was about five feet long with a sail fin sticking up on the top of its back. It looked like an iridescent rainbow as it sparkled in the sun. The deck hand said that Art's sailfish should be about one hundred twenty-five pounds, adding that it was bigger than Bruce's fish.

The boat returned to the dock and a group of people came out to watch the fish being unloaded and put on the scale to check the weights. Art's fish weighed in at one hundred twelve pounds, and Bruce's fish weighed in at ninety-one pounds. There was a noticeable difference in size. The captain of the *Chelsea I* had a photographer take a picture of both fish hanging up with the two fishermen standing beside the fish he had caught.

While the photographer was getting set up to take the picture, Bruce turned to Art and said, "Art, do you mind if we switch places? I'll stand by your fish, and you stand by mine. You've caught sailfish before, and I haven't. Besides I want to have my fish mounted to hang on the wall behind my desk."

Art said, "Please, be my guest."

The two men changed places before the photographer took the picture. Bruce told the deck hand that he wanted to have his fish mounted to hang in his office.

Art said, "That's not for me. Fillet it. I'll take mine home to eat."

The two fishermen thanked their lucky stars that each of them caught a sailfish. Art planned to have a fish fry for his family and friends the following weekend.

The two tired fishermen slept on the way back to Los Angeles. Bruce was ecstatic with visions of his mounted sailfish. It would take about a month to receive it. Art brought the meat back with him.

They landed in L.A., and their wives greeted them when they arrived. Bruce and Art parted company, each going to their separate homes. This however did not end the tale.

Nearly two months later, Bruce called Art. "Let's have lunch, and afterwards I'll show you a beautiful sight."

Art came over at noon and the rest is history. According to the Diamond of Life, the traits that made Art successful were patience and optimism. Bruce, on the other hand was a pessimist, and so it was when it came to fishing. He always talked like a great angler but was very vague when he told fish stories.

After he witnessed the unveiling of 'Bruce's Catch' hanging on his office wall, Art smiled as he said, "Bruce, it is a beauty. Hope you don't mind if I want to show the sailfish I caught. I will bring them over to your office to show them *my fish hanging on your wall*."

Bruce gulped and said, "Of course not, Art."

# THE NAME OF THE GAME IS CHANGE

◆

*The Third Time Is the Charm*

DICK AND GINNY BECAME partners after they graduated from Wayne University. Their Turning Point specifically revolved around two factors. Dick needed a different occupation, and he was looking for an opportunity to change jobs. This happened to be during the Kennedy-Reagan-Clinton-Bush presidencies. The couple lived near the family-owned Gloucester factory in the Northeastern section of the United States.

The question for Dick was whether to keep working in the family business or find a job in another occupation. This became a tale of change in an area that was not noted for change—New England.

Born in Franklin, Massachusetts, Dick met Ginny while going to college. She was a fiery redhead with freckles, and he was a lanky fellow student. It was opposites attract. After graduation and his marriage to Ginny, Dick entered his family's business.

His first career involved the first few years of Dick's business life. He was stuck in a family-owned manufacturing business. It had been in the family for several generations. Working under an autocratic father running the show was not to Dick's liking.

Dick did not like the business or the way his father ran it. Dick did not like the product line because it had to do with polymers and mastic material, which was old hat. The factory made a material that was a staple product sold to the construction industry throughout the United States. It required little salesmanship other than demonstrating its use to homebuilders.

Dick and his father were of opposite temperaments, and that did not work well in a family-owned business. Dick transferred to, and became the manager of the real estate division. This position became his second career. Dick's position was important. He ran all real estate owned by the company. Dick leased and sold land and buildings to major corporations and such companies as Home Depot and Ace Hardware. This real estate activity did not last long. A recession and lack of product caused Dick's failure.

By 2004, Dick and Ginny decided to look for new fields to conquer. Dick quit real estate to see if career number three would be the charm—a winner. Dick and Ginny bought a New England franchisee for a national weight loss organization.

The couple purchased nine franchise-area locations throughout New England and upper New York State.

At last, Dick, the extrovert, loved the feeling that he was satisfying people's needs. He had discovered that being overweight was not fashionable in the 21st century. He had given up on the family-owned business. Selling real estate was not a career. As Dick and Ginny put it, working in the family-owned businesses was like being a stepchild in an orphanage. Nobody paid any attention to him.

Ginny and Dick had reviewed the prospects of owning a franchisee of a weight loss operation. The franchisor offered to sell them nine locations in the Northeast. Prior to closing the deal, the couple compared their traits and abilities with the standards of successful franchisees.

The comparison showed that Dick and Ginny were extroverts. While being family oriented, the two did not like being confined as to the operations controlled by the family. While the two had not been successful, their third Turning Point of owning a franchise might be the path to success.

Dick's conviviality and outgoing personality never wavered. His persistence was proved in trying a third time even though he had failed twice. Finally, being on his own was great. The franchise business was good, even though the United States was entering the 2008 recession.

Dick and Ginny became comfortable with the adage 'The Third Career is a Charm!'

## NECESSITY IS THE MOTHER OF INVENTION

◆

*But Inventing Is Fun*

POOR CHILDREN FIND A way. They play kick-the-can rather than touch football because they can't afford an expensive football. Gerry was a needy kid. He was the son of a building window washer who drank too much. Gerry found a way to solve his father's always being short of money. To help support the family, Gerry sold magazines and newspapers to bring in cash. He helped his father, Ed, on window washing jobs for stores like Marshall Fields in downtown Chicago. Gerry ran errands for tips.

Gerry's father told him, "Look nobody gave me anything, and I expect to do the same. Remember what Benjamin Franklin said 'Necessity is the mother of invention and you got plenty of need.' I'll be at the State Street Saloon having a beer after I'm done here."

This doing-it-on-your-own atmosphere had the entire family feeling bad about the world. Without knowing why, this downer feeling was influential in Gerry's life.

In 1941, Gerry discovered that he had high blood pressure when he was turned down by the military after Pearl Harbor was bombed. He went to New York and got a job as an installer trainee at AT&T. While working days for AT&T, he went to New York University and after six years of night school, became a registered electrical engineer. This was an important Turning Point in Gerry's life since it provided him a great future, especially in getting better jobs.

Soon Gerry was able to forget about being disadvantaged. He wanted to improve his life, and as luck would have it, he was at Carvel Ice Cream Corporation on Long Island working for AT&T. One of the

Carvel salesman asked Gerry if he knew of anyone who wanted to buy old ice cream machines that the store owners wanted to get rid of.

Gerry jumped at the chance because at last he could start a business of his own. He could repair the soft ice cream units at night. This became a key Turning Point. He was in business for himself.

Then Gerry got a call from his older brother. Did he want come to Los Angeles and go into business together?

This was during the Johnson administration. Since the economy of the country was not the greatest, Gerry worked when he could find it, but it was not anything permanent. Gerry had to decide. Did he want to start his own company or would he hire on with the major firms, such as Lockheed or Northrop—companies who were busy because of the Vietnamese War?

Gerry had his decision made for him. While passing through Chicago to join his brother, Gerry was reading the Chicago American newspaper and spotted an ad by a Carvel Store owner. The ad said, "For Sale—ten used Carvel Ice Cream machines—six hundred dollars each or fifteen hundred dollars for the lot—as is."

Gerry called the store and asked if the lot was still available. It was, and Gerry bought them for twelve hundred dollars. Gerry was very excited when his dad lent him the money and had him sign a note to return it out of the first year's profits. Gerry had become a small business owner. It was the Turning Point of which he had dreamed.

Thus, Gerry and his brother started a service business. It was in central L.A. The older brother was Mr. Inside, and Gerry was Mr. Outside. The two would repair any equipment that had less than a one-horsepower motor. Within two months, the new partnership was in operation. It was tough going. Gerry was very excited when his dad lent him the money and had him sign a note to return it out of the first year's profits. He knew his dad expected to be paid back, so he started selling reconditioned equipment.

The brothers had looked at the lot of used ice cream machines, such as those used in bars and ice cream parlors. They purchased them. This turned out to be an opportunity of a lifetime. The ten machines might not have been new, but they were in great shape, ready to be installed in any soda fountain, grocery store, or other location where there was foot traffic.

Gerry called on all sorts of stores to place the ice cream machines. While he was waiting to see the owner of a bar to get him to use the Carvel Ice Cream machines in their restaurant, Gerry noticed that the bartender used quart bottles of mix for the mixed drinks he made.

Pointing to the open bottle of Coke, Sprite, and other quart bottles in the sink, Gerry asked, "Why do you have so many open bottles in the sink? Doesn't your Coke go flat?"

The bartender answered, "Yeah, but my boss says throw it away and open another bottle."

This started Gerry thinking as he left the bar. "Zounds!" Gerry had it. It was the Turning point of his life. Gerry's life would never be the same again. Gerry developed the nozzle that dispensed flavor concentrate and carbonated water at the same time. It mixed the drink as the bartender filled up the glass. It was sheer inspiration.

Gerry had been able to do as he had said he would. He developed and installed the sample unit and it worked. Gerry had a viable product. Gerry patented the hand-held mix dispenser—the one with a push button on top. From Scotch and soda to gin and tonic—an invention that is used in most bars.

Gerry received the patent and thanked his lucky star that he had the imagination, the drive, and the ingenuity to find a problem and develop a solution. Gerry has retired and has made his fame and fortune.

This Turning Point became such a major one, especially at the age of eighty-five with millions in the bank and a happy, happy wife seeing him become a success and retire in luxury. This demonstrated that, 'necessity is the mother of invention, and a stroke of luck will help it happen.'

# PLANNING IN AMERICA CAN LEAD TO TROUBLE

*An Eight Thousand Mile Mistake*

THE TIP OF THE Malay Peninsula is inhabited by several million people who live adjacent to the Asian mainland. These are the people who live in Singapore. They are accustomed to being crammed together, working long hours at the hardest jobs. This work is primarily in commerce and service industries. The people are always waiting to migrate and will go to any country with better climate, good jobs, and needing immigrants.

Gita's family lived near the Raffles Hotel on the main drag of this metropolis. Gita worked as a duty technician in the Raffles Hotel and received tips for services performed. The population was so dense that walking the five-plus miles to work along the boulevard in front of the Raffles Hotel took her a couple of hours. Gita had wanted to escape from these conditions for most of her twenty-nine years. She saved her money and talked it over with her parents.

Gita waited for an opportunity. She was disgusted—poor transportation, lack of equal rights for women, and the dirty air caused by the taxis and other cars moving at a snail pace.

Gita made plans to escape to America where there was a better climate and more opportunity. Gita corresponded with a girl friend for several years. She heard from her friend that she was recently married. She was very happy and lived near Denver, Colorado. Her friend wrote that 'now was the time to come to the states.'

Gita realized that immigrating to America would be the Turning Point of her life. Gita talked it over with her family. She loved her father, mother, and five brothers and sisters very much. She hated to leave her family behind, but it was time for Gita to make a change.

She made arrangements to go to Denver, Colorado. Once there, she planned to go to a cooking school to learn to be a chef.

Gita had referred to the Diamond of Life while flying to San Francisco. She had planned this major challenge for years. She knew that she had the ability to make the change in life style. She had determined to make it work and hoped her timing was right. Gita looked forward to meeting her friend in Denver. The United Airline plane flew Gita to Denver.

Upon her arrival, she called her friend and was stunned to learn that the friend's husband had been seriously injured in an auto accident. This happening made it impossible for her friend to fulfill her commitment to help Gita. Obviously, being in a strange country was frightening. Gita faced a dilemma—should she return to Singapore or stay in America as planned?

Gita decided to call her parents and give them the news. She would not be able to stay in Denver with her friend but wanted to remain in the United States. She became a worker in a restaurant. She called her father in Singapore, gave him the news, and asked him to forward as much money as he could scrape together. He was to send it by cable to her in Denver.

Upon receiving the funds, Gita went to Houston, Texas. She would attend school and work in a restaurant. The funds from her father, coupled with the money she earned from a job, enabled Gita to support herself and go to school.

After a few weeks, Gita entered a culinary school and she became a helper in an upscale restaurant. She did not know a soul, but with the job and the money sent from Singapore, she could exist, but she could not further her ambitions.

Of course, the inevitable happened. Gita went to purchase a used car. It was a used 1971 Plymouth. This was all she could buy using the rest of her cash. She had an international driver's license and owed nothing on the car. The Department of Motor Vehicles told her that she would need automobile insurance in order to get a Texas license from the DMV.

She proceeded to an insurance agency recommended by the used car company. She went to the center of Houston to see the owner of the insurance company. All Gita wanted was enough insurance to meet the

Texas state requirements to get a Texas license. Gita was told by the owner of the insurance company that the state of Texas would require her to take a driver's test to receive her license. She must have her insurance in hand and visit a DMV office.

Gita got into the car, and as she was leaving the parking lot, her car was smashed. Luckily, Gita was not injured, but her car was totaled.

The police came, heard her story, and said, "There was nothing we can do." They added they would not issue her a citation but advised her to get insurance prior to buying another vehicle.

This incident represented a major Turning Point in Gita's life. It illustrated what can happen when too much of a plan depended upon other people's actions. A stranger in a strange country. Texas was so different from Singapore.

Gita 'shoulda, woulda, coulda' have returned to Singapore rather than going to Houston. She had not followed the advice given by the poet Robert Burns, who said, "The best laid plans of mice and men often go aglee (wrong)."

Gita's plan to come to America without enough money and no occupation skills proved to have dire results. Gita could have prevented this mistake, one caused by her improper planning.

## BECOMING PRESIDENT ELECT OF PIE

◆

*It Is Better to Be Lucky and Smart*

LOOKING OUT HIS OFFICE window at the San Francisco Bay Bridge, Sam could not believe his good fortune. He had been elected president of Pacific Intermountain Express. PIE was one of the largest trucking companies in the United States. Sam thought of the little things that were important in his life.

At forty-six, Sam was a widower with two teenagers. He was a successful attorney with a law practice that included a number of business clients. Many of them included contacts that he had made during his six years at Stanford and Harvard.

As a small town boy in Petaluma, California, he learned that his hometown was the chicken capital of the United States. However, Sam did not want to stay there and be a poultry man. He wanted to go away to university. He went to Stanford to study law. His college days were fruitful. He graduated, passed the bar, and went to San Francisco to begin practicing law. He opened his law office on the fourth floor of the San Francisco Stock Exchange building.

During the Second World War, a stocky man came into Sam's law office asking, "Is Mr. Sam in?"

The receptionist replied, "May I ask who is calling?"

The man answered, "My name is Ken Humphrey. I own a truck line and need an attorney who can handle some of my legal affairs."

Ushered into Sam's office, Ken Humphrey said, "I own Intermountain Express. We operate in Salt Lake City and want to expand our operations to include the Pacific Coast. Can you help me?"

This question became a major Turning Point in Sam's life. A man from Salt Lake City looked at the Tenant Directory in the lobby of the Stock Exchange Building and found an attorney to help his truck line expand.

During the next thirty-one years, the truck line successfully expanded to all forty-eight states and so did the attorney-client relationship. Being a great attorney, as well as corporate counsel for PIE, resulted in a life altering Turning Point in Sam's life. He was appointed successor to Ken Humphreys as President of Pacific Intermountain Express. PIE Board of Directors named Sam as president after Ken Humphrey's death. Being chosen was based on years of calling the legal shots during the growth phase of PIE. Later, he merged operations with Consolidated Truck Lines, which became one of the ten largest transcontinental companies in the United States.

This highlighted how chance, or dumb luck, became a Turning Point in Sam's life. The random selection of an attorney by a growing company, hard work by the chosen one, and luck, pure and simple, led to outstanding success.

# CAN I WORK AND PLAY WITH MY NEW WIFE?

*Two of New Mexico's Finest Take the Test*

TWO SERGEANTS IN THE Hobbs City Police Department fell in love while patrolling their city's streets. Chris and Sue were highway patrol officers and had known each other for several years. As fate would have it, the two were assigned to the same squad car. This new assignment became a Turning Point in their lives.

While performing their policing duties, the pair found out that they had an awful lot in common. They were both promoted to sergeants, and the inevitable happened—wedding bells. It was not a marriage made in heaven, but it was a union by two level headed people having a common occupation.

Chris and Sue were in their mid-forties. It was the first marriage for each. It was not a hasty decision but an important life changing Turning Point—that of falling in love and getting married. Such a union of fellow workers often results in people disliking each other. Remember the old saying, 'familiarity breeds contempt.' Such was not the case of Sue and Chris. Being together at work as well as at home turned out to be a blast.

The celebration of Chris and Sue becoming a couple was postponed until their summer vacation. Both were ardent fishermen, and their honeymoon was spent in Alaska at Angler's Lodge. Neither the bride nor the groom had ever been to Alaska. Both loved to fish and the two were excited that their trip in June coincided with the biggest and best yearly salmon run in Alaska. It was being with each other on the Kenai River that really mattered.

On the jet flight, Sue said she could out-fish Chris. Chris had an opposite opinion, and so the two made a mammoth wager— the one who caught the biggest fish did not have to do the dinner dishes for the entire month of July.

Bright and early the next morning, the two love birds went in a drift boat, fishing together with a fishing guide.

As each put out a fishing line, they smiled at each other, said, "Good luck partner," and started fishing. For the next six hours, Sue and Chris fished their little hearts out. It was not a good day for king salmon fishing. The couple did better than most boats. Sue caught the two kings. Both were over forty pounds.

As they returned to the dock at Angler's Lodge, the guide on their drift boat held up two fingers and indicated that two king salmon had been caught. After the fisherman unloaded at the dock, the guide hung the fish up on the scale, and said that one was forty-plus pounds, twenty inches in girth, and nearly three feet in length. The other king salmon was almost as heavy but was a few inches shorter. It was a female, which doesn't get so big.

The other guests at Angler's Lodge watched as the couple shook hands. They heard Sue say, "I'm sorry, Chris. I caught both kings, and you did not even get a bite."

The other viewers at the lodge smiled, and one said, "This looks like a union that will last forever. If it were my wife, I would be mad at her for a month of Sundays."

The moral of this tale is that getting 'skunked' (not catching a fish), losing the bet, doing the dinner dishes for a month, and having all guests at Anglers Lodge know about it, is humiliating.

Sergeant Chris said as he watched Sergeant Sue have her picture taken between her two salmon. "Well, I'll be damned, and she has never fished salmon before!" He kissed his wife. He turned to the group that watched the proceedings and said, "I can work with my wife and even lose a bet to her on our honeymoon, even though it hurts. But she had better not tell anyone in the Hobbs Police Force how I maintained my 'fishing virginity.' No salmon was caught by me!"

The Traits and Tendencies from the Diamond of Life showed that fairness in marriage does not mean equality. Chris got skunked and Sue got the king salmon.

## THE FIRST SHALL BE LAST
## AND THE LAST SHALL BE FIRST

◆

*David Finds a New Wife, a New Home, and a New Life*

"DAMN, DAMN, DAMN," WAS the voice from the rear of the line waiting to pick up a car rental at the Bend Oregon Airport.

The man in front of the long line who was waiting for his turn said, "Take it easy. The agent is going as fast as she can."

The complaining man replied, "I would if I could. My wife is waiting for me at a realtor's office. She wants to buy a house. We got married recently. This is going to be our honeymoon. Can you help me?"

Stepping back from the counter, the man at the front of the line said, "Here you go. Take my spot, and I'll wait. Congratulations to you."

David, the complainer, was so happy. He would be just fifteen minutes late. He planned to move to the High Country of Oregon behind Mount Jefferson. He was a college professor with a Ph.D. from Santa Fe, New Mexico. He asked his savior for his business card. David planned to ask his savior out to lunch the next week.

Just as he intended, David met his savior for lunch at noon. They went to the Pine Tavern overlooking the Deschutes River. What a lovely spot and a great place to lunch and talk. At lunch, David disclosed what major Turning Points had affected his life. He talked about his last venture—around the marriage track celebrated by his purchase of a new house for her.

The two placed their order, and David noted that the Major Turning Point in his life involved his teaching finance and economics. During the Iraqi War, he was requested by the United States Defense Department to leave his teaching and return to temporary duty, teaching finance and economics to the returning veterans in New Mexico.

David went on. "The reason it was a Major Turning Point was that I had a son who had attempted suicide ten years ago, and he is still recuperating." David added, "This problem bugged me and led to my second divorce."

David said that his new wife had inspired him to make the third time a charm. This time the new couple went to a marriage counselor. The counselor asked them to decide what both liked to do. The choice given was each partner loved the outdoors, especially summers in the mountains to get away from it all. That's the reason the two of them had come to Bend. David added, "The High Country of Oregon is the place to hike. It is summertime, the weather is beautiful, and one can see Sisters from the top of Mt. Bachelor."

David smiled as he said, "My new wife is ten years younger and a lot smarter. The new marriage is a bond that will last forever."

David continued, "My meeting you at the Bend airport was a happenstance. You turned out to be my savior the other day. It was a chance meeting. And every time you come to Bend let's have lunch together. My treat."

The two continued to talk about the prospects of having a happy retirement life. David's plans were not gelled enough to dwell on. He reviewed his plan to stay at the new house for another week before his return to New Mexico to teach and officially retire.

David ended his story by saying that the Diamond of Life concepts could be of great interest to him. David's good luck in finding number three, his intelligence, and his dedication as shown by his teaching was considered. His short temper and impatience were negatives. All in all, David appeared to be on the path to success. It shows that the biblical saying, "The last shall be first and the first shall be last," applies in the case of David, his new home, and his new wife!

9

# PROMOTION

PROMOTION HAS SEVERAL MEANINGS as well as synonyms. It can apply to people, events, objects, or theories. This chapter applies to people, their advancement in life, or furthering a cause. In this chapter, a Russian refugee becomes a success in Australia. An unusual promotion finds a building changing its usage during the 20th century and becoming a haven for millionaire living. A college student joins the United States Air Force and becomes a second lieutenant during WWII. A wide variety of promotional experiences are related in this chapter.

# HERE'S YOUR HAT, WHAT'S YOUR HURRY?

*Morris Was Trained to Remember*

"NO SIR! I DIDN'T forget to give you a hatcheck. I'll remember you. You'll get your own hat back. Yes, Sir! My name is Morris if you need me. See me after lunch."

Morris, the attendant of the cloakroom was a fixture working at the most prestigious hotel in the State of Utah. Morris had become famous in the Great Depression of the 1930s. He was known as the man who could check your coat and hat without giving you a ticket and you would get the right items returned after your meal. Morris's ability to associate a person with a coat or hat became known throughout the United States. Getting this job and exploiting his unusual talent became a life-altering Turning Point in Morris's life.

Morris was born in Alabama around the turn of the 20th century. When he was twenty-five, Morris moved to Chicago, Illinois, because he wanted to become a Pullman porter. He could earn lots of money serving the passengers who traveled on railroad trains. His work saw Morris traveling between New York City and Los Angeles.

Typically, a passenger boarded the train and was escorted by the porter to his seat, where the passenger lived for the five-day trip across the continent. The trains were operated by the New York Central Railroad and the Union Pacific Railway Company. Morris's job was to make the passenger comfortable during his trip on a Pullman car. These sleeping cars were designed and built by the George Pullman Company. They had roomettes with seats, which were made up at night into beds.

As a trained Pullman porter, Morris served his time on the railroads traveling the Union Pacific line from Los Angeles to Chicago and then on to New York City. These trips required extensive service by the porters, so much so, that after several years of such work, Morris decided to look for another occupation. He had traveled through Salt Lake City, Utah, while working as a porter, and he was familiar with the Hotel Utah, which was owned and operated by the Mormon Church.

The Hotel Utah had a restaurant, a number of meeting rooms, and a ballroom called 'The Roof' with dining and dancing on Friday and Saturday night. The Hotel Utah had a cloakroom where Morris worked.

Many of the hotel guests would come in and have lunch or dinner. Upon arrival, they would leave their coats and hats with Morris. The procedure was known as checking your coat and hat. Morris became very capable as a coatroom attendant.

After a few years of operating the cloakroom, Morris developed a secret technique all his own. After customers finished dining, they asked Morris to return their coats and hats. Morris, without hesitating or asking any details, walked to the rack where he had hung the items and returned them with a smile. He never issued a coat check tag. He did it by memory only.

Some nights there would be up to one hundred fifty guests for dinner. But Morris returned each item to its rightful owner. Morris gave each person the right hat, helped him on with the right coat, and received a tip--usually a quarter.

This was so famous a talent that Robert L. Ripley, the "Believe It or Not" cartoonist for syndicated newspapers all over the U.S.A., featured Morris, the "claim-checkless cloak room attendant." It was entitled, "Here's your coat and hat. No Sir, I never make a mistake." And it was true.

Even Ripley himself gave his hat and coat to Morris while he dined. Yes, Ripley received his own hat and coat back. How Morris did it—by memory or by the grace of God—was never disclosed by Morris. It has remained a mystery to this very day.

According to the Diamond of Life theory, Morris was blessed with a unique talent, efficiently used. Morris was born with it, realized its importance in his life, and started a new, much more profitable occupation working in a major hotel.

This Turning Point in Morris's life occurred at the time he quit being a Pullman Porter and got a new occupation. He recognized his capability. Morris realized the potential and seized the opportunity. He changed his life from being Morris, a Pullman porter, to that of a famous checkroom attendant in a major hotel. How? Because he recognized his ability to remember and associate hats and coats with their rightful owners. Such was a Turning Point in Morris's life, and a unique one at that!

## SOL-LEE SUIT MANUFACTURER
## CAN'T MAKE IT ANYMORE

◆

*Henry's Decision*

HENRY COULD NOT SLEEP that night. He had a major decision to make. He got out of bed and went into the den of his home. He had some thinking to do. After getting a warm glass of milk to help him calm down, he got his thoughts in order.

He and his partner Sol, of Sol–Lee Suit Manufacturing Company, owned a ladies ready-to-wear manufacturing business. They had owned this for fourteen years and had been relatively successful. Sol gave Henry an ultimatum, "Either you buy me out or I buy you out. We've had a wonderful partnership together, but I've decided to upgrade our line and sell to a better group of stores than we do now… Sorry"!

Henry recalled how he and his wife Liz had moved to the San Fernando Valley fifteen years earlier. He had come from New York City and had met Sol at a ladies ready-to-wear show in the spring of that year. They had a cup of coffee together. The two men decided to go into business together. Sol was to be the manufacturing head and Henry was to be the sales manager of the organization.

After getting organized, they rented a factory in central Los Angeles and started to market their own line of women's clothes. The line of Sol-Lee was successful. They sold to such Pacific Coast stores as Ransohoffs in San Francisco, Bullocks Wilshire in Los Angeles, I Magnin & Company, and other fancy stores up and down the Pacific Coast.

Henry met his wife-to-be while attending a trade show. They were married within the year. They had two boys and a girl and moved to the San Fernando Valley and lived a relatively peaceful life watching the Valley grow.

Henry was a good salesman. He got to know all the buyers in the fashionable ladies ready-to-wear stores and thought that his future was secure.

Henry faced the unknown. "What should I do if my partner Sol leaves the organization?" Should he buy Sol out or vice-versa? Such decisions were life-shaking and Henry knew it. He weighed the facts for buying Sol out.

The first thing Henry noted was, as the sales manager, he had recruited the sales force. He had made the business successful from day one. He was comfortable in his job, he had developed a great sales force, and the business was making money. He liked the prestige of being president of the firm. He had a wife who was happy raising kids in the San Fernando Valley.

The valley was growing. Their home was near the May Company, one of the largest department store chains, not only in California, but also throughout the United States. All the May Company stores in California were good customers of his.

Henry wanted to buy the business rather than sell out his interest. To do this he needed help from his partner Sol in order to be able to finance his purchase. Henry wanted to have a deal that would make him the sole proprietor of Sol-Lee's. Sol would have nothing to do with it— except to remain a good friend.

Fifteen years later, Sol-Lee was sold to Henry and Sol as selling partner, carried back the paper. While the price seemed high to Henry, he was very optimistic about the future. He felt he would be able to cover the payments to Sol from what would be his business.

Henry, still president and sole owner of Sol-Lee Suits, hired a designer to carry on for Sol and a factory manager to take care of the sewing operations. Henry owned one hundred percent of the company. He remained as the sales manager, which was his niche. The quality of the women's apparel was maintained.

For the first few years, the business continued to run with Henry as president in charge of national sales and the sales force. However, by 1979, the business conditions on the Pacific Coast were bad. The department stores were under attack by firms like Wal-Mart, Target, and other discount operations.

The marketing conditions were completely different for selling and distributing ladies suits of high quality and higher price. Therefore, sales fell, profits fell, and Henry looked at his cash flow. He came to the realization that he would be dipping into his cash reserves in order to continue paying Sol.

Also, Henry's personal living expenses had risen. He was fifteen years older; he was in fairly good health, but travel had become extremely burdensome, and being away from his wife and his kids was no fun. And last of all—his business was failing!

Thus, Henry faced another major Turning Point in his life. Should he retire at sixty-five or should he look for another business position? He was a great salesman, but he had passed his prime. This Turning Point was almost as important as when he decided to buy Sol out.

Henry looked at his situation and realized his life was a seesaw. During the first twenty-eight years of his life, it was up, up, up. He had formed a partnership with a credible partner, and at the end of their time together, he had bought out his partner, Sol.

Then the seesaw started its downward move. By the time Henry was seventy, he had lost his vigor, he had lost his will to work, he had lost his business, and he had hit bottom.

Thus, the Turning Point in Henry's life came at the apex of his career. The purchase of the other half of a business was a mistake of proportions from which he would never recover. Such is life. No matter who it is or what it is, timing is a key factor, and in Henry's case, it was everything. Sol-Lee Suit Manufacturing Company could not make it any more.

## DRYING OUT FOR THE NTH TIME

*Dennis Tells All*

S ITTING ON THE SIDEWALK, he leaned against the wall of the Bank of America, near the door to PIP (People in Progress), a non-profit group who weaned drunks off the sauce. He was waiting for the office to open. Dennis ignored the looks of the passersby. He realized that he had faced the tortures of the damned during the past two days. Only an alcoholic knows the feeling. He had been 'drying out.'

The door opened, and Dennis walked in. He said, "Where's the sign-in sheet?" Dennis had reached his Turning Point—he was going to change his ways. He knew in his heart that this was his last chance. He knew it was either the PIP program to make a new man out of him or suicide.

Born at the end of WW II, Dennis had lived in New York City for most of his early life. He was a creature of the streets. He remembered his family—his father, mother, and two brothers— all drinking and popping pills.

Dennis saw no service in the Army. Having left school at fourteen, it was a difficult task just to stay alive. He took any jobs he could get, from being a delivery clerk to shining shoes in downtown Los Angeles. He lived in community after community, from Santa Monica by the beach, to Pasadena near Cal Tech. He begged, borrowed, and stole just to exist.

His schooling had terminated in tenth grade. Dennis liked people; he could make a great leader if he only could dry out. He could speak well, think well, and when sober, act as any twenty-five-year-old would act. He went to church as often as he could to ask for forgiveness. He finally ended up in Sun Valley at PIP willing to give it one more chance. He was dedicated. He knew that it would be recovery or suicide.

PIP was a state funded organization made especially for giving substance abusers a chance to straighten out their lives and become productive citizens. PIP had several locations. The one that Dennis wanted to go to was out in the San Fernando Valley with open space, a small community, and a special facility that would get him on the right path.

The six months flew by and Dennis ended up in the kitchen after many other jobs in the seventy-man recovery center. Reggie Salzburg headed the Board of Directors, and they met nearly every month at the Sun Valley facility. Dennis impressed the director of the facility with his ability to do almost any job they had, from cleaning the bathrooms to cooking for seventy people.

Dennis talked to Eric H., the facility manager, about how to get his position once he left. Dennis did not want to return to the streets. He knew how difficult it was for someone with substance abuse to find an occupation and succeed. He wanted to improve his life as he tried to gain experience.

Eric said that he was leaving the organization to take another job, and he would recommend Dennis as his replacement. The effect it had on Dennis was surprise. He had some concerns. Dennis felt that he should have some training before the change-over took place. Dennis and Eric met with the board and its chairman to tell them of the situation and that Eric was requesting Dennis as his replacement. It would require six months of training with Eric. The Board said, "We will consider it and get back to you, Eric, within a week."

The two left the meeting. A week passed, and Reggie Salzburg met with the two men. Their training plan had been accepted, and Dennis would go to work at the minimum wage of $6.50 an hour plus benefits. After the six-month training period was completed successfully, Dennis would receive Eric's salary. Dennis and Eric gleefully accepted this offer and were excited about the prospects. Eric would postpone his leaving for six months, and he wished Dennis a successful new career.

Dennis spent the six-month period serving and learning each step of the functions that were required. He went to the monthly PIP board meetings and was asked to give reports to the Board about his training and how it was coming along. This Dennis enjoyed. He knew in his heart that this was the opportunity he had been looking for. It would be a Turning Point in his life.

When asked by the board about other Turning Points in his life, he told them about growing up in New York City—that it was possible to live on city streets, although having shelter every night in the summer and winter had been a problem. He told about his exit from New York and hitchhiking his way to California. He explained that the experience of coming to California was indelibly etched in his mind. Dennis said it was a shock for a New Yorker to find out what life was like in California. It was an enlightening Turning Point in Dennis's life.

Finally, Dennis had another major Turning Point after he had been managing PIP for several years and taking on more and more of the overall responsibilities. The Board of Directors even asked him to become familiar with the other locations and operations of PIP. This Dennis did willingly. He spent one day a week in a different location to talk with the manager and see how the facility operated.

At the end of this period of time, Dennis asked the board if he could get involved with the Sun Valley Chamber of Commerce. They heartily agreed and would pay for the membership, as long as it did not interfere with his operation of PIP. The board would appoint him as their representative to attend. This was done in the late nineties. Dennis did the 'grunt work' for the chamber, including their major project—an anti-graffiti program sponsored by the City of Los Angeles. After checking with the board of directors, Dennis planned to maintain graffiti removal in the Sun Valley area. It did not interfere with the main functions of PIP, which were substance abuse and its treatment.

At the end of 2005, the Chamber of Commerce Board asked Dennis to become their 2007 president. Dennis accepted but said he would have to get approval to do so because he had observed the outgoing Presidents during his period on the Chamber Board and noticed that they spent more time on Chamber business than they did on their own business.

The PIP Board gave Dennis the go ahead as it would benefit their organization and give them exposure throughout the San Fernando Valley. It would also highlight activities provided by the City of Los Angeles.

Dennis campaigned little and was elected president of the Sun Valley Greater Chamber of Commerce, which represented the twenty-five hundred businesses in its area. Dennis suggested a project that gained citywide attention—to beautify the railroad tracks. Dennis did this by planting oleander bushes, some one thousand of them each year. This project became well known throughout the entire City of Los Angeles.

At the end of Dennis's first year of his presidency, he was asked to stay on for an additional year. Dennis agreed. He notified the board that at the end of his term he would be sixty-five years old and wanted to retire from being the manager of the Sun Valley branch of PIP. This was another Turning Point of Dennis's career. He was applauded for his work and given honorary recognition from all the other chambers in the Valley through the United Chambers of Commerce.

Thus, Dennis was able to climb from the very depths to the peak of success. He had conquered the 'demon rum.' He had reached a position where he had the respect and admiration of men of the PIP organization, state leaders, and his Chambers of Commerce peers in the San Fernando Valley. Dennis acknowledged that he, manager of People in Progress, had dried out for the final time.

## ANNE FINDS THAT A STITCH IN TIME SAVES NINE

### *The Quilting Question*

ANNE OWNED THE STITCHING Post located in Sisters, Oregon, a small, mid-state country town of about one thousand people. Anne displayed handmade quilts of all sizes, types, and descriptions. Her store provided an outstanding exhibit of pioneer quilting.

As part of Anne's promotional efforts, she was the unpaid executive director of the National Quilting Society. She put on the annual National Quilting Show, where nearly two thousand quilters displayed their quilts to visitors who came from all parts of the United States.

The question before the group was whether or not the National Quilting Society should postpone the 2010 convention in Sisters, where its member's quilts were on display, or hold it as usual despite the declining attendance.

Anne had been involved with the convention for fourteen years. She knew that once it was postponed, the society would be sorely pressed to restart the show in Sisters. In addition, she felt that as owner of Stitching Post, she might have a conflict of interest if she wanted to continue to have 2010 show in Sisters. If the show did not go on in 2010, the lack of participants would reduce sales in her store to lower than they were in 2009.

Anne thought that the directors of the Quilting Society would be looking for a new location even if the attendance did not go down. The organization felt that changing the location to a different part of the western United States would stem the loss of attendance.

Anne met for breakfast with the leaders in the National Quilting Society. Some of the directors of the organization felt that Anne was the problem. The opinion was that National Outdoor Quilting Show would be improved if there were a change in location and management. They wanted Anne to resign and so they could take a fresh look at curing the problem. It was a Turning Point requiring action. The question posed was simple—vote to decide whether to move or to stay in Sisters.

The Stitching Post and Anne would suffer if the society board voted to move the location. It would be a Turning Point in Anne's life because of her fourteen years as president. Was there a conflict of interest between Anne and the society? Should she resign, withhold her vote, or support the change in dues structure?

As Anne was picking up the check for breakfast, she made up her mind. The trouble and discontent were pronounced. It was better to quit than leave in an uproar. She would talk to the society's directors over the phone and tender her resignation.

While reviewing Anne's Traits and Tendencies established in The Diamond of Life, it is apparent that she had the courage to face the Quilting Society's declining numbers head on. She showed good judgment in deciding to resign her position. With the business conditions in Sisters tanking and the hierarchy unhappy, it was the right timing for her to fade into the past. Too many problems and too few solutions.

Anne realized that the coin of promotion had two sides. Her resignation was a demotion. She had her health and a business that was struggling. The Quilting Society would have to get a new location or die. Anne's Turning Points depended upon many factors, but they were Turning Points and they represented major decisions in Anne's life. She had been the National Director of the Quilting Society, and then it became a bad dream.

# COMMUNITY ACTIVIST CHANGES HER TUNE

### *How a Loser Wins the Game*

IT WAS MARCH 2007, election time, and the City of Los Angeles was holding its municipal elections for mayor and seven of its fifteen city council seats. Mary, fifty-nine, married with two grown children, wanted to have some of the municipal laws changed to benefit the local horse owners and other people who lived in the Second District.

With this thought in mind, Mary felt that she had reached a Turning Point in her life. It was whether or not she should run for the council seat in the second council district that covered the eastern portion of the San Fernando Valley.

The benefits were important, and they would influence her action. Winning the post as city councilwoman would strike a balance. She was middle of the road in her past, present, and proposed activities. She was environmentally conscious, but she did not believe that the current no-growth policies benefited the City of Los Angeles. She believed that the business owners and the valley horse owners could get along together, especially if she won.

Her experience in politics was scant, but that was counter-balanced by her drive and enthusiasm.

It was springtime in Sun Valley, California, and Mary was vice chair of the neighborhood council, a volunteer organization in a small community near Los Angeles. This position had given her an opportunity to get involved with local horse owners who kept animals in a large city.

It was the fall of 2006, and she was considering running for the city council. If she won the election in March 2007, she would be able to introduce municipal laws to help the district keep political peace in the area. This was a Turning Point in Mary's life—to run or not to run for office.

On the negative side of her running for councilwoman was her age of fifty-nine. She felt that was old in terms of starting a political career. She was not wealthy as far as politics were concerned. Running for office was costly. But Mary was well known throughout the Second District because of her frequent appearances on the local TV show, "Harry Hughes Here." She appeared as a community leader and political guru of the area. She felt that belonging to community groups would offset her having limited funds.

During the fall, Mary learned that Councilwoman Marsha Gruel would not run for re-election. The Second District would not have an incumbent running. Mary knew how difficult it was to win an off-year election without enough money. However, she was willing to give it a go.

In reviewing the necessary statistics to run, Mary found out that each of the two favored candidates had raised between two to three hundred thousand dollars to prepare and publicize their candidacy for the seat being vacated.

Mary started her campaign. She visited all the Chambers of Commerce of the cities in the Second District of Los Angeles and became a viable candidate. Nine people were running for the same office.

Mary belonged to many organizations in her district and went to their meetings religiously. She was the featured speaker for many of them and also appeared on public television a number of times, setting forth her program to reduce the Los Angeles City budget by ten percent.

Getting this message across to her voters would take a major effort if she decided to run. She realized that to do this she needed adequate financing, TV advertisements, and continued speaking engagements throughout the Second District. She realized at the inception of her campaign that she did not have enough money to match two of the candidates.

Mary decided run. She campaigned like a veteran. Speaking engagements and public television were her specialty, but without adequate funding it was an impossible task.

Election Day came, and the results showed that Mary came in third out of the nine candidates. She was not on the runoff ballot.

Thinking about the future, should she run again? She knew that she had leadership capability, a great attitude, and persistence to enter the 2011 Los Angeles Council election. All of the attributes found in her Diamond of Life indicate the possibility of success.

Mary received a phone call from the winner of the council seat. He said, "Mary, I have intended to call you, but I have been bogged down. Could we have lunch together say next, Tuesday? I need to replace my Chief of Staff as Wilma gave me her notice. Can you meet me at Dimion's for lunch at noon?"

"I'll be there," Mary said.

This phone call, and resulting employment offered by the winning candidate, proved the old saying, "So goes the life of a Community Activist."

# RUSSIAN ROULETTE

◆

## *From Immigrant to Tycoon*

T HE JEWS FLED RUSSIA during World War I. It was to escape the
Czar at all cost. This was a Turning Point in the lives of Norman
and his wife, Suzee. They were Jewish, and they were tired of being
considered the lowest of the low.

Then a miracle happened, which Norman considered awesome.
Norman had heard of a philosophy called the Diamond of Life. It
considered everyone on planet earth was a part of a grand game. Norman
and Suzee were peasants. They were in love. Instinctively, Norman knew
he had the skills and the courage to make their escape from Russia. He
wanted to become successful.

The couple made a plan. The two were excited about going to
another country. It was now or never. Such an escape was a form of
Russian roulette. It was a serious venture of go and never look back, or
get caught and be executed.

Norman had a friend who lived in Melbourne, Australia. The
friend had made his escape from Russia several years before. Norman
planned to duplicate his friend's method. He would leave Russia, spend a
year in England, and then apply for entry into Australia. He would go to
Melbourne, meet his friend, get a job, and send for Suzee to join him.

Norman was an impatient man. The year's wait for an entry
permit seemed like an eternity. He spoke little English, and the
immigration into Australia was to be a major Turning Point in his life.

Australia was a strange new country. Norman was very poor, and
he needed a job to survive. In desperation, Norman went to the Menzies

Hotel in Melbourne. He applied for a job. The only opening available was as a bootblack, shining shoes in the barbershop while men were having their haircut. This was the first work he had in Australia, and it gave him a start.

Since Norman had a job, he sent for Suzee. She arrived safely. She watched Norman work seven days each week. After the barbershop closed, Norman worked as a janitor in the hotel. Norman had jumped at the chance of working in the hotel because it was a wonderful place to learn English.

During the next few years, Norman and Suzie had three sons and a daughter. The couple learned to be as Australian as the kangaroo. Norman's major goal in life was to become a businessman. He read the Melbourne newspaper want ads looking for a better opportunity.

He found one. It was an American chain of moderately priced women's dress shops looking for potential storeowners. Norman took the money he had brought from Russia. It was money he had saved, and money he was able to borrow from wealthy émigrés. This risk-taker bought the American ladies ready-to-wear store. He called it Mode O' Day (Fashion of the Day). Although it required Norman to spend all the capital he could beg, borrow, or steal to make it work, it gave him a chance to show his entrepreneurial skills.

Norman grew his one store into twelve. It took five years and many sleepless nights, but it was a worthwhile sacrifice. It gave Norman access to the necessary capital to organize many other ventures. This move became the key to Norman's entry into real estate development. It was his little acorn that grew into a might oak.

Norman's life changed. Instead of working for the hotel or looking for another job, he started his own small business. It had become Mode O'Day Australia. Once he had become successful, he wanted new fields to conquer.

Norman sold this infant chain and used the Mode O' Day sale as an entry into shopping center developments. These included banks, a Florida-like development named Surfer's Paradise, and Australian government buildings. His company developed and owned the 'must-be-in' shopping center, the largest in Melbourne.

Norman had reached a great Turning Point in his life. Norman wanted the ultimate Turning Point to be his becoming a public leader. He decided to specialize in community improvement. He wanted it to be added to that of his business successes. Norman needed public recognition, too.

His children had matured. His eldest son became a farmer in the outback. His second son went to college and, upon graduation, went to Wharton Graduate Business School in America for his MBA. He then went to work as the future leader of Norman's companies.

Norman's daughter went to France, got married, and lived in Paris. His youngest son, who felt the urge to become a playwright, went to Greenwich Village in New York City and wrote away. The jury is still out on the children—except in the case of number two son, Irvin.

The next Turning Point of Norman and Irvin was the formation of a father and son business. They worked as a team—Mister Outside (the Tycoon) and Mister Inside (learning the business). It represented the classic father-son problem of when the reins should be turned over to the younger generation. Norman was investing in community ventures, mostly real estate donations, and Irvin was directing business activities.

Then Norman started to look abroad, mainly at the U.S.A. He wanted to diversify and spread the risk over two continents. He traveled to Los Angeles.

In Los Angeles, Norman went to Coldwell Banker, where he met a real estate agent who was more than happy to find investments that met Norman's requirements: (1) he would continue to live in Australia, and the property would be in the United States; (2) he would not have any management responsibilities; (3) he would be only an investor and owner; (4) he would buy something that was very secure; and (5) he would get his cash and profit back within seven years.

Colwell Banker found him just such a property. Norman made a visit and looked at the property, looked at the signed leases, which included two banks, the telephone company, (then Pacific Telegraph), and an insurance company named Prudential Insurance. Also, there were three or four other tenants.

All in all, half the building was leased to key tenants of stature, and the other half was in the process of being leased. This, of course, was a Turning Point in Norman's life because it was one of the first investments in the United States of major proportions.

As far as his personal Turning Points were concerned, Norman's son, Irvin, at thirty-two, was elected to the city council and then became the Lord Mayor of Melbourne, the second largest city of Australia. Norman loved the fact that his son had reached this level of status. It was another Turning Point in Norman's life.

The next of Norman's crowning achievements, Turning Points if you will, was his development of a first class, outstanding hotel in the center of Melbourne. It was a monument to himself, which he called The Regency. It took him four years to have this building completed. The building was occupied at the end of the 20th Century.

This review of Norman's career shows that major Turning Points involved the relocation from one foreign country to another and the choice of location—staying in England, moving to United States, or moving to Australia.

As to Turning Points, he wanted a monument to himself and to live long enough to witness it. Being a Russian immigrant, Norman has been rumored to say, "It is my way of playing Russian Roulette."

# GOD'S GIFT TO MANKIND
# GOES TO NEW YORK CITY

◆

*Ending a Marriage and Starting a New Career*

A RTHUR HAD CONTEMPLATED THE big move for several years. Young, married, and returning from serving in World War II, he realized that the big move would be a major life change for him and his family. It would be a change from a placid life to a hectic one in an environment that surrounded a large city. It would also be a major change in lifestyle, as money did not go as far in New York City as it did in Texas. His lifestyle in Fort Worth was modest but comfortable. He lived the life of a family man in a middle class community.

On his thirty-ninth birthday, just like radio comedian Jack Benny, Arthur's persona was changing. He had felt that he was reaching the period when he was no longer God's gift to the human race. His face was no longer that of a high school class president. His hair, once jet-black and shiny, was becoming grey around the temples. Suddenly, the country style of family life seemed to become dull and boring.

Arthur had operated a special section in Fort Worth's leading specialty store carrying high fashion apparel and other department store merchandise. It was his father's business. After his dad passed away, Arthur took over. He had been the heir apparent, and for ten years, he had managed the china, glass, and gift store extremely well, showing that he was an outstanding manager.

Arthur loved the hustle and bustle of New York City! Twice each year he went to New York City to buy his new spring and fall merchandise. These buying trips were the highlight of his life. He went to all the showrooms in the china, glass, and gift building named 225 5$^{th}$. It was the center of the gift industry. It was a place where manufacturers had central offices with showrooms. The purchasers retailed these new items and developed ways to sell the gift items they bought. It was the heart of wholesaling gifts for gift shops and department stores. They in turn resold Christmas goods at retail.

Arthur relished going to market. He had developed the idea of business and pleasure together. He did this instinctively. Every time he went to market, he loved being wined and dined while he was in New York. It was entertainment, as was purchasing his china, glass, and giftware to be resold in Fort Worth.

Arthur was much married and a family man. But this buying trip was different. Arthur was staying at the Waldorf Astoria. He had completed his buying for the day. He had been invited to see the newest products from Corning Glass Works, a famous American glass company. Also, a famous importer of Swedish crystal, Brodegard, would be there. He knew that he would be among the most important retailers in such stores as Bloomingdale's, Marshall Fields, and a few others. It was the type of business entertainment Arthur really enjoyed.

As Arthur was shaving, he paused for a moment and pondered. He inspected his cleanly shaven face and thought, "Not bad for thirty-nine, but from here on, it's all downhill." He said aloud, "I made some great buys today. I should be importing on my own. I can do better than these guys."

This was the start of Arthur's moving to the big city. Arthur sensed that the move would be his 'Turning Point of the Century.'

The next few days were hectic. Arthur called his wife and said they must have a heart-to-heart talk. He told her that he would be home in a day or two. Then he listed the most important items on his agenda. These included his marriage, separation, and talking with the manager of 225 5th Avenue about a position as salesman with one of his major tenants.

Arthur was part of the WW II generation. Well educated, well situated, and while not filthy rich, affluent. He was always looking for new fields to conquer. He knew that his selling at the wholesale level could be more rewarding than running his store on the mezzanine of the A. Harris & Co. He did not like the detail in running the entire operation. Arthur's plan was to keep selling china, glassware, and gifts—but at the wholesale level. Arthur was willing to learn another aspect of sales— how to sell at wholesale and make a living doing it.

Financially, Arthur was in fair shape. His father had died just after divorcing his mother. His jewelry and gift concession in a major department store had provided a comfortable living for her. This concession was the inheritance that Arthur had received from his father. Arthur knew that he needed to sell the concession rights before he left Texas. Once that was done, his financial ties to the area would be gone.

In the meantime, Art polished his selling skills. He knew instinctively that the saying 'too soon we get old and too late we get smart' really applied in the case of the wholesale level of trade. In addition, he discovered that the only person who expressed an opinion was the buyer.

The disruption of his career and his married life, the move to New York, and learning a new aspect of selling, resulted in a trip for the fun of it—a three-week tour to see the Far East. While in Hong Kong, Arthur attended a conference of travel agents who were visiting principal cities of Japan, Korea, China, and Hong Kong.

Arthur's pleasure trip to Hong Kong resulted in his staying in the Peninsula Hotel. He spent three days wandering around 'the micro city.' He remembered his Fort Worth years of retailing as he climbed the hills of the island of Hong Kong. He was viewing retailing at its best. It resulted in his referring to his Diamond of Life capabilities. They were exceptional.

The Traits and Tendencies in Arthur's life pointed out that the timing of his move was good. Arthur had ambition and planned ahead for the changes. He had the imagination to merchandise at the wholesale level. The challenge of the misty future excited him. It made Arthur accept the inevitable. If he did not change, he would always regret not altering his career and making his move. The three days in Hong Kong had clarified his thinking about his future. Arthur was going to end his marriage and start a new career.

# 10

# *RELIGION*

M ANY PHILOSOPHERS CONSIDER THAT a superior power governs the beliefs and actions of the world's inhabitants. Religion is a spiritual expression of this belief. The federal authorities wanted the freedom to practice a religion with gospel that read, "In the United States, a person can believe anything he wants to and it will be an unalienable right."

A self-appointed savant from Asia, the Bhagwan Rajneesh came to the state of Oregon and brought several thousand followers with him. For three years, he tried to have this church and its followers buy land and establish a new nation with its own constitution. He was the leader. The courts ruled that this was not allowed by the United States Constitution. The Rajneesh was served with papers, taken into custody, and expelled from the country. It was a Turning Point for both the interloper and the United States. No one can evade the law and establish its own rules by forming his own country. It is one of nine stories that illustrate the cause and effect of religion.

# ESCAPE FROM THE NAZI'S IN 1936

*Bad News Travels Fast*

B AD NEWS! UPON HEARING the voice over the radio, Hans talked to his wife. They lived in Berlin, Germany. Hans's face was grim, and his voice was sober, "It looks terrible for all of us."

The two concerned German Jews talked of the Nazi book burning and the destruction of all literature written by the Jewish people. These happenings were described in detail by newspapers and were broadcast constantly over the radio. The two discussed what might happen next and what they could do about it.

The couple decided that they should contact distant relatives who lived in the United States. Hans called a second cousin and told him that he was an engineer for a small motors factory. Hans talked directly with the president of this firm. They discussed how Hans would be an engineer who would design new products.

The United States factory manufactured appliances using less than one horse power motors. This included appliances such as refrigerators, vacuum cleaners, etc. Hans had helped design such items and sold them throughout Western Europe.

Hans also asked his relative to find out if Jews could still move there and live in a country that was not in turmoil. He knew that the Great Depression was worldwide, but Hans's profession made the move worth a try. The relatives asked Hans if he and his wife had worked out an escape plan. Hans said that he had, and he would leave his family at home while he went to the United States. As soon as it was possible, Hans would send for them.

With the plan in mind, Hans went to the United States. He went through Belgium and England to Canada. It took him two years to make the trip to Los Angeles.

Once in Los Angeles, Hans contacted his second cousin, Bert, who owned and operated Given Manufacturing Company in south Los Angeles. Hans called Bert upon arrival and, in broken English, explained who he was and why he called. Even though business was very slow, this phone call resulted in Hans being employed as an engineer.

This job became Hans's key Turning Point— moving from Nazi Germany to the States and becoming employed where his engineering skills could be utilized. What luck!

The Diamond of Life review of Hans showed he was innovative (developing a new product), self-sufficient (escaping from Hitler), and resourceful (meeting his own needs in a foreign country). Hans's Turning Point was escaping from Germany before Adolph Hitler got him! This Hans did. He had decided that this was his chance of a lifetime, and it was!

During the next couple of years, Hans learned English and assisted the Given Manufacturing Company in developing the Waste King Garbage Disposal. Part of the developing process was the design and testing of this new household product. Hans ended his career as an executive of the Given Manufacturing Company, a manufacturer of many home appliances.

Hans and his family escaped the Nazi persecution of the 1930s. Had they stayed in Germany, they would have been victims of the Holocaust.

# HOW ANTELOPE CITY DIES A DREARY DEATH

*A Spiritualist from India Ruins the High Desert
for All Oregonians*

THE OREGON HIGH DESERT swallows its dead. So it did in 1985 when the owners of all the small stores in Antelope City, Oregon, closed their doors, boarded up their buildings, and left. Everything the storekeepers couldn't carry they left behind as they looked for greener pastures. The one person left was the United States Postmistress.

The postmistress was a seventy-year-old woman with dusty grey hair. When asked about Antelope City and the famed Spiritualist Bhagwan Rajneesh, she replied that she had lived in the Antelope City long before Rajneesh came to town. She said that he had purchased the entire city from its owners. And from the local ranchers, he purchased twenty-five square miles of the surrounding desert ranch land, including the cattle and horses that fed on the sparse vegetation.

The Bhagwan Rajneesh had become the 'Emperor of Antelope City.' It became a desert town of one hundred twenty-seven Oregonians and about two thousand five hundred settlers from the East Coast, the West Coast, and all the states in between. The new settlers were vagabonds who smoked pot and used other drugs at will. The only thing they didn't do was work.

The postmistress was the only federal official in the area. Her post office was a forty-foot travel trailer with a ramp leading up to the door. The trailer had a customer area in one-half and an employee service area in the other. Also in the trailer were a service window, a bank of individual mailboxes, a stamp-dispensing machine, and several wanted posters.

After going up to the window, a rancher came into the post office to get his mail, and I asked him if he remembered the Rajneesh.

The rancher said, "My dad knew him as our spread was bought by him and we bought it back after the feds came to take him and send him back to where he came from. I remember that the Rajneesh, as he was called, was living in Madras, a small town twenty-four miles away. He was rumored to own fifty Cadillacs and Rolls-Royces! He was driven to and from Madras in a chauffeur driven car. Every day he inspected his troops. He wanted them to wear red robes when they lined up along Main Street."

The postmistress said, "Hi, Franky. We just put up some mail for you."

As Franky left, she turned and said, "I remember now. The Bhagwan invasion was a period of time like no other I remember. His three-year 'occupation' was limited to his daily visits. He wanted a valid visa giving him the right to stay in Antelope City as his permanent residence. It never came!"

She continued, "In the meantime, the entire community, as well as the surrounding twenty-five square miles of ranch land, was tied up. You can look around and see the city. It was nice then, and now it is trashed. The only thing he didn't buy was the post office you are standing in."

Asked if she saw the Rajneesh and his disciples, she said, "Yes, when he bought a new Rolls-Royce. Every day after the purchase, he stopped to see if Washington had sent his residency permit. Then he returned to Madras. Rumor had it that the Bhagwan's spiritual theory had ten rules as its basis, just like the Ten Commandments, the most important of which was that anything was permitted in his new independent community.

"This included free sex, any place at any time. Smoking pot was O.K. too. I didn't come here after dark because of the shenanigans going on."

I thanked the postmistress for her help and left the tiny post office. She had suggested a walking tour of what remained of the deserted community. All the streets were dirt and gravel, and the few homes were rundown. There was abandoned equipment and broken down cars scattered about the yards. Inspection of Main Street took imagination.

It turned out that the town died in 1985. This was the year when the Rajneesh was deported back to India, where he remained until he died in 1989. The real estate in Antelope City was re-purchased by a rancher for far less than what the Rajneesh had paid for it. Everyone left town except the postmistress.

It should be noted that the United States government did not object to the fact that the Bhagwan Rajneesh had purchased the whole town. It was the local ranchers who objected because of the 'anything goes' policy, such as smoking pot and having illegitimate sex openly in the street at night.

So it goes. "America the Beautiful" was despoiled by an invader from India. This bit of Oregon's history included an Indian interloper causing the death of a community. It was a Turning Point in the lives of those who lived in the town while it died a dreary death. The Diamond of Life pointed to failure. Antelope City has never recovered, though the rest of the high desert communities have done so.

# ISAAC AND HIS AWAKENING

*A Sincerely Spiritual Man*

ISAAC AROSE IN THE November morning. It was spring. He thought about his continuing to attend medical school in his hometown of Johannesburg, South Africa. He was just nineteen years old. He realized that he didn't want to be a medical doctor. Training to be a physician as his father hoped was not for him!

Isaac looked out the bedroom window and saw a pink cloud in the morning sky and remembered the old saying, "Pink sky at night, sailor's delight; pink sky in morning, sailors warning." He thought a moment and realized that his pink cloud in the morning was his father choosing medicine for him and Isaac not making his own choice. Isaac realized, as he looked out the window, that he wanted to quit his pre-med studies and tell his dad that he could not follow his father's hopes of having a doctor son. This was a major Turning Point in Isaac's young life, and a very tough one at that.

Isaac's family emigrated from Lithuania, every European country was in turmoil. Adolf Hitler was ascending to power. They wanted a safe haven, so they immigrated to South Africa and settled in Johannesburg, a small city at the time.

Isaac was born in 1950 and spent the first nineteen years of his life growing up in poverty. His family did the best they could to survive. Apartheid was still rampant in the country, and Nelson Mandela was just coming into power. All the whites in the country found themselves without the labor of those who had had no civil rights. The roles had been reversed. Seeing this change had a major impact on Isaac.

Isaac saw the turmoil that was caused by a group of people struggling for their dignity. This greatly influenced Isaac's life. This was a Turning Point in itself—seeing a country go from a two-class society to a classless society and the impact that it had on both groups.

Having quit medical school, Isaac knew that he must do something to earn his living. He spent several years in South Africa trying to find himself. After much soul-searching, he decided he wanted to get back to basics and become a 'kibbutzim,' so he moved to Israel. He joined a kibbutz that produced fruit and vegetables. It was north of Jerusalem. He saw that such an organization had a classless society.

After Isaac arrived, he was assigned to run a tractor—literally tilling the soil of the 'promised land.' He did this for the next four and a half years, after which he had his 'second awakening.' It was an inner feeling that the Israelis were destroying the natural state of the land, even though they were providing food for his fellow Israelis. What he wanted was to pioneer— to find a home where he could start his own community and become a spiritualist.

He sent for information about New Zealand and its North Island. It had just three million citizens. It was Isaac's Promised Land, and when he saw what New Zealand was, he wanted to immigrate there.

This became another Turning Point—leaving Israel. Isaac checked with the authorities in New Zealand. Could he go to New Zealand to test the water? He learned that he must spend one year in England before he could immigrate and receive permanent residence in New Zealand.

The next step in Isaac's plan was to move temporarily to London. He proceeded to put in his year there as a 'fix-it' man, doing anything and everything to earn his keep while waiting to go to New Zealand.

While he was in London, Isaac met a lady and asked her to go to New Zealand with him. She agreed to go down under. He felt that this was the perfect life for his persona. His new country was gorgeous. He observed this as he flew into Auckland. The hillsides were shamrock green and had little white dots all over them. Those white dots on the ground were part of the millions of sheep raised by the New Zealanders. It was a beautiful panorama!

The English lady became Isaac's first wife, spending six months in New Zealand and six months in Britain. Isaac had wed her and taken her with him on his first visit.

Isaac purchased a thousand acres of land on the North Island of New Zealand and proceeded to establish a colony of followers. He divided the land into individual lots. He planned to build houses and then sell the homes as part of a major development. Isaac felt that he would build a new city that would provide jobs for those who bought the houses. This development would be self-sustaining. It was to be his new community.

Isaac's move to New Zealand to establish a development was a Turning Point. It was the start of a ten-year plan. Isaac and his wife had three children. However, the project of subdividing and selling off the property had lost its luster and was not, in itself, fulfilling enough for Isaac.

Isaac began philosophizing about what he wanted out of life. It was a period of developing a following in New Zealand. It was the basis for a future existence. Isaac dwelled on the future. Where should he go and what should he do when he got there? He became fixated on ideas about his future, and since he had family obligations, Isaac pondered the imponderable!

To find answers to these questions, Isaac took his family to Maui, a Hawaiian Island, and spent the next sixteen years there, educating his children, being together, and developing his philosophy. Isaac was in his fruitful forties. By then he had several children, a second wife, and a live-along 'companion,' all of whom provided inspiration.

It was the major Turning Point in Isaac's life. He developed his own philosophy based on his theory that the past cannot be changed, that the future is an intangible, and that one should live in the present. This spiritualistic alteration in his life was one of Isaac's most important Turning Points. He believed that one should live and enjoy the 'now' because it is the only thing one can change.

During this period of time, he became a spiritual leader. He also had changes in his family life with two divorces and a new relationship. These changes in his personal life and his thinking carried on for the balance of his fifty-nine years.

Isaac found himself to be a spiritualist who began concentrating on the present—a philosophy that was real and was based upon enjoying the moment and getting others to follow his lead.

He frequently said, "The past is cast in concrete, the future provides an intangible dream, and the present is here and now."

It represented the concept of the Diamond of Life Traits and Tendencies that would continue to lead Isaac toward success— his attitude (upbeat thoughts), his ambition (always thinking success), and his know-how (using common sense that made success a probability). All of these personal traits stimulated Isaac's spiritual awakening in the first decade of the 21st century. Isaac had spent ten years enjoying the moment and helping others follow his path. He began traveling the world presenting his views to old friends and new contacts alike.

Isaac is welcomed when he revisits and renews those who embrace his concept of 'Now is where it's at!' While this is not a unique view, it is certainly self-fulfilling. It is introspective and has met Isaac's spiritual needs. It is a true 'awakening.'

## PASTOR STRIKES GOLD

◆

*A World Wide Copyright Service*

A DAY WITHOUT RAIN is a beautiful day in Portland, Oregon. One such Sunday found a pastor with a compelling idea. It was a special plan to license religious songs and music. Before his discovery, the common practice was the copying of religious works, such as sheet music or recording songs, from the airways without permission from the writer of the music.

Rozen was the pastor who thought of this novel idea. He researched copyrights as a way to increase member participation. The plan was simple. The pastor investigated copyrights that could be registered. The intention was to get a license from the person who wrote the music and license it to prevent the copyright from being violated.

This process of licensing copyrighted works and leasing the use of same was a Turning Point in the lives of Rozen and his wife, Marta. Rozen intended to contact the originators' religious music publishers in the United States and get them to copyright religious music that they published and have it distributed through Rozen's organization. This was a new idea and would represent an important Turning Point in Rozen's life. It would become his life's work.

Rozen established his organization. This new company was called CCLI the registered name for Christian Conservative Licensing Incorporated. Rozen started organizing at the end of the 20th Century. Rozen had researched this possibility, as it would prevent copying of religious music without CCLI signing a licensing agreement.

From a small beginning with about one hundred music publishers and two thousand churches, Rozen saw his concept explode. No one had realized how needed this efforts were. By the year 2008, some twenty years later, the licensing would be operative in twenty-six countries.

This was a Turning Point in Rozen's life. It meant a huge amount of effort and the element of luck and hard work. This was accomplished by Rozen and his wife Marta. They had developed the principle of copyrighting religious music with the thought that it would be utilized by almost ten thousand churches that were in existence during the beginning of 21st century. The licensing agreement with CCLI is currently available.

This concept has been accepted by the churches, the users, and of course the licensor. This Turning Point in Rozen's life was a major one. The licensing of religious music and legalizing its copying deserves an accolade to its founders—Rozen, his wife Marta, and all the helpers involved in CCLI.

# THE LONG AND THE SHORT OF IT

*A Packager Becomes a Preacher*

OKLAHOMA IS PROUD OF many famous people who were born, bred, and raised as Sooners.* Among them were John D Rockefeller, the multi-millionaire, Will Rogers, the movie star, and Carl Long, the hero of this story. While not as renowned as the other two, Carl had a great number of Turning Points in his life pointing him toward success. These changes in direction were dramatic. Some were high points and others were low points, but all were vital.

Ponca City claimed Carl as its very own even though Carl later lived in Southern California. He grew up raising horses but didn't become a cowboy. He was too young to fight in WWII.

In the early sixties, Carl migrated to the San Fernando Valley, where he married a California beauty and had three sons. Marriage, family, and starting his career were eventful. Carl faced up to new responsibilities. Carl found a job as a night janitor in a cosmetic manufacturing firm. He worked his way up the organization. He became a foreman in ten years.

These events occurred during President Kennedy's administration when the country was frightened by a missile crisis. Carl was interested in getting his own business. Carl raised capital by contacting family and friends—and he succeeded. He started his own business. He would package cosmetics. He also got a start-up loan from a local bank.

He went from a standing start, and in twelve years of hard work, he had saved money and had purchased another small cosmetic company.

Purchasing and operating a cosmetic manufacturing company was a major accomplishment and a Turning Point for Carl. It meant working around the clock. It meant meeting payrolls. It meant overseeing all the functions needed to package for the major manufacturers of beauty products.

After twelve years, he was packaging for Max Factor and other beauty product distributors. Carl was familiar with the company he purchased. Its former owner had retired after one year of working for Carl. In this way, Carl had his dream fulfilled—that of being an entrepreneur in a field that he liked, doing work that he liked, and working harder than ever before. He designed packaging equipment and took packaging jobs. During this time, he met many of the major cosmetic manufacturers who did not package their own products. They had Carl do it.

Carl found this to be a desirable way to turn his life in the right direction. He contacted all the cosmetic manufacturers in Southern California and was successful in having Max Factor give him a spring promotion for Mother's Day. It was by far the largest contract Carl had ever received. This new job was a filling and closure job.

The items that Max Factor wanted to have filled were fruit shaped plastic containers that looked like real lemons, oranges, and apples. The containers would be produced in China, and Carl would fill them with bath salts that smelled like the three fruits.

After filling the fruit containers, Carl would cap them with a specially designed plastic closure that resembled the stem of each fruit. Carl made a test run of a thousand of each of the three fruits. Carl told Max Factor that the order would be $2 million, with Max Factor to pay all shipping costs.

Max Factor delivered the fruit containers in the middle of October. Carl designed and tested the filling and closure production line. He used it to process the initial shipment of fruit Carl received from Max Factor. Carl would have six months to fill, cap, and transport the bath salt filled fruits fifteen miles to be packed for reshipment to Max Factor's California customers. Certainly, this would be a Turning Point for Carl. Max Factor told Carl that he could expect much larger orders for many years to come.

Carl had the filling machine at the ready. During testing, it had worked perfectly. However, the capping machine closure would not seal the plastic fruit properly. The 'fill holes' were not uniform. The sizes were all off. After the bath salts were placed into the apples, lemons, and pears, the fruit had to be capped with their stem tops by machine. The stem tops were not the same size as the fruit openings, and they didn't fit. The shapes were different—they weren't round, and they didn't fit into the holes. The stems couldn't close the plastic fruit. The apple, lemon, and plum stems produced in China could not be used.

This was the beginning of a nightmare for Carl. The first shipment of artificial fruit from Hong Kong arrived in October. Carl had designed and created an automatic filling and closure machine. It worked perfectly on the sample bottles, but as fate would have it, the Hong Kong production run was defective. The holes to close the filled piece of artificial fruit were not standard. It was impossible to close the filled bottles automatically. It would have to be done by hand.

Carl called up the buyer immediately and said that they were having a problem, and to please come over and see what they were talking about. The buyer appeared within a half an hour with the Quality Control man from Max Factor and saw what Carl was talking about. He told Carl to complete the order at all costs, and they would change their price accordingly. Carl agreed, and started his operation to fill the six million units with closures and get the job done a month before Mother's Day. This was just the beginning of the problem. It was the Major Turning Point of Carl's life.

It was an impossible situation. Each unit had to be filled by machine and then the closure added separately by hand. Carl realized that his vision of getting a major customer to utilize his services on an ever-growing basis was doomed. It was a Turning Point in his life that he would never forget. Nor did the bank or Max Factor. Even though it was not Carl's fault, he received all the blame. His production for other customers was delayed. He was forced into bankruptcy.

Furthermore, the Diamond of Life showed that an unpredictable event, coupled with misfortune, would lead to failure. Such was the fate of Carl and his career. This large order and subsequent production problems caused Carl to fail. This one Turning Point converted him from being a profit-making industrialist to a bankrupt one. Carl lost everything he owned. He became a nonprofit preacher.

The Diamond of Life review showed that Carl was ambitious, dedicated, and capable. He did not have judgment, financial strength, or technical knowhow to make his career a success.

These characteristics were not required in the nonprofit area. This is the story about Carl, a packager who became a preacher bringing religion to his flock.

*Sooners* was the nickname given to the Oklahomans who left the starting point of the land rush staged by President Cleveland at the end of the 19th century. The name has stuck and is currently used for the University of Oklahoma football team and the residents of Oklahoma.

## A PRODUCER OF RELIGIOUS FILMS
## IS SAVED BY THE BELL

*He Died Before His Time*

B RAM ROOS DIED WITH his boots on, but his reputation remained
intact! Chairman of the Board of Directors, Dennis racked his brain
as he called the special meeting of PIP (People in Progress) to order. This
was an emergency because PIP was funded by the State of California and
other government agencies. As such, the organization's operations had to
be 'as clean as a hounds tooth.' Such was not the case with the office
manager who signed all vouchers for payment. She had absconded with
money—the amount of which would be discovered. PIP's investigation
of cash shortages was being supervised by Director Roos.

PIP, a residential facility, housed ninety-two male 'street people'
who had become clean (non-users) and were transitioning to everyday
life. The residents of this nonprofit agency received support for their
struggles to keep living a drug free life. Not using was the only condition
of living in this state-supported facility.

PIP's board was discussing whether to appoint a co-manager of
the facility. With the investigation going on, a board member dead, and a
potential splitting of management being considered, PIP, as an
organization, was facing a major Turning Point.

The board was considering appointing Wayne as co-manager.
His duties would include the review of PIP's books and records,
supervision of the office staff, preparation of the annual financial reports,
and management of office operations. Lance O'Brien, a senior staff
member, would be the other co-manager handling operational functions.

Taking part in this selection process was Bram Roos, a board member for six years. To his credit, Bram Roos served as vice chairman of the PIP board because, as a recovering substance abuser, he could lend his drug-dependency experience to target the board of director's efforts and keep it on the right track.

Chairman Dennis said that PIP needed to have a typical line of authority and staff organization with two co-managers running the facility. The two men selected as managers were Wayne, a new employee, and Lance O'Brien, a seasoned manager of PIP's Sun Valley's California location. The vote to approve the concept was unanimous.

The Turning Point in this instance was the introduction of split management. The consensus was to create a mini-study setting forth:

(1)     Current activities
(2)     Division of management responsibilities
(3)     Assignment of each manager, including duties and responsibilities
(4)     Submission of a report to board for approval
(5)     Submission of a report of irregularities—directly to Chairman of the Board

The details, developed as a team effort, and the mini-study prepared by the two co-managers, were reviewed and approved by the PIP board. The board approved the suggested plan of divided responsibilities, the study was completed, and the appointment of the two managers, O'Brien, and Wayne, was in the offing.

The Diamond of Life method was used to select the co-managers. It found that both men had the traits of experience in their respective fields. Each was intelligent, and each had college degrees.

Lance O'Brien was shown to be lax in his supervisory skills and tended to be laid back and somewhat indolent and undisciplined. On the other hand, Wayne had leadership traits (former positions with Chambers of Commerce) and PR capabilities, having served as staff to various local elected officials.

After a few weeks on the job, Wayne found fraudulent entries in the financial records of PIP. It was during his review of the books and records just after his assuming his duties. He reported this fact to PIP's

Vice Chair Director Roos. Such action became a Turning Point for Bram Roos.

Wayne told Director Roos what he knew about the fraud. He said that he had discovered that Maria, the employee keeping the books, was stealing money from PIP. Wayne found that vendors' invoices were paid, but that the amount entered in the books did not agree with the amount paid. Wayne came to Bram because the two of them had known each other for years. Bram Roos told Wayne to notify the Chairman of the Board, but Bram Roos did not follow-up to see that Wayne had done it.

This was an error on Bram Roos's part since the fraud became a major Turning Point to the extent that it was more extensive, and that there were several other employees and outsiders involved, including Lance O'Brien, people at the bank, and other lesser PIP employees.

The fraud investigation by PIP's accountants continued until Bram Roos returned from Israel where he was producing a pilot for a TV series. Bram notified the Board of Directors that he was too busy to look into such a serious matter.

Bram Roos faced a decision. After a full disclosure, should he resign from the board or should he remain on the board?

To help him make the right move, Bram Roos remembered that the Diamond of Life's trait of dishonesty could lead to failure. All of the people involved in the falsifications would be prosecuted eventually, despite which action he chose. He shuddered when he thought of the effect on the image of PIP. In any event, the decision that Bram Roos must make was very difficult.

Either course of action had risks and rewards attached. If he resigned from the board, his reputation as being honest, upright and true might be jeopardized because his resignation could be tarnished by implication. On the other hand, if he remained on the board, it would require much more of his time and personal involvement because Wayne had disclosed the fact only to him rather than to the chairman of PIP's board as was required.

Unfortunately, fate intervened. Bram Roos suffered a heart attack and died at the age of fifty-three. Bram Roos's life included happenings beyond his control. Although Turning Points were caused by unusual events, death made the difficult personal decision facing Bram Roos unnecessary.

## TURNING DISASTER INTO A NEW LIFE

*An Odd Combo—Religion and an Independent Publishing Company*

THE DISASTER WAS COMPLETE. Carl watched a major fire destroy his manufacturing facility, plant, equipment, everything. The next morning he discovered that he had no insurance. What was he to do? How could he start over at fifty-plus years old? Except for his personal books and records, it was a total loss. It meant that his custom decorating containers and packaging operation would be closed. He would have to go bankrupt. It was not a pleasant prospect. It was not a pleasant Turning Point in his life. It was not Carl's dream.

This Turning Point involved turning a disaster into a productive life. It meant that Carl could choose one of the following alternatives. The first remedy would involve borrowing money from friends, relatives, or even the federal government, reestablish his business, and do it as quickly as possible.

The second alternative would be to work for somebody else in a managerial capacity, choosing a field in which he was a specialist. Carl did not like this alternative. He felt he was an entrepreneur, a decision maker. He did not take kindly to a superior telling him what and how to do something.

The third possibility was to move to a new location, preferably to southern California.

To accomplish this, Carl wanted to find a small town in need of a newspaper that could be run by an established Christian organization. Carl could be both a pastor and an editor of an independent newspaper. This last idea was the alternative that really appealed to Carl.

Carl felt that his Diamond of Life indicated that his Traits and Tendencies would point him toward success. He had written articles that had appeared in the East San Fernando weekly papers. Also, Carl was a frequent panelist on "Hughes Views," a local TV program. As he was religious, Carl felt that this disaster could be his golden opportunity.

Carl secured as much financing as he could from his parents and friends and headed southeast to the small desert town called Anza. It had about eight thousand residents. Carl jokingly said, "That is counting all the cats and Mexicans." Truly, the population was mostly retired folk and Native Americans who had moved there a number of years ago. Carl saw the city as a potential place to establish his church. Although there were several Christian churches in town, no one had started an evangelical sect in the area. His review of Anza included looking around the city to find out if there were any weekly newspapers being published there. He asked the local bank and found out that closest newspapers were the San Diego Union or the Los Angeles Times.

Carl said to himself, "This is the place." He later realized that he had stolen Brigham Young's words that the Mormon leader had spoken as he viewed the Great Salt Lake in Utah one hundred fifty years before. Carl found a hall that he could rent on Sundays to establish his religious services. His final task was finding a location for his newspaper. It was to be on the main street of Anza, a rental place where he could establish his newspaper, the Anza Valley News.

Being cautious, Carl told his story to many of the sixty-plus business people in town and asked if they would support his efforts. He went to the casino to meet the owner and manager, who was also the chief of the Anza Tribe. He went to the local school and, much to his surprise, found the principal, so he could tell his story. After finishing his survey, Carl decided to move to Anza and start his new life.

In keeping with his word, Carl began his new career. He started by contacting the various politicians located in Sacramento and Washington, DC. His newspaper articles were meaningful, fairly conservative, and to the point. They had to do with the way the state was run, the way the country was run, and what changes should be made in both—if the 'polls' wanted his support. His church flourished, and he built his congregation to almost two hundred people. He had satisfied his major goals in life and felt he had achieved success.

Carl had Turning Points, both favorable and unfavorable. Obviously, the disasters he suffered in the Los Angeles area during the 1970s were major. The fact that he was able to turn his life around by moving to a small community and start over in the Anza Valley turned out to help Carl develop a new life. The Diamond of Life traits of foresight, imagination, and drive enabled Carl to turn disaster into success!

## YOU CAN BANK ON IT

◆

### The Mormon Church Has a Piggy Bank

A WHITE MARBLE BUILDING shone in the summer sun. It was named the Utah State Bank. It sat on the corner of Main and 1st South Streets. It was owned and operated by the Mormon Church and was a showplace for all visitors to Salt Lake City. The local citizens jokingly called it the church's piggy bank. The chief officer of the bank, Orville Adams, was its first vice president. He had been running the bank since FDR became the President of the United States. Orville Adams was married and had six sons.

Orville had a unique problem.  It was difficult to solve and the reason this true story was written. And most of all it was Orville's 'baby!' The Utah State Bank was too prosperous! Here was an example of a bank and its manager doing their jobs too well!

Orville went to Utah State College. Since he intended to be a teacher, he majored in education and religion. He received a BA degree. After graduation, he returned to the family farm near the Utah-Idaho border. Orville's parents had wanted him to come back to their winter wheat and alfalfa farm and take over its management since they were getting old. But after a year or two of actually running the farm, Orville decided he was not cut out to be a farmer. He decided to enter the financial arena and went to Salt Lake City Utah to do so.

In Salt Lake, Orville applied to all the banks. He got a temporary position at Utah State Bank on Main Street. It was near the center of town and two blocks from Temple Square—the center of the universe as far as the Mormon Church was concerned. Moving from farming country to the largest city in the Intermountain West, and getting a new occupation, were life changing Turning Points in Orville's life.

Orville was employed as a teller, one of eight in the bank. He worked hard at this position for two years. He was promoted to being a loan officer. This promotion was a Turning Point in Orville's life. Why? Once a teller was promoted to the 'platform,' he began handling the general business that came through the front door of the bank. These employees were considered likely to fill any of the executive positions that occurred during the bank's operations.

This promotion, of course, became a Turning Point for two reasons. The first was that he had found a role in the financial world that could lead to executive banking. The second was the fact that he belonged to the Mormon faith. Orville believed that his faith in Brigham Young's church had been the cause of his getting promoted by the Utah State Bank.

Four years later, he was promoted to vice president in charge of the platform group. This was a great promotion because it meant that he was to report to the current president of 'The Church,' which belonged to the Latter Day Saints Sect of the Mormons.

At one point, Orville became the employee of the year. He had shown the officers of the bank that he was executive material and deserved this promotion. It had taken him six years to accomplish this because he had been filling 'dead man shoes.'

According to Orville, his marriage was made by Jesus. The couple had wed very young. They had six sons, approximately a year and a half apart. At each birth, Orville felt he was achieving a lifelong goal of having a large family. After the sixth son was born, he realized having a girl child was not a probability. He accepted this fact as the will of the Lord.

At this juncture of his life, Orville decided to purchase a home in a Salt Lake City area called Federal Heights. Such a purchase was another Turning Point in his life. This was a super location, the best in town. It was in an area that was being developed for high-end homes. It was a prestigious house that was close to the University of Utah. It was on Federal Way, the road to Fort Douglas, the second largest army base in the Intermountain West.

This action turned out to be a wise choice. He now was part of the landed gentry of the Mormon Church as well as of Salt Lake City.

Soon, Orville became an elder in the Mormon Church. He was one of its leaders.

Each of his six sons subscribed to the principles found in the Book of Mormon. At eighteen, each son was expected to go on a mission. During this two-year period, the missionary was expected to travel to various areas of the globe, to preach the gospel, and to recruit novitiates to become members of the church. Thus, they spread the gospel of the Latter Day Saints, namely, Mormonism.

Each one of Orville's sons went on a church mission. Two went to England and four went to the Philippines. The success of his sons was his greatest Turning Point. Why? Because he felt he was an icon being a true Mormon example.

As each son became eighteen, Orville endowed them with the Mormon philosophy. The Mormon Church financed itself by tithing. Each member of the church did so. Tithing meant giving ten percent of one's annual salary to the church. Orville was more than happy to do so, and he expected all of his sons to follow his lead.

The second tenet was to read the book of Mormon, the Mormon Bible. It became the main instrument by which the Mormon faith was practiced.

The third action that Orville expected of his sons was to adopt the limitations of pleasure—they were to refrain from smoking, refrain from drinking alcohol, and refrain from cavorting with women. They were expected to be good Mormons.

How did each son measure up? Here is what each son achieved.

His firstborn, Alan, had been a football star and inherited the family farm. Number two son, Lane, was an excellent student who specialized in math and engineering. After he returned from his mission abroad, Lane became an accountant for a bank in San Francisco, California. Son number three was Heidi. He was an excellent sportsman.

Heidi had the misfortune of riding his horse on a country road. As Heidi galloped along, the horse shied into an automobile, and Heidi was killed on contact with the car.

Son number four was Ted. He was not nearly as intelligent as he might have been. But Ted became an excellent electrician. He worked for the Utah Power and Light Company after he returned from his mission. Son number five, Preston, liked the church. After his mission, he did not want to become a minister so he became a professor of religion at Utah University.

Orville's sixth son, Webster, was the wildest one of the group. He became what is known in Salt Lake parlance as a 'Jack Mormon.' He did not adhere to the tenet of deprivation, especially of alcohol. Webbie was a 'rounder' and a great disappointment to his father, who practically disowned him. This success story was backed up by referring to the Diamond of Life portrayal of his raits and Tendencies . Orville had character and moral strength. He was persistent in following his precepts. He stood tall in facing life.

Orville had made his mark in banking. He showed that with sweat, tears and good fortune one could face Turning Points, make sound decisions, and live a good and successful life. His cohorts said that if Orville said something, 'you could always bank on it.'

**Note:** Orville Adams is deceased. The information is true as recalled by his close friend and next-door neighbor who lived on Federal Way.

# 11

# SEX

IT WAS ONLY A matter of time before sex reared its ugly head. The incidents in this chapter have been segregated as a group. Mankind has been involved with sexual activity since Adam and Eve. Sex follows religion in importance for those who live in the here and now. The stories related include youths playing doctor, a toss in the hay, and a rabbi 'playing patty-cake' with a member of his congregation. Who did what to whom is told in a fascinating way because having sex can't be made unpopular.

# RABBI GORDON GOT CAUGHT

◆

*An affair to Remember*

T HE LOCAL GOSSIP WHISPERED in Salt Lake City, Utah, was, "Have you heard the latest? Becky and the rabbi are having an affair. Don't tell anyone I told you!"

The background of the affair showed that the rabbi came from Cleveland sometime in 1926. Upon his arrival in Salt Lake City, he contacted the mayor to learn about the Jewish community in an area that was seventy percent Christian and belonged to a sect called the Church of Jesus Christ of the Latter Day Saints. This faith is commonly called Mormon.

While the Jews numbered fewer than four hundred fifty adults, Rabbi Gordon had decided to form a congregation of Reform Jews. Their place of worship was in a synagogue (temple) which was located in the center of town, near Temple Square.

The religious services were conducted by the rabbi and included the reading of the Torah and discussing the history of the Jews since the year 2000 BC. He would talk about being a Jew, about the Mormon faith, and why both denominations frowned on extra-marital sex and how polygamy was banned by federal law.

At the end of Friday night services, the congregation would leave the temple, stand around outside, and talk with each other and the rabbi about what happened the previous week and what they were planning for the upcoming week. Those outside numbered twenty to twenty-five people at most. The rabbi would discuss anything that affected the Jewish religion and Salt Lake City activities. This was on a very informal basis, and it depended on there being good weather.

One beautiful Friday evening, just before the Fourth of July, the rabbi discussed infidelity in his sermon. He talked about women who were unfaithful to their husbands. It was an interesting service, and Rabbi Gordon laid it on the line. At the end of the service the people flocked outside to have a cigarette and talk with each other.

The rabbi stopped to talk to Rebecca (Becky) Samuels, a married thirty-five year-old with two children. She was smoking a cigarette, and when the rabbi stopped by to talk to her, she asked the rabbi if he cared for one. He said, "Yes, that would be great." This was the start of an interesting relationship.

Rebecca and Rabbi Gordon soon became very engrossed with each other. They met publically for lunch at the Hotel Utah. They spoke about Salt Lake City politics, the weather conditions, and what was going on in the Jewish community, particularly activities that affected the rabbi's congregation.

As they came to know each other a little better, the rabbi asked Rebecca to have dinner at the Hotel Utah. At this dinner they enjoyed a quiet meal. Becky told the rabbi that her husband was watching the kids. The two talked about the Beehive House, which was where Brigham Young kept his fifty-three wives during his stay on this earth. The beehive is the symbol that is used by the State of Utah on their state seal.

During this dinner, the rabbi spoke about his past—coming from Cincinnati, Ohio, and his rabbinical studies in the state of New York. The rabbi told Rebecca how he met his wife and what it was like to be a rabbi. He asked Becky to tell him a little bit about her life.

Rebecca smiled and said, "Well, now let me see. I was a girl born in San Diego and came up here as a young girl of twenty. I got a job at Tracy Loan and Trust Company as a platform officer's Secretary.

"I met my husband, John, several years later at a party given by Tracy Collins Trust Company's President for the entire bank staff employee's and their guests. John and I went together for six months, enjoyed each other's company, and got married a year after that. We have two children about two years apart.

"John has continued to do well in his produce business. It has been successful, especially with what's going on in the stock market. We had been relatively happy with our children—a little boy and a little girl.

"John has been in the produce business; he buys from farmers and sells to store such owners as Dickenson's and other small grocery stores throughout the Salt Lake Valley. It's been a good life but a little boring for me. There is very little to do in Salt Lake City now. With what's going on in Europe and basically the American economy, it's affected our business in Utah."

The rabbi said, "I have been hearing this from a lot of the people in our congregation, and I know how difficult it must be for independent merchants such as your husband to get along these days."

The rabbi looked at his watch and said, "Oh my goodness, it's almost 8 o'clock. I have an appointment I must meet. I'll see you on Friday night?"

She replied, "Yes, John and I will be there. We usually are. It's one of the things we like to do."

After the rabbi had paid the bill, each went their separate ways.

This was the first of several meetings at the Hotel Utah and the Hotel Newhouse four or five blocks down Main Street. They were casual meetings during the day and rewarding conversations took place for both of them.

Then the inevitable happened. The congregation at the temple had noticed the attention Rabbi Gordon was giving to Rebecca after the services, especially during the informal discussions on the sidewalk in front of the temple. People started talking and gossiping about the two of them and the interest that the rabbi was showing toward Rebecca, even with John present.

One Friday night, when Rebecca's husband was on a business trip to Boise, Idaho, Rebecca came to the service alone. After the service, the rabbi came out as usual and mingled with the crowd in front of the Temple. He ended up talking to Rebecca.

After talking over a few inconsequential topics, the rabbi suddenly said, "What are you doing for lunch tomorrow?"

Rebecca said, "Well I've got the cleaning lady coming and the two kids will be around. I promised them that I would take them to the movies. It is at the Centre Theatre, and it is ideal for kids. But after one o'clock, I'll be able to have lunch with you. Where shall we meet?"

The rabbi thought for a minute and said, "Let's meet in the dining room of the Newhouse Hotel."

The next day, the two met after one o'clock and had lunch in the dining room of the hotel. As the two were leaving the dining room, the rabbi said, "Becky, they are remodeling the fourth floor of the hotel. Let's go up and see what the rooms look like."

She said, "I'll have to pick up the kids by three o'clock because the movie will be out."

He said, "Fine, we'll look at the new rooms, and you'll have plenty of time to get there."

They went upstairs, looked at the new rooms, and the inevitable happened. They made mad and violent love. At quarter to three, Rebecca said, "Oy vey! I have to go over to the Centre Theatre to pick up the kids."

The rabbi said, "Thanks very much for a wonderful afternoon. I'll see you on Friday night at our services."

The two lovers went down the elevator together, and just as they were leaving the elevator, one of the rabbi's congregants saw the two leaving together. She spread the word far and wide. This gossip was all over town before the sun went down.

At the Friday night services, the rabbi finished his sermon and went outside to mingle with the portion of the congregation that stayed around to talk with the rabbi. As he went from group to group, he noted that there seemed to be a change in their attitudes toward him. He felt certain hostility, especially on the part of the women. He wondered what had happened.

He sensed that something was wrong, and it probably involved Becky, himself, and the hanky-panky at the Newhouse Hotel. At home, his wife was her old self. The two kids read to him and went to bed. The rabbi wondered if he was making a wrong assumption. Did somebody in the congregation know? Was the truth out?

He got up the next day, and after breakfast the telephone rang. He answered the phone. It was one of the senior members of the congregation. He told the rabbi to be at the Synagogue at eleven o'clock am—sharp. He said the directors of the temple wanted to talk to him.

At eleven o'clock the rabbi arrived, and the grim-faced men were sitting at a table in the rear of the temple. Just as he suspected, the senior member of the group told him that somebody had seen Rebecca and him leaving the Newhouse Hotel elevator together.

The rabbi was asked, "Was the gossip true?"

The rabbi decided that honesty was the best policy and he said, "Yes, but it won't happen again."

The head of the group said, "You bet your life it won't, rabbi. Don't send your laundry out." The rabbi knew the jig was up, and that he would be given notice of termination of his services at the temple.

The rabbi left the room shaken. He realized that this could a major Turning Point in the scheme of things. Should he tell his wife the truth or should he lie?

The rabbi talked to his wife. He told his wife a lie as to what happened. He left making a complete disclosure of the truth for another day. The truth was another matter that he would face in the future.

He analyzed the situation using the Diamond of Life as a gauge. His character was at stake favoring that he tell the truth. His ambition, his sexuality, and his stupidity had led him to lie. The bad luck of being caught by his peers and telling them the truth shows a lack of judgment. It made confessing his sins an impossible alternative. It would be difficult to explain why he was fired.

The essence of this story demonstrates that if you play 'hanky-panky' and are married you better not get caught! Rabbi Gordon was the one who got caught. The inevitable happened. He lied to his wife and she believed him. Rabbi Gordon lied to the leaders of his synagogue. They were certain the rabbi was lying and told him so. It was a vital Turning Point, one that Rabbi Gordon will never forget!

## A FARMERETTE GETS A TOSS IN THE HAY

### *A Silent Soliloquy*

KANSAS IN JULY IS as hot as our kitchen stove. As a farm girl of eighteen, looking out my bedroom window at the winter wheat just peeking out of the ground, I am excited. I hope to go to an eastern college to become a teacher. I like kids and figured that this would be a temporary career until I found Mr. Right and married him. I applied to several schools and hoped to get in Bennington. I liked thinking about what it would be like to be away from my parents.

It was the summer before I was to start college. I went out to the Air Force base on Saturday nights to a dance. I felt it was a wonderful time to be a young girl, single, and looking for fun and excitement.

At that time during WWII, Kansas had an Air force base near Topeka. It was teeming with pilots and enlisted man flying the B-17s that were bombing Germany.

Before I tell you of the Turning Point in my young life, let me explain a little bit about Topeka during 1943. It was a town of fifty thousand people, all vitally interested in the Second World War and how it was going. The building of the Air Force base in the early part of the war indicated that we would have more personnel stationed there. Also, there was an influx of farmers from Nebraska and other states.

We lived on a farm on the outskirts of town about ten miles away. I went to school on a school bus during the week and looked forward to Saturday night. This was when there were dances at the officer's club the enlisted men's gym. The dances were exciting to a schoolgirl of eighteen. As I said before, Topeka, Kansas, had about fifty thousand people, not counting those at the air base. At five feet, six inches tall, one hundred twenty pounds, with blue eyes, red hair, and freckles, I was probably one of the most popular girls in my class and, for that matter, in town.

Topeka had a main street, a drug store with a soda fountain, a hardware store, a chamber of commerce, and three high schools. Within the county, all the rural roads were gravel. The only paved roads were in town.

My father farmed all his life, as had his father. My grandfather worked the six hundred forty acre spread in the twenties, as did my dad. I learned how to milk the cows, take care of the horses, feed the chickens, and help my mother. We had no help on the farm other than the people who lived there. It was a rough life style, especially since I was going to school from eight a.m. to three p.m. I did chores in the morning, such as milking the cows and feeding the chickens. I helped by doing the washing and hanging up the clothes. We had no driers. We had a rudimentary washing machine for our clothes, and that was about all.

My Dad was proud of his 'Old Tin Lizzie.' It was made by Ford and painted black. We were one of the few families in town with a car. If you have ever ridden down Main Street you would understand the situation in a farm town.

Every Saturday my Mom, Dad, two younger sisters, and I went downtown to the general store to buy items that we needed to run the farm and keep us for the next week. Everyone wore Levis or coveralls to work on the farm. We girls wore cotton dresses and bobby socks to do our chores in and wear to school. I remember it was wartime, and gasoline was hard to come by.

During the war, there were a lot of items rationed, and I can remember my mom treasuring our ration stamps to buy coffee and items that we did not grow on the farm. My Dad had a hired hand who helped plow the fields. In the late summer, he would mow the hay. I remember at Christmas a pair of roller skates given to me on my fourteenth birthday. I used to go downtown on Saturday and take my skates. As my parents were shopping, I would skate on the sidewalk in town.

I remember that my dad told me how he had met my mom. It was at the Baptist Church on a Sunday. He had gone out with her for a year before he proposed marriage. Of course the three of us, me and my two sisters were born during the ten years following the marriage. Because I was the eldest, I helped Mom do the cooking for the five of us plus the two hired hands.

I'd get up in the morning, help with the house chores, milk the cows, and get ready for school. I'd get dressed in a plain, everyday dress that we bought at the general store. I'd be picked up by the school bus and taken to a high school that was about ten miles away. It would get me home about four o'clock in the afternoon.

After school, there would be the evening chores, which I did, and then I studied for an hour after dinner. After homework was done, I got to listen to the radio. I went to bed between nine or ten o'clock.

Our whole family listened to President Roosevelt's speeches, as well as Kaltenborn, the announcer and news commentator. Basically, that was the extent of our listening, especially during the week when we had homework to do. As I remember it, we had Saturday night music from Glenn Miller. I wanted to learn ballroom dancing so I could be the belle of the ball at the Saturday night dances.

This was especially true after the Air Force moved into town and officers and enlisted men came to our dances. We also went out to the Officer's Club once in a while. The date would take me to dinner and we would go to a movie that the Air Force provided the troops. We saw such movies as those produced by the Marx Brothers, like "A Day at the Races," and movies with Bing Crosby and Bob Hope.

I loved to go swimming as a means of entertaining myself, and on Saturdays we used to go down to the river when it was warm enough and the mosquitoes weren't too bad to go swimming. It was great fun.

Growing up I had a number of Turning Points, which everyone has. Mainly starting grade school, becoming a woman, and my high school romances. I will tell you of a special one.

I went to a high school dance. I think it was around the first of June when I was eighteen, and there were a few young military men dancing with the girls. These were the kind of dances where the girl sat on one side of the dance floor and the boys sat on the other. The boys would ask the girls to dance, and the wallflowers would continue to sit on the chairs. These dances were 'cutting in dances,' meaning that if you were dancing with one boy and somebody tapped him on the shoulder, the first boy would leave, and you would start dancing with the guy who cut in. I was very popular at these dances.

I was dancing with one of the high school boys at my school when my partner was tapped on the shoulder. I started dancing with this young second lieutenant, a pilot out at the Air Force base. He was about six feet tall and of slight build with jet-black hair—a good looking dude.

We danced a couple of dances, and he said to me, "My name is Mike. What can I do to meet you again?"

I said, "Well, I can't go out on week nights, but we usually come downtown on Saturdays. I could go swimming and meet you at the swimming hole. Next Saturday if it's possible."

He said, "If it's good weather, and I get a pass, I'll meet you there at 1:00 pm."

I was thrilled to death, and I looked forward to the next week's Saturday and prayed for good weather.

That Saturday turned out bright and shiny, and I eagerly awaited going downtown to see Mike. My Dad came in and said, "I'm going to take your Mom and the other two girls to the movies. Do you want to come along?"

I said, "No, I'll stay here. I've got some stuff to do, and that will be all right."

Just before the appointed time, one o' clock, I went outside, and there was Mike in front of my house in an army truck. We met at our gate and walked on back to the house. We went through the house, and he commented that he loved this and he loved that. He liked the kitchen and the living room and the dining room where we ate dinner. Then we went outside to look at the rest of the farm. He looked at the fields of the wheat growing and the Lucerne fields.

We went to the barn and saw the cattle and the horses, and I showed him the mowers for the hay. We walked around to the back of the barn, and there was our haystack fourteen feet tall with newly laid up alfalfa hay. The old dried hay was underneath but the new hay had been thrown on trop.

Mike looked at the empty house and said, "Let's go up to your room, I'd love to see that."

I said, "I can't do that. If my parents came home they'd kill us— me and you, too."

With that, he said, "Come here," It was then that Mike kissed me for the first time. Also, it was the first kiss I'd had in my life other than my family. I was shaking I was so excited.

He said, "Well, since we can't go up to your room or in the house, let's go up on top of the haystack. I'd love to smell the hay and be there with you."

So we climbed to the top of the hay and the smell was wonderful. I was really enamored. He kissed me a number of times and fondled me, and of course you know what happened. He and I became intimate. I won't go in to the details, but it was an exciting afternoon to say the least. It revolved around the haystack and enjoying each other's company in the nude.

I have no idea how long it was, but we saw a cloud of dust coming down the gravel road. I said, "Wow! We better, hurry. I think my parents are coming home early. They may not have gone to the movies, or maybe they left early to come back here."

Mike said, "My god if I get caught with you, it will be curtains for me because I'm sure your father will not only give us hell, but he'll call the commandant at the airbase and complain about what has happened."

We slid down the haystack in a hurry. I straightened my clothes and combed my hair as best I could with my fingers. The second lieutenant arranged his uniform and tied his tie. He looked fairly presentable.

My Dad, Mom, and sisters drove up to the house. We were waiting on the front porch, and I introduced him to my parents. He said, "Hi, I'm glad to meet you. I am from the Air Force Base. I've been dating your daughter, and she wanted me to meet you."

In late September, I was in my senior year and the military continued to have dances, which I attended. Mike came to the dances and danced with me, but I was afraid that something would happen again, and that he would either want to come out to the farm or find some other place to play hanky panky. So, even though I was madly in love, I was afraid to do anything.

That's the story of my first love and one of the Turing Points in my life. It was the foolish moment when I surrendered to passion. What more can I say except, "Thank God I did not get pregnant." This affair was when I lost my virginity. This was the major Turning Point in my young life.

# PLAYING DOCTOR

◆

*Four Adolescents Find out about the Birds and the Bees*

IT WAS A BRIGHT, shiny day during summer vacation in Salt Lake City. Four teenagers–Kelly, Dane, Dane's sister Virginia, and her friend Marigold—were looking for something to do. The young men, Kelly and Dane, were about to enter university. Virginia and Marigold were still in high school.

It was after lunch. With nothing else to do, Dane, the eldest, suggested that the four of them visit the new athletic stadium at the University of Utah. He was planning to go out for freshman football when he attended the university that fall, so he wanted to look around.

As they were leaving, Kelly said, "It's hot today. We better get some water or we'll die of thirst walking over there."

Dane said, "That's a good idea, Kelly. Have you got a canteen or something we can use?"

Kelly nodded, went into his home, and came out carrying a canteen with enough ice water in it for the four of them. He swung it over his shoulder, and they walked a block or two to get to the university campus.

On the way to the campus, there was a large alfalfa field that had not been cut. The alfalfa was about eighteen inches high. It looked like a green velvet cover had been spread over the entire field. It was a lush pasture that was about one-half a square mile bordering the university. The four started to walk across the field in single file toward the new football stadium.

About half way across the large field, it was so hot that the four stopped for a minute to rest, take a drink of water, and get their bearings.

While they were waiting around, Dane said, "You know I'm going to the university this fall. I will be a freshman, and I plan to go to medical school after I graduate."

Kelly said, "I wish I were going to Utah with you, instead of going down to Brigham Young."

Dane said, "Well, why don't you talk to your parents and see if you can change to Utah."

Rested, Dane stood up and added, "Just a minute—let's look around while I take a piss."

As Dane left the group and relieved himself, the others tramped down the alfalfa and sat in a circle, had another sip of water, and talked about what each one of them would be doing that fall.

The two girls, being fourteen and fifteen, said, "We're going to go to high school. We're planning to go to Bryant, and since most of our friends from Wasatch are going where we are, it will be fun."

Kelly said, "Well as you heard from Dane, I'm going to BY in Provo. That's where I want to go, but I sure wish I was Dane and was going to Utah. He's lucky to be starting his pre-med, while I will be getting ready to work in my dad's business."

Dane said, "Well, I've looked at my watch, and it's about two o'clock. The football stadium closes at three thirty—I think—so we've got plenty of time to meander over there or do anything else we want."

Kelly said, "It's okay by me. What about you girls?"

The girls said, "It's alright with us. We'll loll around for a while and then go to the stadium and see what's going on as far as football practice is concerned."

After another sip of water and a stretch, Dane got up and looked around. Dane smiled, winked at Kelly, and said, "You know in my first year at Utah, I'm going to be taking pre-med courses. I want to get ready for school. One of freshman courses is learning about our anatomy. You know, I will be learning to be a physician, an internist."

The girls said, "What's that?"

Dane looked at Kelly and said, "Gee Kelly, I guess these girls are young, and they do not know about medical school."

Dane pointed to Virginia and said, "You lie down in the cool alfalfa, and I'll examine you." He started to examine her from the top of her head to the tip of her toe.

The other two looked on as Dane continued, "Please take down the shoulder of your dress, and I'll continue looking you over." He proceeded to go down her body and said, "Okay, now I'm going to look at your insides. I'll do as much as I can without my medical instruments."

So he had Virginia spread her legs while he examined her. Dane motioned to the other two and said, "Basically what the docs do is examine externally and then as much as they can to see internally."

Dane then said, "Turn over on your back Virginia, and I will finish my exam. Now that didn't hurt did it?"

Virginia shook her head as he proceeded to finish his internal examination. He began to get excited himself.

He said, "This playing doctor is great fun and very helpful to me."

The other two were interested spectators.

However, the two young men, being human, got excited. One thing led to another and the four had sex. After satisfying themselves, Kelly said, "Well, let's switch partners and do it again."

This meant that Kelly had sex with his sister. Both the boys enjoyed the encounter. After another few minutes, the young men were thoroughly spent. The girls were concerned with how hot it was getting and had tired of playing 'doctor.'

The four of them stood up, rearranged their clothing, and went on to see the stadium.

Of course, it's obvious that this was a Turning Point in the lives of all four youngsters. All four discovered sex as teenagers. Neither of the girls got pregnant. All four continued their schooling, and the young men boasted of their sexual prowess to the rest of their contemporaries.

According to the Diamond of Life analysis, the opportunity (where they were and when), curiosity (the desire to know), the ages of the four (timing), and human nature (sexuality) were the Traits and Tendencies demonstrated by this anecdote.

Five years after this incident, Dane was attending the University of Utah. He decided to join the U.S. Air force during World War II. He became a bombardier. He was sent to the European Theater. He was flying in B-17s, bombing Northern France and Germany. He was killed as his plane was shot down by the Luftwaffe.

The others went on with their lives. Certainly, being killed in the service of his country was the ultimate Turning Point in the life of Dane. The others survived discovering sex, incest, and growing up without harm to their psyche. Playing doctor, curiosity, and sexuality were irresistible during World War II. Sex and the single girl is as old as time.

## SEX AND THE SINGLE DUDE

### Arthur and His Unusual Career

ADAM HAD DESIGNED products sold by department stores throughout the New York City area. Among his customers were such stores as Bloomingdales and wholesale showrooms like those at 225 5$^{th}$ Avenue, The Gift and Art Building. Hal was personable (had lots of business and personal friends), had a good track record (was successful throughout the New York area), and was dedicated (loved visiting and working the showrooms). Adam spent a lot of time at 225 5$^{th}$ Avenue.

During one of his visits, he met Steve, a salesman in a first floor showroom. The two became fast friends. In fact, Steve and Adam became enamored with each other. The giftware buyers there found Adam's designs wondrous. A number of stores were anxious for Steve to get his own designer and go to Europe to buy merchandise for sale in their stores. It was logical for Steve and Adam to become a partnership and open their own location at 225 5$^{th}$ Avenue.

The suggested name was Steve & Associates. Adam would be a candidate for the designer job. Adam was interviewed. He talked to Steve and said, "I have some great ideas, but it will take a trip to Europe to get them made." If Steve would send him to Italy, France, and Spain, he would design items that would make history.

Steve sensed that Adam could and would be his designer. He said to Adam, "Your ideas complement my own. I think a showroom is a wonderful idea. However, if you go to Europe, I want to go along with you to help with the selection of merchandise and the new lines."

Steve made plans for the two of them to go to Europe. Adam would sketch the items and Steve would arrange to buy them or have them made.

Both men felt that the new items from foreign manufacturers would sell. The selected merchandise could develop a completely new niche in a showroom operation.

The two men flew to Italy. It was then that Steve became what was known as an 'AC-DC Lothario.' He discovered his sexual leanings toward both men and women. He was approached by Adam. Of course, it happened. Love was in bloom. Such goings on did not prevent Adam from designing gorgeous items to sell in the United States.

Steve went to an area in Italy that manufactured pottery, and he selected some patterns and items that were not available in the U.S. The two men returned to New York after placing large orders for new designs.

During the next nine months, the liaison between Adam and Steve became stronger and the two decided to move into the same apartment in upper Manhattan near Central Park. By May of the next year, the merchandise had arrived from Italy. The showroom modification was completed, and a few more men were added to the staff. The new showing was a tremendous success!

As always happens in strange relationships, Steve became interested in a woman who came to market at 225 5th Avenue. Steve met her and wanted sex with this woman. She was a customer of the new showroom and made a liaison with Steve, much to Adam's dissatisfaction. This was another Turning Point in the life of Adam. His paramour had a triple header in mind. Steve told Adam that the buyer from Dallas came to market three times a year. He added that that was the way it was going to be.

Steve found an apartment in the same building in which Adam lived. Steve would lease it himself. He would see his Dallas girl friend when she came to New York three times a year. Steve told Adam, "That's the way it's going to be. It is my way or the highway." Adam reluctantly agreed. A triangle in the same building but with different players.

This was the beginning of a Turning Point in the lives of all three participants: Steve who was having an AC-DC relationship, Adam who was being shut out during the visits of this woman buyer, and the woman who became involved with Steve during buying trips.

Adam secluded himself and let this new temporary arrangement continue. Steve pondered whether being bi-sexual would ruin the lives of any or all of them. It was the climax of a love triangle.

Later in the year, this drama came to its end. It had become impossible, so much so that Adam jumped out the window of his tenth floor apartment. Steve was completely shocked at this occurrence. Steve went into a deep depression. When they heard the news, the staff in the showroom could not believe it. Steve could not find another designer with Adam's talent and with whom he got along so well.

The showroom business declined. The realization of all who knew Steve—his history and its end—became convinced that 'into each life some rain must fall,' and the final Turning Point was Adam's death.

## SOUNDING OFF FOR WOMEN'S RIGHTS

*The ACLU Fights the Battle of Norton Sound*

THE EXECUTIVE OFFICE STAFF of the ACLU (American Civil Liberties Union) was listening to the United States Defense Department Legal Officer saying that they would close the Norton Sound Destroyer matter. The armed services had eliminated its restriction on having women serve on vessels when they were out to sea.

It was thumbs up and a happy day for Sybil. She was an ACLU staff attorney, instrumental in representing the sailor involved. The sailor, a young woman, had joined the United States Navy during the war of Vietnam. She had volunteered and qualified to become a Wave.

She went through the training program, passing all the physical and mental requirements to serve her country. After a year of active duty, this Wave requested a transfer to serve on a ship for sea duty. She was assigned to the destroyer, Norton Sound.

The Norton Sound operated under a policy that limited Waves to non-combat duty while on the high seas. The Wave had requested to be assigned as a member of the gun crew, which was combat duty. Her request was denied. What concerned the United States Navy was the fact that Sybil, an attorney for the ACLU, took the matter up the line asking for reconsideration.

The Norton Sea matter finally landed on the desk of the Secretary of the Navy. Sybil had to go to Washington as counsel for the Wave. The Navy called it the 'Norton Sound Incident.'

This was an example of sexual discrimination of the gun crew on the forward five-inch cannon on the destroyer.

The Wave had requested this duty specifically from the commanding officer. He told her that it was against Navy rules to have a women serve in any capacity other than non-exposed duties, such as working in the kitchen, painting the ship, and other such non-dangerous duties.

The captain of the destroyer told Sybil that if she was not satisfied with his interpretation of the rule, she should appeal the rule to the U.S. Navy Department in Washington D.C. It was said that only this way could the appellant serve on a gun crew.

Sybil was assigned the case. She proceeded to research the equal rights statute under the Constitution, and decided this was a Constitutional matter. The navy's position was contrary to the First Amendment of the U.S. Constitution. Sybil wrote a brief of her findings and presented it to the Attorney General of the United States.

The Attorney General looked at the case carefully, and told the Department of Defense that they had a losing case. This ruling did violate the First Amendment, which guaranteed equal protection under the law. The ruling went down the line to the captain of the Norton Sound, and he notified the sailor in question the he would allow women to serve in any capacity on the Norton Sound. This was a victory for women's rights.

In looking at the success story, and seeing how it played out in the Diamond of Life, the Wave and Sybil were persistent in presenting the Norton Sound case to the Department of Defense and the United States Attorney General. They wouldn't take no for an answer. Sybil was so successful in having the rule changed that this became a Major Turning Point in both of their careers.

# A COUNSELOR TELLS ALL ABOUT
# THE BIRDS AND THE BEES

◆

### Puberty and Sex Affect All Boys

WHEN ASKED ABOUT MAJOR events in his life, Andrew, 'Andy,' smiled and said, "I have always been interested in languages. At a young age of thirteen, I was just entering high school and talked to my advisor about my future studies." He said that he remembered being thirteen.

"I was starting my pre-college career. It involved four years of learning a foreign language. The advisor told me that Latin was the basis of many European languages—such as Italian, Spanish, French, and of course English. Everyone knows that many English words come from Latin.

"As your counselor, I know you have been hearing from me that thirteen is a wonderful year for teenagers. They become very rebellious, uninhibited, and difficult for a teacher to handle. This happened to me, and of course, it was a Turning Point in my life. It was namely about finding out about sex—not physically, but mentally.

"I entered junior high school and immediately took Latin. I was just following the advice of my counselor. The Latin class that fall was taught by a young lady named Miss Caffey, an attractive young woman of twenty-eight. She was very well proportioned and had a wonderful smile.

"Miss Caffey had us take our seats. Once seated, we put our names on an attendance sheet that was passed around the room. As we were doing this, Miss Caffey pointed to a pile of books and said, 'Before you leave, please pick up your book, and put your name on it. Take it home with you, and read Chapter One. We will not have a class today. I just wanted to get acquainted with you. So I will ask each of you to stand up, state your name, and tell what your major will be in college—if you know it now.'

"This the class did, and after fifteen minutes of introductions, Miss Caffey said, 'I'm letting you go a little early. Please be on time tomorrow. You are in the ten o'clock class, so be on time.' We left.

"The next morning, the class reassembled at ten o'clock. Miss Caffey asked us to take our seats, and she said, 'Take any seat you want.' As I remember, most of the boys sat in the front row of seats, and everybody else sat as close to the front of the room as they could.

"Miss Caffey took a piece of chalk and wrote the words *Allia Gaulia es deevisa en tres partes*. This is the best I can remember it, and as I recall, she said, 'This is the first sentence of Julius Caesar's book. It was written in the first century BC, and it means *All Gaul is divided in three parts.'*

"With this she walked back from the blackboard, and proceeded to sit on the top of her desk facing the class with her legs crossed in a very casual manner. Then she said, 'We take up the first chapter of Julius Caesar and start learning vocabulary.' Following this train of thought, Miss Caffey said, 'This was written in the first century by Julius Caesar and reported his experiences as a general leading the troops in the Gallic Wars.'

"She added, 'When I ask you to stand, please stand, listen to my pronunciation of the word, repeat it, and I'll ask you to repeat it again. This is a word drill. I'll call on the next student after you have been seated. We will discuss the next word going through the same process.'

"And the first student, Arnold, stood up to face the teacher just as she crossed her legs. As she did so, she exposed the upper part of her leg. She was not wearing panties. The boys in the front could see this was the case. Arnold, being first, blushed a little bit and proceeded to repeat the Latin word she had said, and after doing this twice, sat down.

"This exercise continued until the entire class had gone through the same process. As I remember it, the drill continued, and it was embarrassing to say the least. Several times during the drill, Miss Caffey changed her position—sitting on the desk, standing up, and crossing and uncrossing her legs as she did so. In essence, she exposed her private parts to all of the boys sitting in the first row in the classroom.

"Since my last name started with W, I was the last person to stand and get a view of Miss Caffey. I recall experiencing sexual arousal—excitement—because of its novelty. This, I think, was a Turning Point in my life. It was the first time I realized that there was an inner fire in every one of us boys in the class, all teenagers and experiencing such sexuality.

"I was only thirteen. I had a glimpse of what it was all about. Yes, I was stimulated. Yes, I was embarrassed. Yes, I found out that puberty and sex were Turning Points in my young life."

This is a story of a counselor telling it all to a young boy of thirteen. It was an event the young boy will never forget.

In revealing an experience of thirty-five years before, Andy divulged that sex and puberty go together, just as salt and pepper, and once experienced, become a Turning Point never to be forgotten.

## A STUDENT IS NOT A SLOW LEARNER

*Too Soon You Get Old, Too Old You Get Smart*

THE DOCTOR LOOKED AT Barbara and said, "Good news and bad news. The good news– you are young and very healthy. The bad news – you didn't behave yourself. You are going to have a baby."

Barbara started to cry. As she sobbed, she said, "No, no don't say that."

Barbara phoned Hank, her high school steady, and told him about her visit to the doctor. Barbara told Hank that he was about to become a father at the age of eighteen. Hank was stunned. He knew that he had been doing the wrong thing when he seduced Barbara, but as their relationship continued, they had become careless, and the result was a pregnancy.

What was Barbara to do? Her choices were limited. She could marry Hank, she could abort the baby, she could put the baby up for adoption, or she could have the baby out of wedlock. This would be the Turning Point of her young life.

Hank, a Mormon, was about to go to England on his mission. As far as his religion was concerned, he was devout. He was stunned to say the least. Hank thought to himself, "This will disrupt my immediate future. My family will want to know why I will be turning down the experience of a lifetime."

He wanted to be a Mormon missionary. It involved going to a country, teaching Mormon principles, and trying to get them to join the Mormon Church.

What was Hank to do? He told his folks of his problem, and they urged him to marry the girl and take her with him.

Barbara was about six months pregnant and desperately in love! This was a major Turning Point of her life. The decision had to be made within a week.

Hank decided that Barbara was half-wrong and his obligation would be to support the baby, but he wanted to go to England and complete his mission. He would be two years out of the country and away from Barbara. He did not want to get married at eighteen and told Barbara so.

The Turning Point of Barbara's life was having the baby. She now had a family of two to manage.

Hank told her that he was not going to marry her. She contemplated suicide, but decided she must bear the brunt of her being foolish. She had the baby alone. Hank would provide a payment each month. She would stay out of school for at least two years while the baby grew to an age that she would be able to use a babysitter. This would allow Barbara to return to school.

Barbara knew her family would be discredited by this act and certainly disappointed in her, to say the least. All her friends would shun her as she had shunned other girls at East High school who had been as foolish as she was.

This Turning Point in the life of Barbara would not go away. She would be ostracized by all those of her peers who heard the gossip. On the other hand, Hank was getting off lightly. Money to support the baby couldn't solve all problems. His male contemporaries might envy him.

The Diamond of Life indicated that Hank was both careless and irresponsible—two traits that could lead to failure. Barbara had been distracted from her studies by Hank. Her parents had not controlled her free time. They had had too much confidence in her ability to keep her virginity. How many young girls go through this experience of having their lives disrupted by unwanted children?

The die was cast, and Barbara had a little girl. The baby would grow up knowing that she was unwanted, was unplanned, and had ruined her mother's future. Barbara, an outstanding student, had committed an act of passion, one that had deprived her of two years in the prime of her life. Barbara, not a slow learner, would regret her stupidity forever while Hank got off scot-free.

# PROVING LEFT CAN BE RIGHT

*A Navy Brat's Life Unfolds*

"YAH! YAH! YAH!" JEERED the six-year-olds—first grade children in the school in Coronado Naval Base. All the other schoolchildren on the island had made fun of the latest first grader to enter class. The first memory she had was being moved from one navy port to another. Cindy remembered it as the first phase of her life, namely from birth to twenty years of age.

As a 'Navy brat,' she went from port to port with her father, a captain in the Navy. His service to his country took the family from Coronado in the San Diego area to various other naval bases. This constant relocation continued until Cindy reached the tender age of twenty.

In retrospect, her 'Go Navy' heritage stemmed back to her grandfather and his being an admiral. As she was growing up, she lived, learned, and played near San Diego at the Coronado Naval base. She moved often. She changed schools every few years. This fluidity meant new friends and new environment.

When Cindy reached the age of twenty, she started going to college to finish her education. She attended Western State College of Law. This was where she received her Jurisprudence Degree. She became an attorney, passed the bar examination, and was ready to practice law.

She witnessed the Eisenhower years, the election of John F. Kennedy, and the defeat of then Vice President Richard Nixon and his "this is my dog, Checkers" speech in 1960. She became a 'libber' of the sixties, interested in left wing policies. She was a very liberal lady. She married at the age of twenty-six and had two children before the age of thirty-three.

In the 1970s, Cindy witnessed the resignation of Lynden Johnson, the gay rights movement in San Francisco with its candlelight marches, and the Market Street parade. This phase of her life was awe-inspiring. It was exciting enough to make all those liberals proud and happy. However by 1975, she was approaching the end of this part of her life.

Inherited raits and Tendencies , according to the Diamond of Life, were the need to be the best (drive), not doing the proper thing (dysfunctional), and acting without giving thought to the consequences (impulsive).

At that time, she was living with her husband where he was finishing his education. The couple lived in the upstairs apartment of a duplex. During this time, she met Joan, the woman who lived downstairs. As neighbors, Joan and Cindy took care of the kids, 'coffee-d' together, and became very friendly.

Suddenly the friendship turned into passion. It was as if Joan and Cindy were watching a very lousy movie. This rapturous love continued to consume them for over a year. It was a matter of choice. Joan and Cindy were cheating on their husbands and afraid of getting caught. After a lot of soul searching, the two of women decided to divorce their husbands and dedicate themselves to each other.

Obviously, this changing of sexual orientation on the part of two married women became Turning Points in the lives of all concerned. The husbands were astounded and dumbfounded, the kids were so young they were oblivious as to what was going on, and Cindy's father, a naval officer was heartsick.

However, divorce was an out. Cindy received a law degree, passed the bar examination, and became a liberal attorney working in Washington D. C. She got a position with the ACLU. In this second phase of her life, she was single, and her ex-husband received custody their kids.

With this Turning Point rose a fascinating question. "Why, at a time of one's life, when she could have become a successful attorney in diplomatic law, did she want to take on sexual discrimination cases for the female members of the military?"

Her answer was, "I feel an uncontrollable need to do so!"

The Diamond of Life approach to understanding the actions so foreign to Cindy was found by just accepting what 'was done was done' in the heat of passion.

The action itself belies explanation. Bias (public approval of this action by very few people except gays), notoriety (the general public loves a spicy story), and intelligence (the action appears to be, in a word, dumb).

This Turning Point in the life of Cindy shows that this occurrence in the lives of the two women, although much to the left of center, can, in certain circumstances, be right. Thus, 'Left Can be Right!'

# 12

# *RETIREMENT*

L IFE CAN BE VIEWED as a game, the objective of which is to become a success. In the case of real life, it is to be productive in a chosen field, be it 'a butcher, a baker, or a candle stick maker.' Even the goal of a 'worker bee' is to make enough honey (spelled money) to retire in the lap of luxury and live to a ripe old age.

Many people approach retirement with trepidation. Others can't wait and take early retirement. This Turning Point is varied and so are the incidents that have been selected. Be sure to read "WHO ME? NOT AT NINETY-THREE," as well as the background information related in each story.

# WHO ME? NOT AT NINETY-THREE

*Just Existing*

THE ROTARY CLUB OF Sun Valley stood up, and the oldest member of the club, Jack, said, "Hi guys, let's start our weekly meeting soon. At ninety-three, I may not be around at the end."

Sixty minutes later, the Rotary Club meeting was over. Jack added a final thought, telling all those who would listen, "When a widow lady comes to visit me, she usually carries a freshly baked cake in one hand and a mattress on her back. I smile and say, 'Who me? Not at ninety-three … and besides I lost all my spending money!'"

Being the star for a day caused a flood of recollections. Jack recalled how upset he had been when he had reached a point in his life that had required him to move from his home of seventy-one years to a so-called assisted living facility. It had caused Jack to be remote and to look at the future with a jaundiced eye. He had lived to be ninety-three years old, and he was still active, but he could not live alone anymore. Nevertheless, he was the idol of all of his friends and acquaintances.

The major decisions in Jack's life had been few and far between. The first and foremost occurred during World War II. He had enlisted in the army as a grunt—a private. He received a couple of months of training at Fort Ord, California, before being sent to the European theatre.

His infantry company was heading toward the German border. Along the way, his outfit had a number of skirmishes but continued to move ahead. They crossed the Rhine. Jack's company came upon a group of German soldiers, and they had a 'fire fight.' The man next to Jack was killed when a mortar shell exploded.

Jack was wounded in two places, treated behind the lines, sent to a French hospital, and given notice by the medics that his hospitalization would be for a short period of time while his wounds healed.

After a month or so, the doctor treating Jack said, "You're in good enough condition to rejoin your unit in Germany or return to the states. This was a big decision for Jack to make. Did he want to stay with his outfit? Or did he want to go home? He'd given his all serving in Europe. He knew that the war was winding down. He felt that it would be best to return to his home in Southern California. Entering the Army, serving his country, being wounded, and being given this choice of duty was a Major Turning Points in Jack's life. He never forgot it.

Jack felt that he had had the courage to face the enemy, had the good judgment to realize he was wounded under fire, and the good sense to request being sent home. The Diamond of Life confirmed his decision—enough was enough.

Falling in love became a Major Turning Point for Jack. After his return to Southern California, he played baseball. He was a catcher on the Sun Valley baseball team. Sun Valley was playing the City of Burbank's team. One of the fans in the bleachers had been rooting for Sun Valley. She approached Jack after the game and said, "Great game."

Jack replied, "Thanks. Did you go to Poly High school? I'd like to hear more about you. I know all about me already." This banter started a romance. Pauline became the love of Jack's life!

After dating two years, Jack asked her to marry him, and the two became one. This was a dream marriage. They lived for fifty-eight years as husband and wife.

Another Turning Point in Jack's memory was the family hardware store burning down. He recalled that it forced him to make the most important choice he ever had to make. It was to take the money and run or have the store rebuilt.

Jack was seventy-three years old. He received the telephone call at three in the morning. Disaster had struck. Someone had broken into the store and ransacked it. After taking all the valuables they could steal, the vandals torched the store.

Jack had insurance, but at his age, he didn't have the energy to rebuild. He had two sons, neither of whom wanted to continue working in the store. Selling nuts and bolts for a living was not for them. They told Jack, "Take the money and run!" Jack decided to follow their advice.

There were three Turning Points in Jack's life. He was drafted and served in World War II before being wounded and discharged. He met and married his lovely Pauline. His hardware store burned down.. His insurance covered the loss, but to rebuild at age seventh-three? No way!

Jack's Diamond of Life showed that he had good judgment. At twenty-seven, one 'bit the bullet' and got married (lonesome). At seventy-three, one retired after a major event. He did not rebuild a retail store (good judgment). At ninety-three, one did not get a new bride (proper perspective). And at ninety-three, one realized that the game of life was in its final inning, and one faced the truth. Jack knew that he found a sound answer—*Not me at ninety-three.*

# MARV'S CHEVY ONLY HAS PARTS GALORE

*An Entrepreneur Revolutionizes the Auto Parts Industry*

MARV'S CHEVY ONLY PARTS had a large inventory of used and reconditioned parts stocked at his facility in Sun Valley, California. He specialized in marketing this inventory nationally. His wife, Judy, stuck with Marv and helped him operate through thick and thin. Marv had driven his own off-road Chevy for years and had expanded his activities by developing the selling of Chevrolet auto parts. Marv's business was one of the Sun Valley California Chamber of Commerce prize members. But he had a major automobile accident in Baja California that left Marv partially paralyzed but very active. Judy managed to keep the business going during his recovery.

Marv's contribution to the secondary marketing of Chevrolet auto parts industry became well known. Marv became involved with a nationwide system utilizing electronic communication to connect dealers of Chevy parts from all areas of the United States. Expansion was amazing at the time. The network became countrywide. Thus, Marv's Chevy Only Parts was the leading light in developing a new industry. He proved that he could market reconditioned Chevrolet Auto Parts system all over the United States.

At the age of twenty-five, Marv's son, Sam, bought Marv's Chevy. Using and expanding the business substantially allowed Sam to become a well-known racecar owner and driver. Sam took over and became the prime mover of the family business, expanding it substantially. Marv moved to Nevada and began enjoying the good life, and best of all, Marv's Chevy Only still had parts galore.

# A COUPLE CAST IN CONCRETE

*The End-all of a Business Operation*

A FTER SLAVING FOR TWELVE years as yard manager, Jack managed to become owner of the Blue Sky Concrete Company. It was one of the smaller ready-mix concrete companies found in the San Fernando Valley. His office manager was Gloria. The two worked as a team.

Shortly after the business was Jack's, he and Gloria were married. Wonderful relationships are often said to be cast in stone. In the case of Jack and Gloria, theirs was cast in concrete.

The test of their marriage came on a Friday afternoon ten years after they were married. The intercom barked, "Jack, phone—Jack, phone! It's important."

Jack returned from the yard. He went to his private office, and as he did so, said, "Thanks Gloria. I know it's Pete on the phone, and I haven't made up my mind yet."

Gloria smiled and said, "Take your time, honey. We've been together for ten years. This is an important decision. A few days more or less will not make any difference. I'll let Pete know about your delaying until next week. We will decide over this weekend at home."

That night Jack recounted his actions during the Korean War and the post war building boom. He remembered what his labors meant to Blue Sky's concrete's business. The couple recalled their meeting at Mr. C's, a restaurant in Sun Valley, California. It occurred prior to Gloria starting to work as Office Manager at Blue Sky Concrete.

Then, Blue Sky marketed ready-mix concrete to the entire San Fernando Valley. Their product was made as the cement trucks were delivering it to many tracts of new homes, industrial building sites, and commercial properties under construction.

This cement business had grown with Jack as its owner. He had become an important figure in his community. He was a spokesman for the Sun Valley Chamber of Commerce. He belonged to Rotary and other service organizations. The couple realized that working together, falling in love, and getting married were important times in their lives.

It should be noted that during this time, Sun Valley was a growing community and business was very good. In addition, Lockheed Aircraft Corporation, with fifty thousand young workers, was within five miles of what is now called Bob Hope Airport. Many builders constructed tracts of lower priced homes for the aircraft workers.

Jack was in his middle sixties when he became foreman of a concrete batch operation in the booming building industry of the San Fernando Valley. He operated this concrete batch plant in the Valley, an area in Los Angeles that was experiencing a tremendous expansion of industrial and commercial building activity.

For the uninitiated reader, Blue Sky Concrete operated the big ten-wheeled trucks that traveled Los Angeles streets. Jack, as general manager, was responsible for his plant making money. He kept the big, open-mouth drums turning as the trucks rolled along the highway delivering concrete.

During the early seventies, President Nixon had the U.S. Congress put on price controls. However, concrete companies with fewer than sixty employees would be exempt from these price control regulation. Therefore, a smaller operator such as Blue Sky Concrete could price its product as it wished. Such a system of pricing led to open competition for all the new projects in the San Fernando Valley.

During the late eighties, competition from much larger concrete companies affected Blue Sky Concrete. This situation caused United Concrete to want to buy Blue Sky Concrete. Its offer was made during President Reagan's second term. The U.S. congress had removed price controls from American manufacturers with sixty or more employees and competition was getting fierce.

Jack and his wife had enjoyed working together. However, Jack was in his sixties and began thinking about when, where, and how to retire. This offer was a fair offer and it came at an ideal time in Jack's life. He had worked hard, maintained his health, and, as is true with most small businessmen, Jack had not vacationed as often as he should have. The sale of his business would be a Major Turning Point in his life.

There were pros and cons to selling Skyline Concrete. The price was right. It was from a substantial firm. It would include all the assets, such as the company name and any patented rights that Jack might have. It would be payable in three annual installments and all in cash. This sale would enable Jack and Gloria to get out of the rat race and enter their golden years well financed and with no financial problems.

On the other hand, this sale would mean lack of activity. Jack had always been busy. He was approaching the so-called golden years. He wondered if travel, rest, and relaxation, such as getting away from his life's work, would be difficult for him. He was relatively young, in good health, and in a happy marriage. He enjoyed doing what he was doing. To walk away from this, even though he would be well compensated, would be difficult.

Thus, the Turning Points in Jack's life were related to growing old and deciding what to do before and after retiring. Such a move was major and irreversible!

Both Jack and Gloria had personal Traits and Tendencies shown by the Diamond of Life. These can lead to either the success or failure of their retirement. Factors coming into play were Jack's financial stability, his ambition, his courage in recognizing a golden opportunity (buying Blue Sky Concrete), and the judgment needed in deciding when to sell his business.

Jack's indecision could have led to failure. Jack's age could have resulted in misfortune He was relatively young to retire. But, on balance, Jack and Gloria found that retirement was wonderful—a 'happy couple cast in concrete.'

# TO RETIRE AT HOME OR TO RETIRE AFAR

*There Is No Rest for the Wicked*

BOB AND HIS WIFE, Fonda, were on their way to Montana. They wanted to escape involvement with Hurricane Katrina and enjoy a long overdue vacation. During the drive, Bob's impending retirement was discussed. Reminiscing, Bob and Fonda talked about his career and their chance meeting at a computer sales conference nearly thirty years before. It was the instant that they had discovered each other and knew it was true love. After a torrid romance and a short courtship, Bob married Fonda.

During the ensuing years, Fonda had become the office manager of Bob's firm. Thus, the two enjoyed a mutual togetherness at both the office and at home.

While the couple was visiting Yellowstone National Park, they found thirty acres of Montana that met Bob's future retirement needs. It was peaceful, away from the big city, and within their budget. It could be a major Turning Point in Bob's future.

The decision facing them was whether to buy and retire in the recently constructed home on a thirty acre spread in Montana or to retire in New Orleans, their home for the past twenty-four years.

There was a lot to consider. This would be a startling change for Bob, a city boy. He got his kicks from the Big Apple. He had had a successful career in developing two businesses in two major cities. Could he live a much less exciting existence? Could he enjoy life in a new environment? Bob had reached another Turning Point—retire in Montana or stay put.

This Montana home stay would be on a three-month trial basis. The couple had sixty days before escrow had to close on a house out in a vast wilderness. They were about to have their first weekender in the three-year-old house. The wild rugged Rocky Mountains would be their background landscape for the end of their lives.

There were positive points to making the move. It was close to Yellowstone, U.S.A.'s first national park. The house was tucked in the Southwestern part of Montana. It would be a great buy. The house and adjoining barn had become too costly for the miner/builder to carry any longer. He wanted to sell the ranch, which adjoined other high desert properties in the outback of Montana.

A couple of years before, during a motorcycle trip through Yellowstone, Bob and Fonda had seen the ranch house being built. While it would complement their other city properties in far distant Louisiana, to buy it was still a tough decision. It could be a hideaway for weekend fun and excitement, but as a place to retire to, would become a major Turning Point in the couple's life.

During this time, Fonda fretted about the potential drawbacks that might arise if they bought the ranch. Bob, the visionary, found an answer to each of Fonda's concerns.

Fonda said, "It is too far for us."

Bob's answered, "No, it isn't. By plane and car, it is just five and a half hours door to door."

Fonda mused, "It is too sunny and bright in the summer and too cold and snowy in the winter."

Bob replied, "No, it isn't. The air conditioning will keep it comfortable and filter out the pollen. Besides, the roaring fire will take care of the cold when the wind blows in the winter."

Fonda pointed out, "No friends within fifteen hundred miles."

Bob replied, "Wrong! My talks in New Orleans and New York found that many of our biker friends would drop in on us and buy in the area too. We, as Bob and Fonda, will have a new life and are only limited by how we promote Montana's vast wilderness to our friends."

Then he said to clinch the debate, "Charles Kuralt, the CBS television correspondent, once extolled the surrounding countryside of the Beartooth Highway, U.S.212. He praised that part passing through Beartooth Pass near the house. He noted that it has clean air with scenery to match! It is a scenic experience for us to see time and time again in various seasons of the year."

Fonda said with finality, "It is too costly."

Bob countered, "My analysis starts with compared to what? Cruising starts at several thousand dollars and the time commitment while cruising is excessive. Visiting the many hundreds of national parks and other wilderness areas will take the rest of our remaining years. You know my timing is perfect. I have the money, and biking on the back roads will make me feel like I'm young again. I have the will power to make this move. The thrill of having something to do when I am retired is delightful. Fonda, we will be happy here in Montana—calling it our home away from home."

The die was cast. This Turning Point in their life was special. Finally, they bought the ranch. The ranch was theirs!

Bob told her as they went to bed that night "This house will always be our 'Fondarosa,' our special place for retirement."

# A LEOPARD CAN CHANGE ITS SPOTS

◆

*Chamber of Commerce Manager Resuscitates the Organization*

THE STATIC RAPPING OF the gavel brought the North Valley Regional Chamber of Commerce to order. Over three hundred members were in attendance. Walker, the President, smiled as he said, "Will everybody rise for the Pledge of Allegiance?" Afterwards, Walker said, "This meeting is extremely important because it will be a Turning Point in the NVRCC's life."

Holding up an attractive rendering so all could see it, he added, "It will be accompanied by this new promotional piece and a newspaper called 'The North Valley Community News.' Each of you has received a copy of this first monthly edition. We will be able to accept advertising by the deadline of March 25th."

He continued. "Another feature of The North Valley Community News is a retail and professional service directory. Each of the members will receive one free directory ad, one column inch in size, every fourth month. Thus, all five NVRCC member chambers will get to know the other member firms in your organization. Now, I will turn the meeting over to the Chairman of the Board to conduct further business." With that, Walker sat down to scattered applause.

This meeting was a Turning Point in Walker's career as well as for the NVRCC. Walker was concerned because he had charged ahead with the newspaper without getting the board's approval. After this meeting, Walker would have to sell advertising, pay any cost of producing The North Valley Community News, and use it to increase the prestige and membership. His target group was nine hundred members, but he was gambling on his actions being successful.

Walker was tired of changing positions. He had been oscillating from the public sector to the private sector and back again. His college record showed that he graduated from CSUN in 1971. The job market was dismal. Without missing a beat, Walker, entered graduate school to get his M.S. degree in political science. During 1972, he was ready, willing, and able to tackle his first paid position.

Walker got a position with Ken Spiker, Chief Legislative Analyst for the City of Los Angeles. He felt this was not bad for a recent graduate.

In truth, this was a major Turning Point in Walker's life. While he was teaching a class in city government at Trade Tech Junior College, one of the guests was Ken Spiker. From this casual meeting, Walker received an offer from Spiker to work for the City of Los Angeles in their office. What a break that was!

This was an unexpected Turning Point for Walker. It gave him a chance to meet the various state, city, and county officials. These included Governor Jerry Brown, State Senator David Roberti, and Los Angeles Mayor Tom Bradley.

However, in the 1980 L.A. city election, Walker picked the wrong horse. He was out on the street during 1981. But then he went into the private sector. He organized a public relations firm, which he operated utilizing contacts he had made during the previous ten years. As Walker expected, this became a major Turning Point because he learned one is only as good as the last job—if your candidate loses you are out on the street again.

During the next few years, he worked on various private publications—either as co-editor or as reporter. These included the community paper in Agoura Hills, the Valley Magazine, owned and operated by the largest Ford dealer in the world, and the Valley Industry and Commerce Association.

This allowed Walker to switch to the public sector and become co-manager of a non-profit organization called People in Progress (PIP). He worked as a special appointee of the board of directors. This was a major Turning Point in Walker's life. Why? Shortly after assuming this position, he found that there was an embezzlement scheme occurring. It involved not only the president of the organization, but also a member of the board of directors and the treasurer of the organization.

This incident involved Walker blowing the whistle on the wrongdoers, and of course, the board of directors did not believe the defalcation. Walker was discharged. He learned a lesson he would never forget, which was get your ducks in a row before you take any action.

Each and every one of these occupational changes involved switching from profit-making organizations to non-profit public and/or charitable organizations. It was quite a varied career and filled with Turning Points because such activities were very volatile and, to say the least, temporary.

This took Walker to his post of being President and CEO of the North Valley Regional Chamber of Commerce group. Walker measured up to the necessary Diamond of Life Traits and Tendencies. Those pointing toward success in Walker's career were his attitude, his durability, his leadership, and his diligence. The negative attributes that led to Walker's failures were bad luck, lack of planning, being unrealistic, and having poor judgment in selecting occupations and political candidates.

Like it or not, Walker has been a diligent worker—yet his life so far had shown that Walker, unlike the leopard, could change his spots, especially when it came to choosing jobs and political candidates.

# COUNTDOWN RAN RACES GALORE AND WON

◆

*Kurt Finds His Niche...Jets Rather than 'The Horses'*

"COME ON, COUNTDOWN, COME on." Kurt had entered his horse, Countdown, in a 'claiming race' and heard the track announcer say, "Countdown wins by a head" At the age of fifty-six, Kurt was toying with the idea of getting out of the racing business. He felt he was too old to be a horse owner and needed to spend the next ten years preparing for retirement. It would be a major change in his life.

Kurt wanted to review his past before making his choice. He had entered the military during the Vietnam War. Being from Ogden, Utah, and having the Hill Field, a U.S Air Base, just ten miles from his home, he was assigned to be a maintenance mechanic for the fighter group stationed there.

Kurt became a non-commissioned officer at Hill Field, got married, and had two children. He had a sick uncle living in Logan, Utah, who offered Kurt an unexpected opportunity. The uncle asked Kurt to take over his quarter horse breeding and racing stables and keep it going until his health improved.

This opportunity became a potential Turning Point in Kurt's life. Should he resign from the Air Force to become the manager, trainer, and eventual owner of a string of quarter horses—or not? His uncle would show Kurt the ropes of this new exciting business.

His Diamond of Life analysis showed Kurt that his ambition and financial ability favored joining his uncle and the quarter horse ranch. A distant second choice was staying in the Air Force. Kurt considered the Air Force option because of its stability. In this instance, Kurt chose to take a chance and join his uncle. This was a major Turning Point in Kurt's life.

Kurt spent the next nine years learning and running the quarter horse business. It involved a lot of travel to get Countdown, his best horse, to the racetracks. The races were usually run during the county fairs held all over the West.

Countdown would streak around the track and win over half of the races in which he ran. His winnings kept the rest of the business solvent.

At the end of nine years came another Turning Point in Kurt's existence. He had to decide whether or not to buy Countdown and the ranch or return to the Air Force in his former capacity. This decision was caused by the death of his uncle, which forced his aunt to sell everything she owned, including Countdown and the ranch.

Kurt made his choice. He chose to return to his former position after carefully weighing the positives and negatives of each. While the benefits of continuing to run the ranch, including racing Countdown, were impressive, the less lucrative more stable return to the air base at Hill Field was the life Kurt chose. Therefore, he contacted his former boss, who had become a general.

The general said that Kurt could not be re-employed by the Air Force as a noncommissioned officer in the U.S. Military, but he could become a civilian employee and schedule the maintenance of F16 airplanes at bases all over the world.

Kurt was celebrating his fifty-sixth birthday and jumped at the prospect. Stability had more appeal than possibility. He was at a Turning Point in his life. He chose to return to the Air force Base.

The Diamond of Life Traits and Tendencies chart showed Kurt had the proper attitude (patience) to perform his new Air Force duties. This snapshot of making a life decision showed that, even though there were benefits of a successful business future, a secondary choice can win the race.

# AN ARCHITECT AND HIS MID-LIFE CRISIS

*Peering into the Future*

IN CALIFORNIA, ARCHITECT JOE was sitting on his stool in front of his drafting table. He had a letter in his hand and was reading it for the second time. It was from Colin Grier, his insurance agent and fellow Burbank Rotarian. The letter started, 'Dear Joe,' and continued, 'My date book tells me this is your fifty-fifth birthday, and you should review your retirement needs so that I can update your policy.' Joe mulled over the contents of the letter.

Joe stood straight as a stick, was in good health, and walked a couple of miles to his office every day. He played tennis on the weekends when the weather was good. Married to his high school sweetheart, with his children independent and living in the L.A. area, he realized that Colin was bringing the matter to his attention as a friend.

Joe had reached his middle years, and despite being a very successful designer of buildings, he knew that his retirement would be a serious Turning Point in his life. It would be the when, the where, and even the why to retire since he loved his life just the way it was!

He felt that it was the time to talk it over with his wife of thirty years and decide whether to remain in the San Fernando Valley, a densely populated area, or find a smaller, less stressful, community. This decision would be the most important choice of his thirty-three years in the field of architecture.

Retirement decisions are always stressful, and so it was with Joe. He had become very successful in his current Burbank location. The San Fernando Valley had grown during and after the Second World War. He had watched the valley grow to a metropolis of one million, seven hundred thousand people.

Many of the buildings in Burbank were designed by Joe. He watched them being built to his plans and specifications for over thirty years. Joe had drawn plans for many private and public buildings. He was involved in designing the city hall in Burbank. He had a following of developers of industrial buildings throughout the valley. Ray Sence, a previous mayor and one of the leading developers in town, was a loyal client. Several schools, including the Burbank High School, were his buildings. Joe marveled as he watched the buildings he designed being erected. Upon completion, he went to their dedications with pride.

However, Joe had noticed that the thrill was gone. He had reached the end of his fifties and had seen firms such as Lockheed Aircraft expand their operations and had Joe design new buildings. Plant A was erected to make the Constellation and other aircraft used both in the military and in worldwide commerce. Joe felt that he would want to have retirement in a place where his efforts would not be so demanding—where he could slow down and enjoy his 'golden years.'

Questions came to his mind. Did he want to stay in Burbank where he was well known, but where he was sure that the amount of work demanding his talents would prevent him from quitting? Or did he want to have retirement and no career after moving to the Owens River Valley, an area two hundred miles north of his present location?

Joe had been to Bishop, California, located at the north end of the Owens River Valley. He found it to be a charming town of only four thousand people.

However, the downside of his Bishop-based retirement plan was that it was two hundred miles from Los Angeles and his roots. He also noted that water could be a problem facing Bishop due to the threat of global warming and being in the high desert. Offsetting these disadvantages, Joe expected to enjoy his leisure—fishing in a number of smaller lakes, exploring the High Sierras, and enjoying nature. He would also enjoy a seasonal change in weather.

Thirty years earlier, Joe had found out about California living because he attended the University of California, Los Angeles. (UCLA).

This is where he received his architectural degree. At that time, he was unmarried and only twenty-two. He decided that he would transfer his residency from Pennsylvania to California.

The move to California turned out to be wonderful. But approaching sixty-five, Joe had to decide whether he wanted to stay put in Burbank and attempt to lead a quiet retirement life, or venture to a much smaller community with greater prospects.

All and all, the decision would have to be made soon so that Joe and his wife could prepare for a working retirement in which their lifestyle and needs would change. Weighing the pros and cons, Joe leaned toward the move to Bishop.

The Diamond of life characteristic favored such a move. The environment, the planning, and the love of a less populated area were conditions favoring this plan. He designed a retirement just as he designed a building. It would be a place where he could relax as much as he wanted to and be content with his golden years. Either choice would take care of Joe's midlife crisis of retiring.

# TO RETIRE OR NOT TO RETIRE, THAT IS THE QUESTION

*A Career-Altering Event*

A YOUNG-LOOKING BOB was considering retiring after twenty years of doing the sanitizing and cleaning of the swimming pools and spas at an Oregon high-desert, posh resort. He had to make an irreversible Turning Point decision.

Bob and his wife were hired to clean swimming pools and keep them spotless in a major recreation community near Redmond, Oregon. Bob was the foreman of a five-man crew. He had been working twenty years at this occupation. His wife was part of the team that cleaned three swimming pools, one indoor pool, and six hot tubs. It was Bob's responsibility to inspect the pools daily and check the chlorine count and the filtration equipment of the swimming pools three times a day.

Bob was finishing his twentieth year working for the Eagle Crest Resort. He was sixty-eight years old. Being a youthful sixty-eight, he had maintained his physical condition, by, of all things, using the Resort's swimming pools and gym equipment.

Bob was born in Salem, Oregon, about one hundred miles from Redmond. He worked for twenty-six years for a plywood manufacturing company, which used trees that proliferated on the Oregon coast. He worked as a salesman, and he started this in 1972 because President Nixon put price controls on any firm manufacturing plywood that had more than sixty employees.

Bob quit his job at a major mill and, with a friend of his and fellow worker, decided to start selling his own plywood because the prices they could charge were higher than the price controls put on plywood made by major manufactures who had more than sixty employees. Bob's friend and partner were 'jobbers.' They bought plywood at the price-controlled price and sold it to homebuilders—or anybody else who would buy it at any price because he was a small company. This proved to be a very profitable business for fifteen years until another president, President Reagan, in 1987, had Congress remove price controls on all products, including plywood.

Congressional action put jobs such as his out of business. Thus, Bob and his wife desperately needed jobs. While he had saved some money, he wanted a new occupation. He was only forty-nine and his kids were grown. So he went to the high desert and found his swimming pool sanitation job at Eagle Crest.

Both he and his wife were employed. This continued for nineteen years, and as he approached his twentieth year as the major domo of the sanitizing team at Eagle Crest, he considered a Major Turning Point in his life. Should he and his wife retire, although she was not of retirement age, and enjoy the balance of their 'golden years' traveling and doing things that he had not been able to do while working for Eagle Crest?

This was a major decision and there were factors to consider. First and foremost, he liked the job. He enjoyed being foreman, and of course, bossing his wife around. He liked the atmosphere and weather at Eagle Crest. They had expanded during his twenty years to where they had three major golf courses, two indoor swimming pools, two outdoor swimming pools, and six hot tubs that were located throughout the residential areas that encompassed the resort.

On the other hand, there were positives to retiring. The first was he and his wife would be able to do anything they wanted. They could get up at the time they wanted. They could each go their separate ways. They could buy a second car and travel—together or separately, as the case might be.

They were in beautiful Oregon, close to the Deschutes River, which paralleled one of the golf courses. Bob was an ardent fisherman. The trout fishing was unbelievable, and it was a way of his relaxing and enjoying his leisure.

As one can see, Bob was facing a tremendous decision that would be irreversible. He had not made his mind up as to what to do at the writing of this episode, and the major decision of retirement facing all workers and others who had arrived at the age of sixty-six. What should Bob do?

*Bob died in 2010 on the job having made no decision.

## JERRY GETS A CONCRETE IDEA

*Discovering That Shooting Gunite Brings Success*

JERRY REMEMBERS HIS FATHER'S advice about life and his future. "Becoming a success depends on both inspiration and perspiration." While Jerry was only seventeen years old, he took such advice seriously. Jerry realized that living one hundred miles east of Bend, Oregon, and ranching cattle and sheep would not be the life for him, even though Jerry had the traits necessary for success.

He had a vision of a life not so lonely and in an occupation he could relish. He had the drive to do it, and he had the self-confidence of youth. He felt that living the ranch life, one he'd known for his entire time on earth, would not be exciting, but leaving it could be! Thus, he had the courage to go to Texas and look for a way to make a fortune.

The decision to move rather than stay was a Major Turning Point in Jerry's life. He headed for Texas during World War II and went to work in the oil fields as a common ordinary laborer. At that time, re-working the old oil fields was keeping the oil industry very busy. In addition, the companies like Texaco were drilling new wells all the time. He learned how to pour and finish concrete slabs that were placed around the wells after they were in production.

The next Turning Point in Jerry's life was his decision to quit his laborer's job and move to California to find work in the housing boom that was occurring in the San Fernando Valley. Once in the San Fernando Valley, he got a job as a concrete finisher. Jerry worked for a concrete swimming pool installer. After the concrete started to harden, it was his job to finish the concrete by smoothing it out.

After a few years of this work, Jerry became foreman of the crew and developed a new technique called 'gunite.' It revolutionized the construction industry because it reduced the labor in the pouring of concrete by forty percent. As a result, Jerry's company became the leader in the building construction. He formed the California Gunite Company, a life altering Turning Point. Jerry was a business owner rather than a worker. This happened at the age of forty.

By the time he was fifty, Jerry had over fifty employees. He was getting such projects as the L.A. Music Center and the 'islands,' concealing oil derricks in Long Beach harbor. Jerry had arrived. He was a success.

'But into each life some rain must fall,' and so it was with Jerry. At the age of fifty-one, without notice, Jerry had a serious heart attack. The doctor told him that he should not be in a business where he worked twelve hours a day, had a great deal of stress, and had demands that needed his immediate attention.

The next six months were a nightmare for Jerry. He was restless. He was wealthy, but he was not able to utilize his wealth to satisfy his desires. It looked like he must retire at the age of fifty-two. This news was such a downer that literally he faced the Turning Point of his life!

Jerry went to his doctor and said, "I can't stand it any longer— tell me what to do."

The doctor said, "Change occupations, or retire and start enjoying life."

Jerry thought it over. He decided that half a loaf was better than none. He would become a consultant in the field of guniting.

This was a Turning Point in his life, and it worked out fine. He joined a neighboring construction firm and agreed to supervise the inspections required to complete different phases of small commercial structures. It was a firm called Convenience Shopping Center Properties that built Seven/Eleven-type stores and were springing up all over the United States. This Turning Point saved Jerry's sanity, health, and marriage.

Thus, Jerry met the requirements of his golden years in that he could wind down his career, travel the world, and enjoy the benefits of his outstanding success. Guniting was the bridge between stress with a possible heart attack and a humdrum life while waiting to die. Jerry did it on his own. Jerry was an expert when it came to concrete! The Turning Point that saved his life was his heart attack at the age of fifty-two, far from his golden years but early enough for Jerry to exclaim, "Thank the Lord that I had my heart attack while I was young enough to enjoy it— Life that is."

# MERGER-MANIA IN REAL ESTATE

*What to Do in Life's Tarnished Years*

JACK WAS ENTERING MEMORY lane. The golden years passed before his eyes. His career began before WWII as a real estate broker. Real estate in the San Fernando Valley was a feast or famine business. To level the peaks and valleys, Jack acted as an appraiser and became a headhunter and property owner before he retired to rest, relax, and enjoy retirement.

His life's major Turning Point happened during the merger mania at the end of the 20ᵗʰ century. Jack's life had many twists and turns. The Valley had grown exponentially, having a million and a half people. It had spawned substantial industrial companies, one of which was the Glenway Company. Glenway had used Jack to find industrial space so its warehousing company could grow. The company had asked Jack to find a larger building to lease. It took a year, but an ideal space was found and would be available at the end of the year.

Jack had told Glenway that he located a one-hundred-thousand square feet of warehousing space to replace the forty-five thousand square feet that it was using. The leasing commission would be enough for Jack to make his retirement possible.

In the late 1970s, during the Carter presidency, Jack was working as a real estate broker for Grubb & Ellis Company. Unfortunately, the company over-expanded and had to let Jack go after just ten months.

This lay off was caused by two factors. The first was that the company involved was acquired by a larger company in the San Fernando Valley. The second factor was that in such mergers, certain positions were consolidated, and Jack was a victim of this consolidation. Even though he had worked continuously for eighteen years building a good following, he was on the street. He had a bad case of 'merger-itis.'

This was a Major Turning Point in Jack's life. It was no fun to be merged out of a position. Jack was forty-eight years old and found that, because of his age, most positions that he looked at were not available.

Then Jack was recruited by a large recruiting company. He was hired as an executive recruiter— a headhunter. Jack found himself suited in both personality and past experience for this new occupation. He was successful.

After Reagan became President, Jack was among those who were terminated by the recruiting firm—not because of ability and service, but because the economy tanked during President Reagan's second term. This Turning Point in later life was hard to take, but being over sixty-five, Jack thought to himself not again! It meant starting over as a real estate broker in a new area in his own company, a start up.

The area he chose appealed to him. It had the best three advantages: location, location, location. The Burbank Airport became very important. Also, Interstate 5 connected Los Angeles to the eastern valley. It provided great access for trucks and personnel. Finally, the Southern Pacific Railroad gave all the industrial companies in the area a low-cost shipping method of distribution throughout the entire United States.

So, it was start all over again, and he associated himself with Lee and Associates, a large brokerage firm in industrial Real Estate. In later life, he discovered merger-itis was not deadly.

This Turning Point allowed Jack to continue being active in his tarnished years. He was winding down his activities in real estate. He suffered setbacks because of wars, because of the internet, because of the recessions, and because of 'Merger Mania,' a crippling disease of the 21st century. He looked back at his life and its Turning Points with pleasure. This final one, retirement, proved that perseverance and hard work made Jack's life a successful one!

# 13

# UNCLASSIFIED

THIS CHAPTER OF *LIFE'S Turning Points* presents an assorted group of vignettes that do not easily fit into the categories of the previous chapters. But these stories are so unique, they cannot be ignored.

# THE WOW BOYS

### *Stanford Indians 1940 Football Season*

IN THE LATE 1930S, an appraisal of the Stanford University's football team showed it was the laughing stock of the Pacific Coast Conference. Stanford was a very small college. The school's student body was fewer than eight thousand students. Little wonder that football was not highly regarded in the eyes of either the students or the alumni.

The 1939 Stanford football team had lost most of its football games. Called the Stanford Indians, one of the sports writers nicknamed them 'The Indian Maidens.' This type of belittling was what Stanford students faced in their years at the university. The year 1940 seemed that it would be more of the same, another disastrous football season.

In 1940, the Stanford Indians had to play ten football games. The football team had a new coach. They played their first game in mid-September and trashed their opponent. The reason for the team's success was the professional team approach to the game, which had been adopted from the professionals by the new coach, Tiny Thornhill. Thornhill called this approach the 'T- formation.'

The 'T' simplified the game. Each time the team lined up to start a play, the formation had the four men who could carry the ball positioned so they could be handed the ball rather than having the ball thrown to one of them. The football was handed to the quarterback rather than have the action start by the ball being thrown to him. It was a simple change, but it completely altered the college football game. The quarterback would have the choice of passing the ball, running himself, or handing it to one of the three players who had lined up in a straight line six feet behind the quarterback. Stanford won eight other games using the 'T' formation.

It was 'The Big Game'—Stanford against the University of California at Berkeley. They were playing to win the Ceremonial Trophy—'The Axe,' which was to be kept by the winner until the 1941 season. Also, the winner of the game would get the bid to be the league representative playing in the Rose Bowl on New Year's Day.

It was the end of the season for both California and Stanford. Not only was this game the Turning Point for the Stanford team and its use of the 'T- Formation,' it was also a Turning Point for college football throughout the nation. Winning the Cal game resulted in a ten-team victory string by the Stanford Indians and a trip to play in the Rose Bowl.

On January 1, 1941, Stanford played the University of Nebraska in the Rose Bowl. They beat Nebraska soundly and were declared the national champions. According to the football writers who observed the Stanford team in action, the coach and the team were daring to use a new untested football system in such a game. They were skillful in that the Stanford quarterback took control of the big game, the Rose Bowl game, and college football in just one year.

This Turning Point in America's favorite sport was a feat that may never be duplicated. In changing the football system at Stanford and introducing the 'T' formation to the Pacific Coast colleges in 1940, made the Stanford football team the 'Wow Boys' to the entire country. It was an unbelievable athletic success!

# POLIO EPIDEMIC POSTPONES
# NATIONAL CONVENTION

◆

*FDR Holds Jamboree for Boy Scouts of America in 1937*

"**M**Y FRIENDS," SAID THE voice from the radio. "This is your President speaking from the White House. I am having a fireside chat with you. I have some bad news and some good news for all of the people in our America..."

It was a Sunday night in 1935. A polio epidemic was sweeping the country. This crippling disease was affecting the lives of many. The President, did not want to have many thousands of Boy Scouts visiting the nation's capital until the epidemic was under control.

His broadcast concerned a meeting that he named a Jamboree. It was based on his own bout with polio, which had left him unable to walk without assistance.

This speech would be a Turning Point in the lives of over a million young boys from all sections of the nation. Should the Jamboree be cancelled? FDR, the President of the United States thought so. Whatever he did would affect the lives of many thousands of teenage boys who belonged to the Boy Scouts of America.

One of the Boy Scouts, a fourteen-year- old, was listening to the president speak. He had reached the rank of Eagle Scout, the highest rank possible in the scouting movement. He had managed to save enough money for his round-trip railroad ticket from California to Washington, D.C. The trip included a week's stay in the nation's capital.

During the Jamboree, the Boy Scouts would have the opportunity to meet with the president along with all the other scouts who were planning to attend. This group was expected to number nearly fifty thousand young men from every state in the United States.

David had convinced his family living in Los Angeles, California, to match his dollars that he had saved by working part-time in a Piggily-Wiggily Market. David had stocked the shelves as needed. At fifty cents an hour, it was a tough way to save eight hundred dollars. It was a major achievement that had taken three years of working full time in the summer and part-time during the school year.

The scout troop to which David belonged was located in a church. The group was relativity large in number. David, along with several other members of Boy Scout Troop Fifty-one, was to attend the Jamboree. It was led by an assistant scoutmaster. The summer scouting event was to coordinate with the July 4th activities held in the capital.

The Jamboree was deferred two years—until the last week of June 1937. Then, a train was to start from Union Station in Las Angeles, travel through Chicago, and then on to New York City. After a couple of days in New York, it was to go to Washington D.C. This was the tentative revised schedule of the jamboree.

The group of boys boarded the train on June 26, 1937. They joined other scouts as they traveled throughout the West. The train would pick up scouting members as it proceeded across the country.

In 1937, the trains were not air conditioned. The only means of beating the summer heat was to open the windows and allow the warm air to circulate throughout the train car. David splashed his face with cold water  to cool down and remove cinders from the smoke of the coal-fired engine that pulled the train along the rails.

It was a long and tedious trip, and the scouts sang songs and ate in the dining car. They were hungry and all ate three hearty meals a day. To give them some relief, the scouts drank cold water and slept a bit.

It took five days and nights to cross the United States and reach New York City, where the boys visited several famous spots, including the Empire State Building, the Brooklyn Bridge, the theater district, and Central Park. The scouts even had enough time to go to Herald Square and meet with other scouts who were on their way to the Jamboree in Washington.

This trip to Washington D.C. was a Turning Point in most of the Boy Scouts' lives. During the year, an estimated crowd of fifty thousand Boy Scouts and their families met to hear FDR give one of his inspirational speeches to those so assembled. He spoke of the March of Dimes program, which he had expanded to stop polio for the youngsters in the United States and especially for those who had joined the Boy Scouts of America.

FDR spoke of the problems he personally had with recovering from polio. He told of contracting the disease in 1921 when he was in his late thirties. He told them that he would help the movement all he could. He said that he had started the March of Dimes to stamp out polio.

It was early morning and the visiting Boy Scouts tenting arrangements made the area behind the U.S. capitol building look like a military battlefield. There were campfires every night. The cooking was done by the scouts themselves, with food provided by D.C. grocery stores at substantial bargain prices. Songs went on through the night. Many skills and activities were presented, such as starting a campfire, erecting tents, establishing sanitary conditions, listening to experts in the field of hunting and fishing, and other outdoor activities.

The scouts visited all the federal buildings to see exactly where the politicians ran the country and passed laws to do so. The group visited such places as the U.S. Senate, the U.S. House of Representatives, and the U.S. Post Office. They met with workers of the Labor Department and the Departments of the Army, Navy, and Interior.

The weather was not ideal because of the heat, but at least there was no rain during the time spent in Washington. Upon conclusion of the five-day event, the President of the United States commended the Boy Scouts of America for holding such an inspirational and educational conference. He concluded his speech with the words, "May God lay a hand on each and every one of the Boy Scouts assembled here, and make them into the men. Bless such a meeting as the Jamboree."

On July 5th, the tents were struck. All the baggage and items used during the five-day period were put into the same railway cars that had taken them to Washington. The carloads of scouts proceeded to return to their homes.

David, who had scrimped and saved and had received matching funds from his parents, took the train back to Los Angeles.

On the trip back, he realized that this jamboree had been a Turning Point in his young life.. The President, FDR's efforts had helped stem the polio epidemic, Meeting the President had made it an awesome trip. The two-year postponement had taken a boy and made him an adult. For David , the Boy Scout Jamboree had been a stupendous success.

# A TEACHER TAKES A CHANCE

*When a Middle-School Teacher Proves It's Right*

"GET UP, GET UP! We're landing in Baltimore. We have to be in the D.C. by 10:30 a.m.to meet with Senator Feinstein," said the teacher, Steve, as the jet landed in Baltimore some fifty miles from the U.S. Senate Office Building.

To Steve it was old hat as he watched his three assistants shepherd the twenty-three Sun Valley Middle School students from the jet. The educators were guiding young men and women who were interested in Steve's leadership training program. This trip would provide a springboard for a career when they finished their education. It would be a Turning Point in the lives of all twenty-three!

Steve was a youngish teacher of thirty-seven. He developed this novel leadership development program for middle school students. Steve wanted to highlight the importance of the trip in the minds of his students. He did this by going to the seat of the nation's government in Washington, D.C. He wanted them to observe the nation's legislative process in action.

In 2007, Steve felt he had reached a Turning Point because of the recession. Steve was counting on a grant from the Bush administration. The retail business in Los Angeles had affected budgets for all Californians. It had severely hampered the raising of funds. Steve had cut the length of the trip. They would travel to the East Coast and visit Washington D.C and New York City but not stay as long in either city.

The Turning Point that Steve was facing was a money problem. The annual trip was costly. He didn't know where the money would come from and whether or not the trips could be continued. This would affect Steve's career, his life, and his future.

Steve was a hometown man. He was born, raised, and educated in Los Angeles, and he became a teacher there. He loved the city, he loved teaching, and he loved the idea of leadership training.

Steve was unmarried. He was vital and alive and had developed this program during his ten years of teaching thirteen and fourteen-year-olds at Sun Valley California Middle School. Most of the students had never been out of the State of California or even Los Angeles County. They were primarily Hispanic children who were born in California. They were a bright group. They worked hard—both at school and at home. Each paid part of the cost of the three-week trip.

This program was started in the early 2000s and increased every year. It was sponsored by the Governor of California and business through the Chamber of Commerce and the Sun Valley Rotary club members. Steve had received the 'Teacher of the Year' Award for the L.A. Unified District of Los Angeles in the years 2004 and 2005. He felt that he had received the award because of developing this annual trip.

Whether the annual trips should be cancelled or changed would be a major Turning Point in Steve's future. Steve's plans included running for political office—that of L.A. City Councilman. As one of fifteen such members, it was a prestigious and powerful position.

The publicity of his annual trips to see the federal government in action would be a major benefit to his career in government.

The Diamond of Life review showed that Steve's imagination (developing a new idea), persistence (eight trips in a row), ambition (going for political office), and planning (thinking ahead as to his future) favored Steve's continuing on with his trips.

The negatives were profound. The trips were time-consuming, costly, and risky, as they might generate dissatisfaction from his superiors. Steve decided that the Turning Point should be 'give it a go.' He took the chance and kept the trip in place.

# A TEACHER LEARNS A LESSON

◆

*Tina's Dream House Becomes a Nightmare*

"**I** COULD LIVE IN this house the rest of my life," whispered Tina to her realtor during an open house. The year was 2006. Tina was a special education teacher for the Los Angeles Unified School District. She had been looking for a house to buy. It was to be located in mid-San Fernando Valley. Her hunt had been going on for well over a year. She had inherited money from her father that would enable her to purchase an expensive house. However, Tina was very particular. Finding just the right house, the one for her, had been almost in vain. Finally, she found her home. She bought it!

The only fly in the ointment was a neighbor who lived across the street from her who had trees that spoiled her 180° view of the San Fernando Valley. Did she want to continue to own this house if she could not get the neighbor to trim the trees that blocked a portion of the view? Or did she want to resell the house and look for something else? This was a Turning Point in Tina's life.

Tina was nonplussed. She approached the offending property owner. He said, "No" to her. She approached him again and offered to pay for the cost of the work. He refused. She offered to buy his house. He said, "I'm not interested." She collected names of all other property owners within one thousand feet of his property and petitioned the city to make the change mandatory. The offending owner was not willing to change his stand. He told Tina to quit harassing him. He asked her, "What part of NO don't you understand?"

A Diamond of Life review prior to Tina's dream house purchase would have shown she was naïve in thinking she could change a neighbor's mind. She was impulsive in making a decision to buy without looking at the negatives and frivolous in ignoring the old saying, "Look before you leap."

The Turning Point alternatives in Tina's life looked to be unsolvable. None of the alternatives seemed plausible. Tina looked at the positives and negatives of buying another house, trying to resell hers at a loss, and giving up the dream house without a view. She considered ignoring the problem of not having her view. Tina stayed put. Her Turning Point was related to a 'dream home becoming a nightmare.' But she wanted time to think it over!

Time was on Tina's side. Upon the current owner's demise the house would be sold. Tina was fifteen years his junior. The grave was Tina's last hope. Death became a solution. It would preserve her dream house and make it house with a view!

## PRACTICE MAKES PERFECT—
## ESPECIALLY IN A DOCTOR'S LIFE

◆

*A Country Lad Becomes a Successful Dermatologist*

ACCORDING TO SHAKESPEARE, HUMANS can divide their lives into seven stages. Doctor Brown first saw the light of day in the bedroom behind the kitchen of a small café owned by his parents. He had all the benefits of being an only child.

In the second stage of his life, his youth, he worked both before and after school cooking for the customers of the tiny café. Brown slept in the loft over the restaurant. He went to school and did his chores during his free time. He dreamt of better things and swore to himself that he would escape from the drudgery he experienced while growing up.

The third chapter of Brown's life occurred after he graduated from high school. He talked to his father and told him that he wanted to go to university and get his degree. His father said, "Brown, you will have to work your way through school. You know our money is hard to come by. We can't help you at all."

This was certainly a Turning Point and a major one in a young man's life. He solved his money problem by getting a part-time job as a detailer (salesman) for the Roche Company, a major drug manufacturer. He worked his way through college by selling medicines. This double duty enabled him to solve one of the most difficult problems—finding a first job.

Brown entered the fourth stage of his life by having Roche continue his detailing work after he graduated from Minnesota with a BA degree. Having continued his employment with the drug company, he had found out the hard way that being a detailer was shorthand for being a glorified route salesman. Brown called on drugstores, physicians, pharmacies, and the like.

Brown did this for several years. While talking to a pharmacist behind the counter of a drugstore, the pharmacist said, "Brown, you are too intelligent to be a detailer. You should go back to school and become a medical doctor."

Brown thought a minute and said, "You know, I never thought about it, but it sounds like a wonderful idea." That sales call for Roche was another Turning Point in Brown' life. He made a major decision to improve his career.

Returning to the University of Minnesota became the fifth period in his life. Brown enrolled in the necessary courses to become a doctor and joined the U. S. Air Force Reserve. Such a decision would provide additional funds to allow him to become a doctor.

Brown had heard of the army reserve program to get an advanced degree in the military. He signed up. It was a way or earning extra money to live on. He became a member of the Air Force Reserve with the understanding that he would be trained to become a flight surgeon.

But joining the reserve required him to spend one month a year as a member of the Air Force Reserve. He also had to perform other periodic duties that were required in his final year of college.

After slaving away, Brown gave himself a ten-day vacation in the land of his dreams, the beaches in Mexico. He loved to swim, which was free, but to stay in a hotel was out of the question. He planned to live in his Volkswagen van. He drove one thousand five hundred miles to get to a beach that was to his liking. He planned to spend a week in Mexico.

In Mexico, he had found a private beach where he could park for a couple of dollars a day. He slept in his van. What a way to take a break. It was such a novelty—doing nothing except what he wanted to do!

Brown laughed when he thought to himself, "If my parents could see me now doing nothing, with a bottle of Corona beer in my hand, just to get away from it all… to clear my mind, rest my body, and prepare for my education in Minnesota. What a way to bum around."

It was in the springtime and Brown marveled at the bougainvilleas and the azaleas in bloom. For the rest of his vacation, he planned to swim at the beach, sleep in his van, and tour the country, maybe even visit the local bar. As he was about to get under way, he opened the door to his van, and in the car adjacent to his was a beautiful young woman. Thus, a Shakespearean sixth stage of life became a reality. The two looked at each other, liked what they saw, and spent the rest of their dreamy vacation together.

The young lady was a student at San Diego State. This was her final semester, and she was facing a Turning Point of her own. She had a boyfriend in school. Her parents would not approve of how she met Brown. In spite of these negatives, after meeting on the beach and partying, Brown and Dawn became engaged. The two were married in the States a year later.

Then Brown entered medical school. Poverty stricken, the couple scrimped and saved, waiting for the day he would graduate as a flight surgeon in the U.S. Air Force.

During the following years of studying medicine, Brown and Dawn moved from one air force base to another. Brown finally graduated in1986. He became Dr. Brown, a captain, and a qualified flight surgeon. He had been in school almost ten years. Brown faced a career Turning Point, one of the most important in his life. He must choose the location in which to practice medicine.

Should he go to California? Should he go back to Kansas where he knew people and had grown up? Or should he go to a new place, the Pacific Northwest, where the environment was more to his liking?

Captain Brown consulted his Diamond of Life and found he had the Traits and Tendencies to be successful. He was able to do so by his work ethic (getting his captain's rank, and flight surgeon appointment), perspicacity (choosing to change his career from detailing to becoming a dermatologist), and inspiration (having a family who gave him a goal in life).

It was to be a momentous decision. Without going into to great detail, the old expression, "Ours is not to reason why, ours is but to do or die!" seemed very appropriate. Captain, flight surgeon, and finally civilian medical doctor, Brown chose Portland, Oregon, as his spot!

Brown was about to enter the next-to-the-last stage of man, retirement. The Golden Years. To sum up this story, Dr. Brown has done more than his share for his fellow man. He has proved that 'practice makes perfect,' especially in a doctor's life.

# A WOMAN DELEGATE IN A MAN'S WORLD

*Miss Jennifer Goes to Washington*

TWO CAPITAL POLICE STRODE on the stage wheeling two stacks of documents. Each stack was six feet high. They were placed next to the podium. The audience arose in unison. They waited while President Ronald Reagan and staff reached the podium. The band played "Hail to the Chief." The President smiled and waved to the audience. It was June of 1986 and the opening session of the White House Conference of Small Business (WHCFSB).

The President pointed to the two piles of documents and said that he was honored to greet the delegates and eagerly awaited the recommendations of the conference on new legislation, which would benefit small business. He said that Congress could do nothing less than pass legislation that would do so, and he would sign the bills into law.

Jennifer was glad to be one of the few women delegates in attendance who were recommending the passage of laws that would benefit small business and eliminating the laws that didn't. As far as Jennifer was concerned, the legislators had to 'fish or cut bait.' It was a time in the delegates' lives to lobby for legislation—when the nation's small manufacturing companies struggled to stay alive while foreign imports flooded the United States.

The Diamond of Life review showed that she and her father were unique. They were the two delegates in attendance who worked in a family business. They made a good team as they had characteristics that complemented each other. Jennifer was pessimistic in her views. Her father was optimistic. Jennifer was mild mannered. Her father was brusque.

On the other hand, the two had many of the same features. Both were small, attractive, and intelligent. The familial traits were many and apparent. But they disagreed on ambition, finance, and sometimes about the path to take in solving problems.

The Diamond of Life indicated that careful planning, both short and long range, was needed to avert failure and get back on the path to success. It was for this reason that Jennifer and her father attended the White House Conference.

The two delegates planned to present two issues for consideration by the group. The first was a public relations matter. It was to have the U.S Post Office design a new postage stamp so that the twenty-four million small business firms could spread the word of how important they were to the economy.

The other matter concerned the need for small business protection from foreign completion. Once ranked as to degree of importance by the conference, the President could present legislation so that it could be acted upon by Congress.

On a short-term basis, the addition of tariff legislation should be added to imports, and subsidies should be utilized to make American business thrive. It proved to both father and daughter this making of a competitive United States manufacturing industry required a legislative approach. And as a final resort, Jennifer's family-owned business could use the ancient saying as a guide, "If you can't lick them, join them." They would move off shore where costs are lower.

During the week of the White House meetings, the number of problems and suggested solutions was reduced to the ten most desirable. Unfortunately, the two that were suggested by Jennifer and her father were not part of the ten. However, these were presented to California Senators, Boxer and Feinstein, and they considered them carefully. The two senators indicated that in the next session of Congress, they would introduce legislation to help the U.S. Small Business beat back the foreign threat. This was the first step in a long and arduous process to help small business thrive.

Jennifer enjoyed the experience immensely. The meetings, voting on the issues small business deemed necessary, and lobbying the legislators were unique experiences, especially for a young woman. As part of the father-daughter team, she realized being a woman delegate in a man's world was the next step forward in the woman's lib movement. At the end of the WHCFSB, even President Reagan agreed!

# PUTTING ON THE DOG

*Turning Points from a Pet's Viewpoint*

PETS MUST LOOK AT their human masters as imbeciles. Dogs get housed, fed, and loved perpetually, and the only things they have to do in return is to not bark, not bite, and wag their tails. The following questionnaire was answered by the average dog while he was resting.

1.  Where were you born? When?
    - *6-11-2001*
    - *Redwood City, CA*

2.  Youth interests, i.e. boy scouting, computers, etc.?
    - *Puppy love, rubber ball catching, and milk drinking*

3.  Schooling/Education
    - *Bernie's Dog Training – six months.*
    - *House Training – Learning not to chase cars.*

4.  Tell us about your first job.
    - *Becoming a guide dog for the blind.*

5.  How did you meet your wife? How old were you when you met? When did you get married?
    - *Unmarried, but having a ball at the park waiting for a great mate.*

6.  Who influenced your thinking the most as a child? As an adult?
    - *Playing with other puppies; getting bred.*

7. What did you learn from them?
   - *How to pee on trees and chase cats.*

8. Name three difficult times (Turning Points) in your life or career. How did you deal with them? What did you learn from them? How did they change your life?
   - *To sleep alone and not to pee in the house.*
   - *To live a dog's life.*
   - *To obey my master's voice.*
   - *To heel, to be a watchdog.*
   - *To eat one meal a day and not to lick myself in public.*

9. What would the following four people say at your funeral?
   - Someone from your family. *"Woof, Woof, Woof."*
   - Your friends. *"Woof, Woof."*
   - Your business partner or someone from your work. *"Woof."*
   - Someone from your community. *"He's cute!"*

10. What do you consider your most important accomplishment and why?
    - *Learning to bark—To growl and then bite burglars!*

## SHOWING HOW THE HORSE RUNS A RACE

◆

### *Leland Stanford Wins a Bet*

STANFORD UNIVERSITY, A MAJOR college in the state of California, was located on the property that had been owned by the railroad tycoon, Leland Stanford. The school was located on the bay side of the peninsula south of the San Francisco Bay. It was called the 'farm.' This farm was the basic asset of a trust. It was gifted to Stanford University by Mrs. Leland Stanford, its beneficiary.

The establishment of Stanford University by Mrs. Stanford occurred in the 1890s. It was well funded and became the shining light of the area. Her gift was a Turning Point in the field of education in California. The science department of the university and George Eastman, President of Eastman Kodak Company, are spotlighted in this story.

Leland Stanford was a well-known horseracing enthusiast. Far from Kentucky and the Kentucky Derby, Mr. Stanford had a racetrack on the farm where he trained and raced the equines he bred. He had invited a group of friends for a weekend stay to enjoy the California environment and the wonders of farm living.

After an old fashion barbecue, the gentlemen enjoyed an after dinner cigar on the veranda. The subject of horseracing was brought up. The topic of conversation was a fact that had never been verified.

"Does a racehorse running down the stretch to the finish ever have all four feet off the ground at the same time?"

Half of the guests said, "Yes."

And the other half of them said, "No."

But only one of them said, "I believe he does during the race. However, it will take one week until I will prove my side wins the bet."

Everyone promised to return the following Saturday afternoon, and all the guests left.

The next Saturday, the sun was shining brightly. The last two hundred yards of the racetrack were prepared. It was time to decide if the horse had all four feet off the ground at the same time. Would it be yes or no?

It was a horseracing event that would settle the bet. Leland Stanford had twenty photographic cameras set up on the track. They were spaced ten feet apart and were focused on a straight white chalk line drawn on the track for the two hundred yards to the finish line. Each camera had its shutter connected to the opposite rail by a string that would trip the camera to a take the a picture as the horse sped to the finish line. As the test horse ran the down the track, the photos would be taken.

At two o'clock, the race was run. The racehorse ran to the finish line. The cameras' shutters clicked. Eastman took the film into the barn to develop it.

At two thirty, George Eastman ran from the barn waving the dripping prints in the air, shouting, "We won, we won! All four feet are off the ground during a gallop."

Those who had bet that it was true cheered and clapped. The others were silently disappointed. Leland Stanford was on the winning side.

This incident showed why Leland Stanford had the ability to envision work that could revolutionize travel. The Diamond of Life theory showed the reason that Stanford had joined the group of four who created the transcontinental railroad. His Diamond of Life pattern showed that Stanford reached the pinnacle of success by being farsighted (seeing the need for the transcontinental railroad) and shrewd (becoming wealthy by using Chinese laborers to lay the steel rails to pass through the Rocky Mountains). The experiment and the horse race proved the point that 'seeing is believing.'

# THE KICK OFF

*Discipline, as Well as Truth, Hurts*

IT WAS THE FIRST day of teaching English to his students. Mr. Nelson wanted to get started smoothly so he called the class to order at nine o'clock on the dot. He thought to himself, "This will be the Turning Point of my life." Then he said aloud, "Good Morning, class."

Mr. Nelson smiled as he wrote his name on the chalkboard He turned to face thirty-eight students and said, "I'll tell you my name, and I guarantee that each one of you will always remember it. My last name is Nelson and I am nicknamed 'Half.' For those of you who are not wrestling fans, the 'Half Nelson' is a wrestling hold." Then he added, "But you don't call me by my nickname, I am *Mr. Nelson* to each of you."

Before he taught at the high school, Mr. Nelson had worked for newspapers in several major cities in the United States. He pointed out that he had developed a foolproof technique for students to use when writing papers required in his class. It was to be used in preparing all assignments. It was his preferred way of students learning the facts and then using them in their writing.

Mr. Nelson called it the 'Five Ws and H System.' These initials were the first letters of the factual information Mr. Nelson expected to find in any writing submitted to him as homework.

This system was mandatory. The Ws were for What, When, Where, Who, and Why. The H was for How. Mr. Nelson looked for and evaluated these elements in each student's writing. It was his fetish regarding his teaching.

In addition, on the first day of class, he told the students of his first summer job. It was with the Salt Lake City Telegram, an evening newspaper. Mr. Nelson worked there as a cub reporter. His 'beat' was to summarize the death notices for the paper. It was a section called "In Memoriam." The more important people had their photographs shown. It was great training and he has used his method of writing letters, articles, and papers during his entire career.

That summer, while on the Telegram's staff, Mr. Nelson covered city hall. He discovered why the chief of police, the mayor, the coroner, and the city attorney did what they did. The city officials would talk to him on coffee breaks or when he needed to get the inside story. By the end of the summer, Mr. Nelson was a competent newspaperman. He also realized he had to continue his education, so he looked for other fields to conquer. He chose teaching as his career.

This led Mr. Nelson to the 'Why' of this story. As a green teacher who had not had any experience or met many characters along the way, Mr. Nelson found out that the best defense was to attack. Therefore, he kept a tight rein on his class.

Although it was difficult for both student and teacher to have such discipline applied to education, Mr. Nelson said it best. "You may think my teaching methods are not cool, but I learned early in my career that being strict, disciplined, and truthful hurt both of us at the same time. I hope you have enjoyed my teaching as much as I have enjoyed teaching you."

# PART 3

# APPENDIX

# METHODOLOGY

### Story Research and Selection

THE STORIES IN *LIFE'S TURNING POINTS* were selected, accumulated, classified, and reported in vignette format. An episodic presentation was used to give the reader a glimpse of a person's existence. The incidents were chosen from the lives of friends, neighbors, and acquaintances. They were based on the Turning Point decisions made by real people as they went through life.

The decision-makers came from all walks of life, from all fifty states, and includes both men and women, successful and the unsuccessful. Finally, the age and experience of the person chosen for interview was an important factor in making the study.

The first step in researching for this book required preparing a questionnaire and mailing it to over three hundred prospective participants. Each response was reviewed and a face-to-face meeting was held whenever possible. While these meetings were time consuming on the part of the writer, they were used to discuss as many of the Turning Point decisions as time allowed.

It follows that during the interviews, the participant was asked to recall happenings that are permanently etched on their minds. Although memories fade with the passage of time, incidents could be remembered as snapshots of events that occurred and the decisions made during one's life.

## QUESTIONNAIRE FOR RESEARCH

*I need your help. I am writing a book. Please fill out the answers for my use in writing vignettes of several incidents in your life. Please send it back in the enclosed stamped envelope, OR send it back to me via email to www.artsweetthe1@yahoo.com. You will be grouped with others from all fifty states and will be known as (First name) (Last Name's First Initial) as an example, I would be Art S. Thanks in advance for helping me Art S.*

### *INTERVIEW QUESTIONS*

1.   *Where were you born? When?*
2.   *Where did you grow up?*
3.   *Youth interests i.e. boy scouting, computers, etc.*
4.   *Schooling/Education*
5.   *What were your interests during your youth?*
6.   *Did that change during your high school and college years? If so how?*
7.   *Tell us about your first job.*
8.   *How did you meet your wife? How old were you when you met? When did you get married?*
9.   *Who influenced your thinking the most as a child? As an adult?*
10.  *What did you learn from them?*
11.  *Name three difficult times (Turning Points) in your life or career. How did you deal with them? What did you learn from them? How did they change your life?*

12.   What are your current goals? Now? Five years from now? For retirement? For your Life?

13.   What would the following four people say at your funeral?

   a.   Someone from your family
   b.   Your friends
   c.   Your business partner or someone from your work
   d.   Someone from your community

14.   What do you consider your most important accomplishment and why?

# THE SEVEN STAGES OF MAN

*With Apologies to William Shakespeare*

STAGE 1 FINDS THE infant with a Turning Point. After six months of being in a crib and crying about it, the baby, being a baby, thrashes around, crying and making his parents frantic. They watch him hold his head up and 'presto chango' he finds himself rolling over in the crib. The parents look in awe at the miraculous event. Certainly, a Turning Point in the baby's life. Most of their friends and strangers look at this event with trepidation. Every baby does this, but the parents are astounded, especially if it is their first child. All others sniff and say, "Bah-humbug."

STAGE 2 finds the infant walking, talking, and seeing everything with eyes wide open and a look of wonderment. Of course, this state is a learning process. This stage ends at adolescence when learning about all the strange things he is expected to know as he grows up. It is a wonderful stage because he starts school, he is away from his parents part of the time, and he is under the supervision of somebody other than mom and dad. In the teens, a strange thing has happened, both the sexes mature. This is a very difficult stage of man's life.

STAGE 3 shows the effect of adolescence and approaching maturity where he becomes a young adult. It is fraught with many, many choices because of his starting to appreciate the opposite sex. The high school and college years are increasingly difficult and trying. Decisions have to be made as to which college to go to or even whether to go to college. The vast majority of such maturing adults either enter an apprenticeship or job hunt for a livelihood. Higher education is another alternative.

STAGE 4 has to do with entering the maturity of adulthood. Having graduated from college, having chosen an occupation, or entering the job market without a college education becomes an all consuming task. He is an adult. He is expected to support himself. He is expected to find a suitable mate. Then there are the inevitable children that are now on the way. This stage is the longest portion of man's life. It is a stage to remember.

STAGE 5 is the adult who has found a mate and has a career and/or a position in which he is completely independent of everybody else except those people who really matter—his family, his predecessors, and his contemporaries, most of whom are living in the fourth, fifth, or sixth decade of their lives. He achieves his independence, he reaches his career peaks, and he approaches retirement, all of which consume most of his time except that time spent with his family.

STAGE 6 is retirement and the 'golden years.' This represents a Major Turning Point in everyone's life because the previous efforts are being rewarded by rest, relaxation, travel, or other activities he wants to do. He starts a second career, or he may just go fishing. As he approaches the end of the sixth stage of life, one finds it is the winding down period.

STAGE 7 begins with the 'tarnished years,' and being affected by poor health and troubled finances may be among them. They are those years between his golden years and his approaching death. He, of course, has major illnesses and fewer Turning Points. He loses his mate, his friends, and his complete freedom. One's physical condition deteriorates, and he sees his friends and relatives pass away. The last act in the play of life is the inevitable death...perpetual darkness... the end!

In conclusion, Shakespeare realized that man faces many Turning Points, and that they could conveniently be divided into stages of life that have meaning to all who tread the earth, swim in the sea, or fly high in the sky.

## TRAITS AND TENDENCIES

1. Traits = Distinguishing features (inherited)
2. Tendencies = Attitudes
3. Luck = Fortune; Good or Bad Luck
4. Determination
5. Misfortune = Bad luck
6. Strength = Positive Attitude
7. Knowledge = Know-how or Native trait
8. Drive = Urge to succeed
9. Attitude = Opinion (way of thinking)
10. Ability = Talent or Capacity
11. Ambition = Determination to Succeed
12. Character = Distinguishing Qualities
13. Judgment = Ability to come to reason and conclusion
14. Appearance = Outward Perception
15. Disinterest = Not wanting (boredom)
16. Indulgent = Self satisfying lazy
17. Leadership = Ability to direct
18. Egotism = Self adoration

**Traits:** Distinguishing characteristics most often inherited such as Height, Weight, Health, Stature, Speed, Intelligence, Skill, Vision, Touch. Beauty, Appearance, etc.

**Tendencies:** Insecurity, Heart, Jealousy, Misfortune, Bias, Immobility, Insolence, Hesitancy, Impulsiveness, Anger, Sincerity, Straight Arrow, Honesty, Upright, Luck, Remorse, Joy, Elation, Knowing, Somber, Sober, Down, Up, Ability, Compatibility, Sad, Happy, Moody, Fanciful, Reserved, Talkative, Silent, Active, Inactive, Dumb, Genuine, Careless.

# ROTARY INTERNATIONAL

*A Service Club Providing Life's Turning Points to Those in Need*

THE YEAR WAS 1905. Five men gathered around the desk of Attorney Paul Harris. All were business professionals interested in improving their lot in crime-ridden, downtown Chicago. They were discussing the civic environment in the second largest city of the United States and how each professional would conduct his business in the future. Little did they know that this informal group meeting would blossom into a voluntary association of people and companies that would become a worldwide influence.

All five 'conspirators' agreed to meet again for lunch, rotating each meeting so that it was in a different location. The goal of these meetings was to make new friends and grow their businesses by dealing with each other. There were to be no competitors allowed in this private club—no outsiders joining the group unless invited.

From this impromptu association, Rotary International became very active in the Midwest. The feature of limiting membership by offering it to a person of a different occupation became a Turning Point for the association. When others heard how great it was to have lunch and meet a willing group of fellow non-competitors, the desire to join was the driving force in expanding in the U.S.A.

Several instances of conflicting ideas occurred during the early years. One of these was the objective of Rotary. One group was headed by founder Paul Harris. He felt that serving others was the aim of the movement. The second view was to devote time and energy to make a business profitable so that it was possible to serve the underserved. It was a philosophy best described by the phrase, 'he who profits most can serve the public best.' This conflict became a Turning Point and resulted in founder Harris resigning from club membership.

Another Turning Point occurred after eighty-plus years of Rotary International actively serving the nation. The association saw the 'men only policy' established by its founders challenged by women wanting to be invited to belong to the 30,000-club organization.

The older members wanted no change. They demanded that the executives fight this in the courts but were told by counsel that it was hopeless. At that time the change in membership policy was adopted. Women were invited to attend meetings and join Rotary International to provide "Service Above Self" to the underserved all over the world

Rotary International is still alive and well after over one hundred years of serving the public and facing Turning Points along the way.

www.ingramcontent.com/pod-product-compliance
Lightning Source LLC
LaVergne TN
LVHW011216080426
835509LV00005B/145